CONTENTS

UNIT 6   FOR EAL LEARNERS: A REVIEW OF THE BASICS

PREFACE

Welcome to *The Bare Essentials*, a Canadian text designed for college and university students who need to learn to write for academic and professional purposes. We've designed this book to answer not only the needs of today's students but also the needs of teachers who want a text with simple explanations, Canadian examples, and plenty of practice exercises.

In its print format, this new edition consists of two components: a text (*The Bare Essentials*, Ninth Edition) and a workbook (*The Bare Essentials Workbook*, Ninth Edition). Both are also available as an integrated digital resource: MindTap for The Bare Essentials. To access MindTap, students register at **www.nelson .com/student**. After registration, students can log on at any time to access their work as well as the extensive support material available on the website.

The Bare Essentials, Ninth Edition, presents the fundamentals of English writing skills, moving from words (Unit 1) to sentences (Unit 2) to grammar (Unit 3) to punctuation (Unit 4) to paragraphs and essays (Unit 5). Unit 6 provides a helpful review of some challenging concepts for students who use English as an additional language (EAL). Each chapter offers simple explanations and clear examples supported by copious exercises in the accompanying *Workbook* or in MindTap.

HIGHLIGHTS

Units 1 through 4 and Unit 6 begin with a "Quick Quiz" and end with a "Rapid Review." These tests preview and review the contents of each unit. They also provide practice in editing continuous prose passages. By comparing their results on the initial quiz and the final review, students can see for themselves how far their understanding has progressed.

- Approximately half of the exercises are new. For those working with the print version, most of the exercises can be completed in the *Workbook*, and the answers are easy to find. (Answers to the chapter Mastery Tests are not included in the *Workbook* or in MindTap; they are provided in the Instructor's Manual, along with a set of alternative Mastery Tests.) An icon in *The Bare Essentials* indicates which exercises in the *Workbook* apply to each section of the text. The digital version features embedded exercises. A click of the mouse will open an interactive version of the exercise, often auto-graded, with full explanations. MindTap also offers additional practice exercises for most chapters.

- The *Workbook* pages are three-hole-punched to facilitate peer review or submission to the instructor. Exercises are numbered by chapter and set (each usually with 10 items); for example, Exercise 5.4 refers to Chapter 5, Exercise 4.

- Unit 6, "For EAL Learners," features new exercises that provide hands-on editing, together with suggestions for speaking/listening practice. On pages 318–319 of the print book, you'll find the Time Line, an easy-to-read visual representation of the English tense system. In MindTap, the Time Line is at the end of the Units list on the opening screen.

- Unit 7, "Readings," consists of eight essays, six of them new to this edition. "Career Consciousness" appears first because it is the final product of the essay-writing process through which we guide students in Unit 5. "Readings" concludes with a short documented essay formatted in both American Psychological Association (APA) and Modern Language Association (MLA) styles. Questions for discussion and suggestions for writing follow each reading. Suggested answers to the discussion questions are provided in the Instructor's Manual.

- Appendix A, "The Fundamentals," now includes a section on numbers.

- The "List of Useful Terms" (Appendix B) defines and illustrates terms that appear in bold print in the text, along with other grammatical terms with which you may wish your students to be familiar.

The units in *The Bare Essentials* are independent of each other, so instructors can present them in any order they choose. The chapters within each unit, however, should be introduced in the order in which they appear. The unit exercises are cumulative: those in later chapters often include questions that assume mastery of skills covered in earlier chapters.

We ask students to check their answers as soon as they have completed an exercise so that they will get immediate feedback, learn from their mistakes, and avoid reinforcing their errors. **We urge instructors to emphasize the importance of this procedure.**

On the inside front cover of the print version is a Quick Revision Guide that students can use as a checklist as they edit their work. In MindTap, this guide is located at the end of the Units list on the opening screen. Instructors can photocopy or print out the guide, staple a copy to each student's paper, and mark ✔ or ✗ beside each point to identify the paper's strengths and weaknesses. This strategy provides students with comprehensive and consistent feedback. It also saves hours of marking time.

The Bare Essentials is designed not only for students who need to learn how to write acceptably in college and the workplace but also for instructors who are dedicated to helping their students learn as efficiently and painlessly as possible. While the text can successfully be used for independent study, it works best for students lucky enough to have an instructor who will guide them enthusiastically through its contents, adjust the pace and level of instruction to the needs of each class, and provide regular feedback and encouragement. We hope this new edition will meet instructors' expectations and help them sustain their joy in teaching.

INSTRUCTOR RESOURCES

MindTap® MINDTAP

Offering personalized paths of dynamic assignments and applications, MindTap is a digital learning solution that turns cookie-cutter into cutting-edge, apathy into engagement, and memorizers into higher-level thinkers. MindTap enables students to analyze chapter concepts and apply them to relevant assignments; it enables instructors to measure skills and promote better outcomes with ease. A fully online learning solution, MindTap combines all learning tools—readings, multimedia, activities, and assessments—into a single Learning Path that guides the student through the curriculum. Instructors can personalize the experience by customizing the presentation of these learning tools for their students, even seamlessly introducing their own content into the Learning Path.

OTHER RESOURCES

An instructor's manual and PowerPoint slides are available online at **www.nelson.com/instructor**.

Answers to the chapter Mastery Tests and an alternative set of Mastery Tests are included in the Instructor's Manual.

ACKNOWLEDGMENTS

We are indebted to our reviewers, whose suggestions helped to make this a more useful book:

Jamie Bradley, University of Ottawa
Tim Callin, Camosun College
Kim Cechetto, Fanshawe College
Lynda Garneau, Mount Royal University
Cibylla Rakestraw, Grande Prairie Regional College
Helen Yeomans, Nova Scotia Community College

We owe special thanks to Janet Zlotnik (Vancouver City College), a long-time and enthusiastic user of *The Bare Essentials Plus*. Janet kindly took the time to review the book in detail and provide us with helpful suggestions for the EAL unit. We would also like to thank our supportive team at Nelson Education Ltd., specifically Laura Macleod, publisher; Lisa Berland, content development manager; Natalia Denesiuk Harris, senior production project manager; Cathy Witlox, copy editor; and Amanda Henry, executive marketing manager, whose sales force makes possible the continuing revisions of our *Essentials* series.

Sarah Norton
Brian Green
Nell Waldman

INTRODUCTION

TO THE STUDENT: WHY YOU NEED THIS BOOK

To get a job. To get promoted at your job. To find eternal happiness. (Well, two out of three isn't bad.)

It is a fact: **The ability to write well will be the most valuable skill you learn in college or university.** That's why English composition is part of your curriculum. Curriculum committees know that graduates who can communicate well are hired more quickly, advance more rapidly, and climb higher in their professions than graduates with poor communication skills. Companies from Imperial Oil to IBM, from Canadian Tire to Ford, from the Royal Bank to Bell Canada, not to mention all levels of government, hospitals, police forces, and the Canadian military, all have declared superior communication skills an essential criterion for hiring and promotion.

To any employer, an employee is more valuable if he or she can write well. Fairly or unfairly, no matter what field you're in, your employers, peers, and subordinates will judge your ability—and even your intelligence—on your communication skills.

The good news is that writing skills can be learned. There is no reason you can't write clear and correct reports, memoranda, even emails. This resource will teach you how to write these and other professional documents, just as it has helped thousands of Canadian students before you. All you need is the determination to improve. If you invest the time, effort, and care we ask of you, you will succeed.

WHAT'S IN THIS BOOK?

If you are using the print version of this text, you will discover that it comes in two parts: instruction (*The Bare Essentials*, Ninth Edition) and practice (*The Bare Essentials Workbook*, Ninth Edition). If you are using the online version, you will find that instruction and practice are integrated in MindTap for *The Bare Essentials*, which can be accessed at **www.nelson.com/student**. *The Bare Essentials*, Ninth Edition, divides the basics of English writing skills into seven parts: Units 1 through 4 will help you identify errors in your writing. Unit 5 explains and illustrates how to organize and develop your ideas in effective paragraphs, essays, and reports. Unit 6 reviews those aspects of written English that students whose first language is not English often find troublesome.

Unit 7 contains essays on topics that we hope you will find interesting. These essays illustrate several practical organizational patterns as well as different levels of language, from informal to formal, that writers can use to suit their topic, audience, and purpose.

After Unit 7, you'll find two appendixes. Appendix A covers basic grammar (kinds and parts of sentences and the parts of speech) and shows you how to write numbers. Appendix B defines the technical terms used in this book, along with other useful terms. Whenever you find a **grammatical term** in bold type, you can turn to Appendix B to discover what it means and how to use it.

If you are working with the print version, *The Bare Essentials Workbook* contains exercises linked to the instruction in the handbook; using the two together, mindfully, will help you eliminate errors in your writing. Answers to most of the exercises can be found in the back of the *Workbook*. If you are using the online version, you will find the exercises immediately after the instruction, and answers and explanations are provided automatically. Additional practice exercises for each chapter are also available on the MindTap Learning Path.

HOW TO USE THIS BOOK

In each chapter, we do three things: explain a writing rule, illustrate it with examples, and provide exercises to help you master it. The exercises are usually arranged in sets of 10 items that get harder as you progress. By the time you finish a chapter, you should have a good grasp of the principle you've been practising. Then it's up to you to **apply what you've learned every time you write**. Competence in writing is no different from competence in any other skill: it results from combining knowledge with practice.

THE STEPS TO SUCCESS

1. Read the explanation. Do this even if you think you understand the point.
2. Study the highlighted rule(s) and examples that follow.
3. This symbol tells print users to turn to the *Workbook* to find exercises on the concept we've just explained; those working online will find the exercises immediately below the instruction.

   If you find an explanation easy and think you have no problem with the rule, try the last set of exercises given for it. Then check your answers, either in the back of the *Workbook* or, if you're online, by clicking the Check My Work button. If you've made no errors, return to the instructional text and move on to the next point.

   If you're less confident, don't skip anything. Start with the first exercise and work your way through all exercises until you are sure you understand the point. (As a general rule, getting two exercises in a row entirely correct demonstrates mastery of the skill.)
4. **Always check your answers to one set of exercises before you go on to the next.** Only by checking your results after each set can you identify errors and correct them, instead of repeating an error and thus reinforcing it.
5. When you make a mistake, compare your answer with our instruction to figure out where you went wrong. If you're working online, do the additional practice activities. If you are truly stuck, check with your instructor. Continue with the exercises only when you are sure you understand where you went wrong.

WHAT THE SYMBOLS MEAN

This symbol, with its accompanying instructions, tells you to go to the *Workbook* and do the exercises associated with the point you've been learning. (If you're using MindTap, the exercises appear immediately below the explanation and examples.)

This symbol beside an exercise means the exercise is designed to be done by two or more students working together. Often you are instructed to begin work in a pair or group, then to work individually on a writing task, and finally to regroup and review your writing with your partner(s). (Of course, your instructor may choose to modify these exercises for students working independently.)

The notebook symbol means "note this." We've used it to highlight writing tips, helpful hints, hard-to-remember points, and information that you should apply whenever you write.

This icon indicates a Mastery Test—an exercise designed to check your understanding of the principle covered in the chapter you have just completed. Your instructor will provide the answers to these exercises.

THREE LEARNING TOOLS

- We've included a **Quick Revision Guide** inside the front cover of the printed book and in MindTap. Use it to help you revise your papers before handing them in. This book is meant to be a practical tool, so apply the lessons in all the writing you do. The more you practise, the faster you'll learn! We can identify writing problems and show you how to solve them, and exercises can give you practice in eliminating errors, but only writing and revising can bring real and lasting improvement.
- On the inside back cover of the book and in MindTap, we've provided a list of **Correction Abbreviations and Symbols**. For each error, we illustrate and explain standard marking symbols; we also leave space for you to insert your instructor's preferred symbol or abbreviation for that error.
- The **Time Line**, a quick, easy-to-read chart that summarizes verb tenses, can be found on pages 318–319 of the printed book and in MindTap for *The Bare Essentials*.

UNIT 1

Words

Before you start this unit, complete the Quick Quiz.
Once you have finished this unit, complete the Rapid
Review.

1 Choosing the Right Words

The difference between the right word and the almost right word is

the difference between lightning and the lightning bug.
—Mark Twain

This book is designed to help you overcome two serious problems facing anyone who is learning to write well in English. The first is affectation, which means pretending to be someone you aren't or to know something you don't. Everyone on Facebook can witness the difference between authenticity and phoniness; friends expect to see and hear "the real you." Similarly, when you write in college or on the job, your readers expect to read material that has been written by you about something you know about. The second problem is ignorance of the conventions of written English. You are taking an English course to learn these conventions, which we present in highlighted boxes, like the one below. Of course you will make mistakes; learning cannot take place without them!

Whenever you write, you want your reader to
• understand your message and
• think well of you as a writer

To achieve these goals, your writing must be correct and appropriate. If your readers are to understand you, your message must consist of accurate words, organized into grammatical sentences and arranged in well-developed paragraphs.

The notion of "correctness" in writing has developed over hundreds of years—and is still changing—to help writers create messages that say what their authors intend. Error-filled writing fails to meet the reader's expectation that a message will be clearly communicated. Mistakes in grammar, sentence structure, spelling, and punctuation mean that a message will not be easy to read.

Another reason to ensure that your writing is correct is that our culture associates correct language with education and intelligence. Careless, ungrammatical writing is often considered a sign of ignorance or laziness—or both.

But that's not all. Accuracy alone will not help you reach your goals. A message that is technically free of errors can still confuse or annoy a reader if it contains inappropriate language. Slang; racist, sexist, obscene, or blasphemous language; and even wordiness can interfere with your message. That's why we call them "errors." They divert the reader's attention from what you're saying to how you're saying it. They also lower the reader's opinion of you.

Real estate people say there are three things to consider when buying a property: location, location, location. Good writers know that there are three things to consider when sending a message: audience, audience, audience. Your readers and their expectations—what they need or want to know from you, the writer, should be your constant focus. In this chapter, we provide a brief introduction to choosing language that is correct and appropriate for your message and **audience**. We assume that you are writing for readers in an academic or professional setting. Our goals are to help you convey your message clearly and leave your readers with a positive impression of you and your ideas.

THE WRITER'S TOOLKIT

Before you get started, you need to equip yourself with a few essential resources and an understanding of the levels of language that are available to you when you write.

1. Use a good dictionary.

A dictionary is a writer's best friend. You will need to use it every time you write, so if you don't already own a good dictionary, you should buy a recent edition of a print one or subscribe to an online dictionary. For Canadian writers, a good dictionary is one that is Canadian, current, comprehensive (contains at least 100,000 entries), and reliable (published by an established, well-known firm).

For this text, we have used the *Canadian Oxford Dictionary*, 2nd edition (Oxford University Press, 2004). This dictionary is available online through your college or university resource centre. For those whose first language is not English, we recommend the *Oxford Advanced Learner's* Dictionary (OALD), 9th ed. (Oxford University Press, 2010), available at www.oxfordlearnersdictionaries.com. In addition to most of the information provided in traditional print dictionaries, this resource offers audible English and American pronunciations and helpful example sentences.

A good dictionary packs a lot of information into a small space. Take a look at the *Canadian Oxford Dictionary* entry for the word *graduate*, for example. The circled numbers correspond to some of the numbers in the guide that follows the entry.

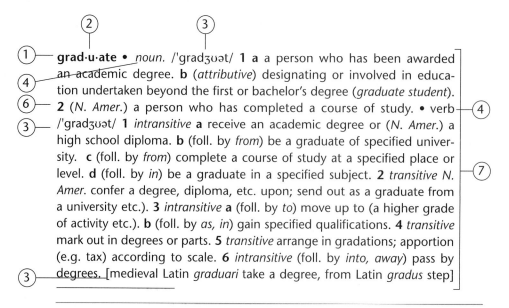

grad·u·ate • *noun.* /ˈɡradʒʊət/ **1 a** a person who has been awarded an academic degree. **b** (*attributive*) designating or involved in education undertaken beyond the first or bachelor's degree (*graduate student*). **2** (*N. Amer.*) a person who has completed a course of study. • verb /ˈɡradʒʊət/ **1** *intransitive* **a** receive an academic degree or (*N. Amer.*) a high school diploma. **b** (foll. by *from*) be a graduate of specified university. **c** (foll. by *from*) complete a course of study at a specified place or level. **d** (foll. by *in*) be a graduate in a specified subject. **2** *transitive N. Amer.* confer a degree, diploma, etc. upon; send out as a graduate from a university etc.). **3** *intransitive* **a** (foll. by *to*) move up to (a higher grade of activity etc.). **b** (foll. by *as, in*) gain specified qualifications. **4** *transitive* mark out in degrees or parts. **5** *transitive* arrange in gradations; apportion (e.g. tax) according to scale. **6** *intransitive* (foll. by *into, away*) pass by degrees. [medieval Latin *graduari* take a degree, from Latin *gradus* step]

Canadian Oxford Dictionary, 2nd Edition, Edited by Katherine Barber © Oxford University Press Canada 2004. Reprinted by permission of the publisher.

In a dictionary entry, you will find some or all of the following information:

1. **Spelling:** If there are two or more acceptable spellings, the most common one is given first.
2. **Syllables:** Small, centred dots (·) in a print dictionary show you where to put a hyphen if you need to break a word at the end of a line. In the online *Oxford English Dictionary*, these syllable breaks are marked with vertical lines.
3. **Pronunciation:** If there is more than one acceptable pronunciation, the most common one is listed first.
4. **Grammatical form(s):** for example, noun (*n.*), verb (*v.*), adjective (*adj.*).
5. Any **irregular forms** of the word, such as the plural form of a noun or the past tense and past participle of a verb.
6. **Usage restrictions:** for example, *slang, informal, offensive, obsolete, N. Amer.*
7. **Definition(s):** The most common meanings are given first, followed by technical or specialized meanings, followed by phrases or sentences illustrating how the word is used.
8. **Idioms** using the word.
9. **Origins** of the word (etymology).
10. **Other helpful information:** for example, homonyms (words that sound the same as the entry word); synonyms (words that are similar in meaning to the entry word); antonyms (words opposite in meaning to the entry word); and special variations in grammar, spelling, pronunciation, and usage.

Here's what the entry for *graduate* looks like in the *Oxford Advanced Learner's* online dictionary.

Definition of **graduate noun** from the Oxford Advanced Learner's Dictionary

graduate *noun*

BrE /ˈɡrædʒuət/ ◀)); NAmE /ˈɡrædʒuət/ ◀))

(*informal* **grad** *especially in North American English*)

(⭐ Add to my wordlist)

1 **graduate (in something)** a person who has a university degree

- *a graduate in history*

- *a science graduate*

- *a graduate of Yale/a Yale graduate*

- *a graduate student/course*

→ SEE RELATED ENTRIES: **University life, University people**

2 (*North American English*) a person who has completed their school studies

- *a high school graduate*

→ SEE RELATED ENTRIES: **People in schools, School life**

Oxford Learner's Dictionaries, Oxford University Press, 2015. Found at http://www
.oxfordlearnersdictionaries.com/definition/english/graduate_1?q=graduate

Unless you have already done so (and most people haven't), begin by reading the introduction or the guide at the front of your dictionary. This information may not be very entertaining, but it is essential to understanding how to read your dictionary accurately. No two dictionaries are alike. Only if you are familiar with your dictionary's symbols, abbreviations, and item-entry format will you be able to use it effectively.

Knowing the information in your dictionary's guide will also save you time. For example, you do not need to memorize long lists of irregular plurals. Good dictionaries include irregular plurals in their entries. They also include irregular forms of verbs, adjectives, and adverbs. And if you've forgotten how to form regular plurals, verbs, adjectives, and adverbs, you'll find that information in your dictionary guide as well.

Read through the guide in the front of your dictionary. Then do Exercises 1.1 through 1.3.

Go to Workbook Exercises 1.1–1.3

After you have checked your answers to Exercise 1.3, go back and look at the questions again. What do the root words in questions 1 to 5 have in common? What do the root words in questions 6 to 10 have in common? How do these similarities affect the way these words are spelled when an ending is added? Can you write a rule to guide other writers who must deal with words like these?

Go to Workbook Exercises 1.4–1.5

2. Use spelling and grammar checkers responsibly.

- Good spell-check programs can find typing errors and some common spelling mistakes. They have limitations, however. They can't tell if you meant to write "clothes" or "cloths," and they won't flag either word, even if it's used incorrectly. (You'll learn more about such words in Chapter 2, "Hazardous Homonyms.") Also, since we use Canadian English, our spellings sometimes differ from the American spellings used in most word-processing programs. If your word-processing program can be set to Canadian spelling, make that adjustment. If it cannot, be aware that words such as *colour, honour, neighbour, centre, travelled,* and *metre*—all correct Canadian spellings—will be flagged as errors.
- Another useful tool is a dictionary app installed on your smartphone or tablet device. These apps contain a large bank of words and will provide a correct spelling if the "guess" you type in is not too far off. Ask your instructor if you can use this device (sound turned off, please) for in-class writing and exams.
- Electronic translating dictionaries are available online. Most of these tools pronounce the word the way a native British or American speaker would.

(Of course, the accuracy of the pronunciation depends on the knowledge and skill of the programmer.) Please do not use the voice feature in class! Most translating dictionaries are limited in their capability, so look for one that is both comprehensive and accurate. And be careful not to seize on the first definition that appears for a word you are looking up. Read through all the options given. Computers cannot grasp ambiguity, irony, or idioms the way the human mind does. Sometimes the convenience of electronic dictionaries can lead to embarrassing language errors; for example, a European vacuum cleaner manufacturer translated its slogan into English as "Nothing sucks like our product." Print dictionaries are usually more reliable than their electronic counterparts, but they won't tell you aloud how to say a word you don't know how to pronounce.

- The best advice we can give you about grammar checkers (they announce their presence by producing a wavy coloured line under words or sentences that your word processor questions) is to use them with caution. No grammar checker has yet been able to account for the subtleties of English grammar. A grammar program is as likely to flag a perfectly good sentence, even to suggest an incorrect "fix," as it is to ignore a sentence full of errors. "I done real good on my grammar test," for example, escapes the dreaded wavy coloured line.

3. Use a good thesaurus.

If you use the same words again and again, you will bore your reader. A thesaurus is a dictionary of synonyms—words with similar meanings. For any word you need to use repeatedly in a document, a good thesaurus will provide a list of alternatives. Note, however, that *synonyms are not identical in meaning*. Only you (or a knowledgeable friend) can decide which of the words listed in your thesaurus is appropriate for your message. Your dictionary will help you decide which terms are acceptable and which are not.

While the thesaurus in your word-processing program will provide quick synonyms for words you don't want to repeat, we recommend you rely on a print thesaurus or on the Oxford English Dictionary online thesaurus, which you will find at www.oxforddictionaries.com/thesaurus. A word-processor thesaurus provides a list of approximate synonyms, but no examples of usage. With unfamiliar or complex words, you need to know if the synonyms offered are nouns or verbs and whether they are in general use or are slang, technical, derogatory, or even obsolete.

Two good thesauruses are available in inexpensive paperback editions: *Oxford Paperback Thesaurus* (Oxford University Press, 2006) and *Roget's Thesaurus* (Penguin, 2004).

Inexperienced writers sometimes assume that long, obscure words will impress their readers. In fact, the opposite is true. For example, what would you, as a reader, make of these statements?

> To fully comprehend an individual, perambulate a league in his footwear.

> In the realm of the sightless, the uniorbed individual is sovereign.[1]

A thesaurus cannot be used to "translate" another writer's idea word-for-word into your own idea. Most readers are annoyed by unnecessarily "fancy" language (see Pretentious Language, page 14).

NEVER use a word whose meaning you do not know. When you find a possible but unfamiliar synonym, look it up to be sure it means what you need it to say.

LEVELS OF LANGUAGE

Good writing involves more than knowing the meaning of words and sentences. It also requires choosing appropriate language. No one would submit a book review that began, "This is an awesome book with, like, ideas that sort of make you think, you know?" It is instantly clear that the language is inappropriate. Similarly, if you were discussing the book with friends over a coffee and said, "This book contains provocative and stimulating ideas that engage and challenge the reader," your language would be equally inappropriate. In the same way that you choose what you wear to suit a particular occasion, you choose a level of language to suit your message. You wouldn't put on a bathing suit to attend a formal wedding, and you wouldn't wear a tux to the beach.

Written English (*Twitter* notwithstanding) is usually more formal than spoken English. Because writers have time to consider what they want to say and how best to say it, they can choose their words carefully, arrange them in meaningful sentences, and organize ideas into logical paragraphs. An appropriate level of language is an essential part of effective writing. Levels of language are defined by vocabulary, by length and complexity of sentences and paragraphs, and by tone (how the writing "sounds"). Choose a level that suits both your topic and your reader. There will be times when you need to compromise: when you send one message to a mixed audience, for example. In such cases, the safe bet is to aim at your highest-level reader and trust that the others will understand (or ask for clarification).

Sometimes it isn't clear what level you should be using. At such times, your reader's preference should determine your choice. Many colleges and universities expect students to write academic papers in formal English,

---

[1] To understand someone, walk a mile in his shoes.
In the land of the blind, the one-eyed man is king.

which requires, among other things, third-person pronouns (*he, she, one, they*). Informal writing, with its first- and second-person pronouns (*I, me, you*), may not be acceptable. (See page 86 for an explanation of "person.") Ask your instructor about your school's policy and follow it.

Similarly, because employers tend to favour formal letters of application over casual ones, if you want to get the job, you will write a formal letter. For a talk you give to your class, an informal, conversational style may be appropriate. Most of what you read and write falls somewhere in the middle. Business documents, for example, are usually written in general-level Standard English.

There are no fixed divisions of English. The three levels we've identified often overlap. In this book, for example, we use a variety of styles, ranging from high-level informal through general (used for most of the text), with a few formal-level passages when they are appropriate. To help you choose the most appropriate level for your message and audience, the table below outlines the basic features of informal, general, and formal written English.

No one level is "better" than another. Each has its place and function. Your message, your reader, and your purpose in writing should determine which level you choose.

	Informal	General	Formal
Vocabulary and Style	Casual, everyday; usually concrete; some slang, colloquial expressions, contractions; written in first and second persons	The language of educated persons; nonspecialized; balance of abstract and concrete; readily understood; can use first, second, and third persons	Often abstract, technical, or specialized; no contractions or colloquialisms; written in third person
Sentence and Paragraph Structure	Sentences short, simple; some sentence fragments; short paragraphs	Complete sentences of varying length; paragraphs vary, but are often fairly short	Complete sentences—often long, complex; paragraphs fully developed, often at length
Tone	Conversational, casual; sounds like ordinary speech	Varies to suit message and purpose of writer	Impersonal, serious, often instructional.
Typical Uses	Social media and some blogs; dialogue (in fiction); zines; much advertising	Most of what we read: websites, magazines, novels, business correspondence	Academic writing, some textbooks, scientific reports, journal articles, legal documents

Unless your instructor specifically says that you may use informal or colloquial language in your written work, use general-level English. The same rule applies to postings to online course discussion groups. Some instructors may be offended by colloquial voice-mail messages, too—especially if they are full of slang terms that teachers aren't always familiar with—and most will not be impressed by cliché- and slang-riddled emails. You and your instructor are not BFFs. Your relationship is a professional one, and your language should reflect your understanding of that relationship.

In the past few years, text-messaging short forms have been creeping into written assignments, reports, and even research papers and resumés. In these contexts, "text messagese" is so inappropriate and reflects so poorly on the writer that we urge you never to use it except on your cellphone. Why? Because these short forms are a code that some people may not understand, using short forms can hinder rather than help communication.

For the uninitiated, this exchange reads: "Question for you. Do you use text messaging?" "Yeah, I sure do. I'm always at the keyboard. How about you?"

The three paragraphs that follow, all on the same topic, illustrate informal, general, and formal written English.

INFORMAL

Rap's getting a bad rap. It's blamed for everything wrong with life in the city these days. Sure, the lyrics make violence sound OK, put women down, talk about people who do drugs, and describe the gangsta lifestyle as cool. But every kind of music has been attacked by the previous generation. Parents, priests, and politicians ganged up to scream about rock lyrics that today seem so tame, and the same groups went after jazz when it was popular. Even waltz music made parents crazy a couple of centuries ago when their kids enjoyed it. I just wonder what the kids of rap fans will listen to that will tick off their folks!

GENERAL

Rap music is being blamed for many of the problems of urban society. True, if you listen to the lyrics, you'll be exposed to glorified violence, women as sex objects, drug use, and the gangster lifestyle, along with other negative aspects of modern life. However, rap is simply following a long tradition of music adopted by young people that annoys their parents. Parents' groups, religious leaders, even the U.S. Congress were outraged by the now-innocent-seeming lyrics of rock music. The same groups spoke out against jazz a generation earlier. Even the stately waltz disgusted and horrified the parents of the 18th-century young people who embraced it. You have to wonder what music the children of rap fans will listen to that will offend their parents.

FORMAL

Rap music has become the scapegoat for many of the ills that afflict contemporary urban society. While it is demonstrable that the lyrics condone violent acts, promote misogyny, endorse the use of illicit drugs, and exalt an unlawful lifestyle, this musical genre is part of a historical continuum of music favoured by one generation that offends the previous generation. Parental lobby groups, religious leaders, and even Representatives in the U.S. Congress were incensed by rock musicians, whose lyrics now seem innocent, even naïve. The same coalition decried jazz in the previous generation, and even the serene and sophisticated waltz was greeted with disgust and predictions of moral collapse when it was introduced in the 18th century. One can only wonder what music the offspring of today's rap enthusiasts will embrace and thereby outrage their parents.

Go to Workbook Exercises 1.6–1.8

"LIKE, I GOT MY DEGREE IN LIKE, YOU KNOW, COMMUNICATIONS."

CAREER COUNSELOR

Jack Corbett/CartoonStock

We've introduced you to the tools you'll need as a writer and to the levels of language you can choose from when writing a message for a specific audience. Let's now turn to the writing errors you must not commit in any message to any audience: wordiness, slang, pretentious language, clichés, offensive language, and "abusages."

WORDINESS

One of the barriers to clear communication is **wordiness**, the unnecessary repetition of information or the use of two or more words when one would do. As a courtesy to your reader, you should make your writing as concise as possible.

Sometimes wordiness results from careless revision. In the editing stage of writing a paper, you should tighten up your sentences and paragraphs. Wordy or awkward phrasing often pops into your mind when you are struggling to express an idea, and it always appears in a first draft. However, there is no excuse for it to survive a careful edit and make its way into a final draft.

Here's an example of what can happen when a writer fails to prune his or her prose:

> In my personal opinion, the government of this country of ours needs an additional amount of meaningful input from the people of Canada.

The writer has chosen impressive-sounding phrases (*meaningful input, this country of ours*) and wordy but meaningless expressions (*personal opinion, an additional amount*) to produce a sentence so hard to read that it isn't worth the reader's effort to decipher. This wordy sentence could be nicely shortened to "In my opinion, our government needs to hear more from the people."

The following list contains some of the worst offenders we've collected from student writing, corporate memoranda, form letters, and advertisements.

Wordy	Concise
a large number of	many
absolutely nothing (*or* everything, complete, perfect)	nothing (*or* everything, complete, perfect)
actual (*or* true) fact	fact
almost always	usually
at that point in time	then
at the present time	now (*or* currently)
consensus of opinion	consensus
continue on	continue

Wordy	Concise
could possibly (*or* may possibly, might possibly)	could (*or* may, might)
crisis (*or* emergency) situation	crisis (*or* emergency)
due to the fact that	because
end result	result
equally as good	as good
few and far between	rare
final conclusion	conclusion
for the reason that	because
free gift	gift
I myself (*or* you yourself, *etc.*)	I (*or* you, *etc.*)
I personally think/feel	I think/feel
in actual fact	in fact
in every instance	always
in my opinion, I think	I think
in the near future	soon
in today's society/in this day and age	now (*or* today)
is (*or* are) able to	can
many different kinds	many kinds
mutual agreement (*or* cooperation)	agreement (*or* cooperation)
my personal opinion	my opinion
no other alternative	no alternative
personal friend	friend
real (*or* genuine) leather (*or* real antique, *etc.*)	leather (*or* antique, *etc.*)
really, very	*These words add nothing to your meaning. Leave them out.*
red in colour (*or* large in size, *etc.*)	red (*or* large, *etc.*)
repeat again	repeat
return back	return (*or* go back)
such as, for example	such as
take active steps	take steps
totally destroyed	destroyed
truly remarkable	remarkable
very (*or* most, quite, almost, rather) unique	unique
8:00 a.m. in the morning	8:00 a.m.

By studying these examples, you will see how such phrases add words but not meaning to your message. Teachers and editors call these phrases "fill" or "padding," and they urge students and business writers to eliminate them if they want to build a good relationship with their readers.

Go to Workbook Exercise 1.9

SLANG

Flink, bag salmon, and *spacker*: do you know what these words mean? Probably not. **Slang** is "street talk," nonstandard language used in conversation among people who belong to the same social group. It's a kind of private speech. Because slang expressions become outdated quickly and are understood by a limited group of people, they are not appropriate for a message intended for a general reader. There are thousands of slang expressions. If you're curious about them, browse through an online dictionary such as www.slangsite.com.

   If you are in doubt about a word, check your dictionary. The notation *sl.* (*slang*) or *inf.* (*informal*) appears after words that are slang or have a slang meaning. (Some words—for example, *house, cool*, and *bombed*—have both a standard meaning and a slang meaning.) If the word you're looking for isn't listed, chances are it's a slang term, and you should not use it in writing. Taking the time to choose words that are appropriate to written English increases your chances of communicating clearly and earning your readers' respect.

Go to Workbook Exercise 1.10

PRETENTIOUS LANGUAGE

The opposite of slang is **pretentious language**: words that are too formal for general writing. Never use a long, difficult, or obscure word when a simpler word will do. Your writing will be easier to read and your message clearer and more convincing if you write to inform rather than to impress.

You can recognize pretentious language easily: the words are long, complicated, and unnatural-sounding. If the average reader needs a dictionary to "translate" your words into general English, then your writing is inflated and inappropriate. Consider these examples:

Before we embark on our journey, we must refuel our vehicle.

The refrigerator is bare of comestibles, so it is time to repair to the local emporium and purchase victuals.

After consulting a dictionary, you could translate these pompous sentences into plain English:

Before we leave, we need to put gas in the car.

The refrigerator is empty, so we need to go to the store and buy some food.

But why would you? It's the writer's job to communicate, and a pretentious writer makes the reader do too much work. Here is a list of some common offenders, together with their general-level equivalents.

Pretentious	Clear
ascertain	find out
commence	begin
conceptualize	think
endeavour	try
facilitate	help
finalize	finish
manifest	show
reside	live
transmit	send
utilize	use
verbalize	say

The cure for pretentious language is simple: be considerate of your readers. If you want your readers to understand and respect you, write in a simple, straightforward style.

 Go to Workbook Exercise 1.11

CLICHÉS

Pretentious writing requires time and effort; clichéd writing requires neither. It is as easy and as thoughtless as casual talk. A **cliché** is a phrase that has been used so often it no longer communicates a meaningful idea.

> At this point in time, we have no choice but to focus our effort where it really counts: on the bottom line.

At this point in time, *we have no choice but, focus our effort, where it really counts*, and *on the bottom line*—all these phrases are clichés. They do not create a picture in the reader's mind, and if your reader cannot "see" what you're saying, no communication takes place. After a few cliché-filled sentences, readers will conclude, "There's nothing new here. It's all been said before." And they will stop reading.

Spoken English is full of clichés—we often use them as shortcuts to put our thoughts into words, and if our listener doesn't understand our meaning, we can always explain further. Writers, on the other hand, have time to plan what they want to say. They also have the opportunity to revise and edit. So writers are expected to communicate with more originality and precision than speakers.

If English is your first language, you will find clichés easy to recognize. When you can read the first few words of a phrase and fill in the rest automatically,

DEPARTMENT OF ENGLISH

"Did you remove all the clichés and slang from your term paper?"   "Like, totally, dude!"

Baloo Rex-May/CartoonStock

you know the phrase is a cliché: *better late than ___; thinking outside the ___; when push comes to ___; a pain in the ___.* If you are an English language learner, a good dictionary or a good friend will identify clichéd expressions for you.

The solution to a cliché problem involves time and thought, first to recognize the cliché and then to find a better way to express your idea. Think about what you want to say and then say it in your own words, not everyone else's.

Go to Workbook Exercise 1.12

OFFENSIVE LANGUAGE

The last thing you want to do when you write is offend your reader, even if you are writing a complaint. As we've seen, some words occasionally used in speech are *always* inappropriate in writing. Swear words, for example, are unacceptable in a written message. So are obscene words, even mild ones. Offensive language appears much stronger in print than in speech. It can shock and outrage a reader. Racist language and blasphemy (the use of names or objects that are sacred to a religion) are always unacceptable and deeply offensive.

Many writers have suffered the embarrassment of having a message read by someone for whom the message was not intended. What may seem when you write it to be an innocent joke or an emphatic expression could, if it is read by someone other than the person you sent it to, prove shocking to readers and mortifying to you. Before you send an angry email, save it as a draft and reread it later. You may decide to tone it down. And make sure you don't accidentally hit Reply All when you intend to reply only to a message's sender. Always think before you click Send.

Language has power. Our language shapes as well as reflects our attitudes and values. People who use racist, blasphemous, sexist, or profane terms reinforce the attitudes represented by those terms and also project a negative image to their readers.

ABUSAGES

Some words and phrases, even ones we hear in everyday speech, are *always* incorrect in written English. Technically, they are also incorrect in speech, but most people tolerate them as part of the casual standard that is common in conversation. If these expressions appear in your writing, your reader will assume you are uneducated, careless, or both. In some conversations, particularly in academic and professional environments, these expressions make a poor impression on your listeners.

Carefully read through the following list and highlight any words or phrases that sound correct to you. These are the ones you need to find and fix when you revise your writing.

alot	There is no such word. Use *much* or *many*. (*A lot* is acceptable in informal usage.)
anyways (anywheres)	The *s* on these words betrays the writer as uneducated.
between you and I	A very common error. Use *between you and me*.
can't hardly (couldn't hardly)	The correct expression is *can* (or *could*) *hardly*.
could of (would of, should of)	Using the preposition *of* instead of the auxiliary verb *have* in these verb phrases is a common error. Write *could have, would have*, and *should have*.
didn't do nothing	All double negatives are errors. Some familiar examples are *couldn't see nothing, won't go nowhere*, and *can't find nobody*. Write *didn't do anything, couldn't see anything, won't go anywhere*, and *can't find anybody*.

good *used as an adverb*	"How are you?" "I'm good." This all-too-common expression is incorrect (unless you mean to say that you are moral or ethical or saintly). If you want to say that you are healthy, then say, "I'm *well*."
irregardless	There is no such word. *Regardless* is the word you may want, but check your thesaurus for other, possibly more appropriate, choices.
media *used as singular*	The word *media* is plural. It is incorrect to say, "Television is a mass media." It is a mass *medium*. Newspapers, magazines, and the Internet are mass *media*. Radio is an electronic *medium*.
off of	Use *off* by itself. "I fell *off* the wagon." Or use *from*: "I fell *from* the wagon."
prejudice *used as an adjective*	It is incorrect to write "She is *prejudice* against teenagers." Use *prejudiced*.
prejudism	There is no such word. Use *prejudice* (a noun): "He showed *prejudice* in awarding the prize to his daughter."
real *used as an adverb*	*Real good*, *real bad*, and *real nice* are not acceptable. You could use *really* or *very* and be correct, but such filler words add nothing to your meaning.
the reason is because	Write *the reason is that*: "The reason is that my dog ate my essay."
suppose to	Like *use to*, this phrase is incorrect. Write *supposed to* and *used to*.
themselfs	Also *ourselfs*, *yourselfs*. The plural of *self* is *selves*: *ourselves*, *yourselves*, and *themselves*. *Theirselves* is nonstandard English and is not used by educated speakers and writers.
youse	There is no such word. *You* is both the singular and the plural form of the second-person pronoun. While occasionally heard in restaurants or retail stores, "Can I help youse?" labels the speaker as uneducated.

Go to Workbook Exercises 1.13–1.14

2 | Hazardous Homonyms

This chapter focuses on **homonyms**—words that sound alike or look alike and are easily confused: *your* and *you're; whose* and *who's; weather* and *whether; affect* and *effect*. Your word processor will not help you find mistakes in these words because the correct spelling depends on the sentence in which you use the word. For example, if you write, "Meat me hear inn halve an our," no spelling checker will find fault with your sentence, yet no reader will understand what you're talking about.

LIST OF COMMONLY CONFUSED WORDS

Below you will find a list of the most common homonym hazards. Only some of the words in this list will cause you trouble. Careful pronunciation can sometimes help you tell the difference between words that are often confused. For example, if you pronounce the words *accept* and *except* differently, you'll be less likely to use the wrong one when you write. It's also useful to make up memory aids to help you remember the differences in meanings between words that sound or look alike. The list that follows includes several examples that we hope you will find helpful.

Make your own list of paired words that cause you trouble and keep it where you can easily refer to it. Post it over your desk, or tuck it into your laptop. Get into the habit of checking your document against your list every time you write.

accept **except**	*Accept* means "t**a**ke" or "receive." It is always a verb. *Except* means "**ex**cluding."
	I *accepted* the spelling award, and no one *except* my mother knew I cheated.
advice **advise**	The difference in pronunciation makes the difference in meaning clear. *Advise* (rhymes with *wise*) is a verb. *Advice* (rhymes with *nice*) is a noun.
	I *advise* you not to listen to free *advice*.

Loren Fishman/CartoonStock

affect
effect

Affect as a verb means "to change." Try substituting *change* for the word you've chosen in your sentence. If it makes sense, then *af-FECT* is the word you want. As a noun, *AF-fect* means "a strong feeling." *EF-fect* is a noun meaning "result." If you can substitute *result*, then *effect* is the word you need. Occasionally, *ef-FECT* is used as a verb meaning "to bring about."

Learning about the *effects* (results) of caffeine *affected* (changed) my coffee-drinking habits.

Depressed people often display an inappropriate *affect* (feeling).

Antidepressant medications can *effect* (bring about) profound changes in mood.

a lot
allot

A lot (often misspelled *alot*) should be avoided in formal writing. Use *many* or *much* instead. *Allot* (*al-LOT*) means "distribute" or "assign."

>   *many*   *much*
> He still has a lot of problems, but he is coping a lot better.

> The teacher will *allot* the marks according to the difficulty of the questions.

allusion
illusion

An *allusion* is an implied or indirect reference. An *illusion* is something that appears to be real or true but is not what it seems. It can be a false impression, idea, or belief.

> Many literary *allusions* can be traced to the Bible or to Shakespeare.

> A good movie creates an *illusion* of reality.

are
our

Are is a verb. *Our* shows ownership. Confusion of these two words often results from careless pronunciation.

> Where *are our* leaders?

beside
besides

Beside is a preposition meaning "by the side of" or "next to." *Besides* means "also" or "in addition to."

> One evening with Tyler was more than enough. *Besides* expecting me to buy the tickets, the popcorn, and the drinks, he insisted on sitting *beside* Ashley rather than me.

choose
chose

Pronunciation gives the clue here. *Choose* rhymes with *booze*, is a present tense verb, and means "select." *Chose* rhymes with *rose*, is a past tense verb, and means "selected."

> Please *choose* a topic.

> I *chose* to write about fuel-cell technology.

cite
sight
site

To *cite* means "to quote from" or "to refer to."

> A lawyer *cites* precedents; writers *cite* their sources in articles or research papers; and my friends *cite* my texts as examples of comic writing.

Sight means "vision," the ability to see. It can also mean "something that is visible or worth seeing."

> She lost her *sight* as the result of an accident.

> With his tattoos and piercings, Izzy was a *sight* to behold.

A *site* is the location of something: a building, a town, or a historic event.

The *site* of the battle was the Plains of Abraham, which lie west of Québec City.

coarse
course

Coarse means "rough, unrefined." (The slang word *arse* is co**arse**.) For all other meanings, use *course*.

That sandpaper is too *coarse* to use on a lacquer finish.

Coarse language only weakens your argument.

Of *course* you'll do well in a *course* on the history of pop music.

complement
compliment

A *complement* comple**t**es something. *A compliment* is a gift of praise.

A glass of wine would be the perfect *complement* to the meal.

Many people are embarrassed by *compliments*.

conscience
conscious

Your *conscience* is your sense of right and wrong. *Conscious* means "aware" or "awake"—able to feel and think.

After Sarah cheated on the test, her *conscience* bothered her.

Sarah was *conscious* of having done wrong.

The injured man was *unconscious*.

consul
council
counsel

A *consul* is a government official stationed in another country. A *council* is an assembly or official group. Members of a *council* are *councillors*. *Counsel* can be used to mean both "advice" and "to advise."

The Canadian *consul* in Venice was helpful.

The Women's Advisory *Council* meets next month.

Brittany gave me good *counsel.*

She *counselled* me to hire a lawyer.

desert
dessert

A *DE-sert* is a dry, barren place. As a verb, *de-SERT* means "to abandon" or "to leave behind." *Des-SERT* is the part of a meal you'd probably like an extra helping of, so give it an extra *s*.

The tundra is Canada's only *desert* region.

If you *desert* me, I'll be all alone.

I can't resist any *dessert* made with chocolate.

"Just de-SERTS" (one *s*) is an expression meaning "what you/ they deserve." It is a cliché; do not use it.

the punishment they deserve.
This government thinks murderers do not get their just deserts.

dining
dinning

You'll spell *dining* correctly if you remember the phrase "wining and dining." You'll probably never use *dinning*, which means "making a loud noise."

The dog is not supposed to be in the *dining* room.

We are *dining* out tonight.

The noise from the karaoke bar was *dinning* in our ears.

does
dose

Pronunciation provides the clue. *Does* rhymes with *buzz* and is a verb. *Dose* rhymes with *gross* and refers to a quantity of medicine.

Josef *does* drive fast, *doesn't* he?

Playing outside provides kids a healthy *dose* of vitamin D.

forth
fourth

Forth means "**for**ward." *Fourth* contains the number **four**, which gives it its meaning.

Please stop pacing back and *forth*.

The Raptors lost their *fourth* game in a row.

hear
here

Hear is what you do with your **ear**s. *Here* is used for all other meanings.

Now *hear* this!

Ranjan isn't *here*.

Here is your assignment.

it's
its

It's is a shortened form of *it is*. The apostrophe takes the place of the *i* in *is*. If you can substitute *it is*, then *it's* is the form you need. If you can't substitute *it is*, then *its* is the correct word.

It's really not difficult. (It *is* really not difficult.)

The book has lost *its* cover. ("The book has lost it is cover" makes no sense, so you need *its*.)

It's is also commonly used as the shortened form of *it has*. In this case, the apostrophe takes the place of the *h* and the *a*.

It's been a bad month for new car sales.

knew
new

Knew is the past tense of *know*. *New* is an adjective meaning "having recently come into being," "fresh," or "original."

We *knew* our *new* pool would attract friends just as surely as fruit attracts flies.

Who would have thought that cropped pants, a style from the 1950s, would be considered a *new* fashion nearly 60 years later?

know
no

Know is a verb meaning "to understand" or "to recognize." *No* can be used as an adverb to express refusal or denial, or as an adjective to express a negative state or condition.

No, we do not *know* the results of the test yet.

Why are there *no* cookies left in the jar?

later
latter

Later rhymes with *gator*, refers to time, and has the word *late* in it. *Latter* rhymes with *fatter*, means "the second of two," and has two *t*s. It is the opposite of *former*.

See you *later*, alligator.

You take the former, and I'll take the *latter*.

lead
led

Lead is pronounced to rhyme with *speed* and is the present tense of the verb *to lead*. (*Led* is the past tense of the same verb.) The only time you pronounce *lead* as "led" is when you are referring to the writing substance in a pencil or to the metal used to make bullets or leaded windows.

You *lead*, and I'll decide whether to follow.

Your suitcase is so heavy it must be filled with either gold or *lead*.

After we changed into our bathing suits, our host *led* us to her private pool.

loose
lose

Pronunciation is the key to these words. *Loose* rhymes with *moose* and means "not tight" or "unrestricted." *Lose* rhymes with *ooze* and means "misplace" or "be defeated."

There's a screw *loose* somewhere.

When Moosehead beer is served, people say, "The moose is *loose*!"

Did you *lose* your keys again?

You can't *lose* on this deal.

miner **minor**	A *miner* works in a **mine**. *Minor* means "lesser" or "not important" or "a person who is not legally an adult." Liquor can be served to *miners*, but not if they are *minors*. For some people, spelling is a *minor* problem.
moral **morale**	Again, pronunciation provides the clue you need. *MOR-al* refers to the understanding of what is right and wrong; *mo-RALE* refers to the spirit or mental condition of a person or group. Most religions are based on a *moral* code of behaviour. Despite his shortcomings, he is basically a *moral* man. Low *morale* is the reason for our employees' absenteeism.
passed **past**	*Passed* is the past tense of the verb *pass*, which has several meanings, most of which have to do with movement on land or water but some of which have to do with sports or games. *Past* describes something that happened or existed in an earlier time. *Passed* is always a verb; *past* can be a noun, adjective, adverb, or preposition, but it is never a verb. George *passed* the puck to Henry, who slammed it *past* the goalie to win the game.
peace **piece**	*Peace* is what we want on **Ea**rth. *Piece* means "a part or portion of something," as in "a **pie**ce of **pie**." Everyone hopes for *peace* in the Middle East. A *piece* of the puzzle is missing.
personal **personnel**	*PER-sonal* means "private." *Personnel* (*person-NEL*) refers to the group of people working for a particular employer or to the office responsible for maintaining employees' records. The letter was marked "*Personal* and Confidential." We are fortunate to have highly qualified *personnel*.
principal **principle**	*Principal* means "m**a**in." A *princip**le*** is a ru**le**. A *principal* is the main administrator of a school. The federal government is the *principal* employer in Summerside, P.E.I. The *principal* and the interest totalled more than I could pay. (In this case, the principal is the main amount of money.) One of our instructor's *principles* is to refuse to accept late assignments.

quiet
quite

If you pronounce these words carefully, you won't confuse them. *Quiet* has two syllables (kwy-et); *quite* has only one (kwyt).

The chairperson asked us to be *quiet*.

We had not *quite* finished our assignment.

stationary
stationery

Stationary means "fixed in place." *Stationery* is writing pap**er**.

A *stationary* bicycle will give you a good cardio workout without stressing your knees.

Please order a new supply of *stationery*.

than
then

Than is used in comparisons: bigger than, better than, slower than, and so on. Pronounce it to rhyme with *can*. *Then* refers to time and rhymes with *when*.

Kim is a better speller *than* I.

I'd rather be here *than* there.

Pay me first, and *then* you can have my notes.

their
there
they're

Their indicates ownership. ***There*** points out something or indicates place. It includes the word ***here***, which also indicates place. *They're* is a shortened form of *they are*. (The apostrophe replaces the *a* in *are*.)

It was *their* fault.

There are two weeks left in the term.

Let's walk over *there*.

They're late, as usual.

threw
through

Threw is the past tense of the verb *throw*. *Through* can be used as a preposition, adjective, or adverb, but never as a verb.

James *threw* the ball *through* the kitchen window. When he climbed *through* to fetch it, his mother angrily told him that his days of playing catch in the yard were *through*.

too
two
to

The *too* with an extra *o* in it means "more than enough" or "also." *Two* is the number after one. For all other meanings, use *to*.

It's *too* hot, and I'm *too* tired *to* go for another hike.

There are *two* sides *to* every argument.

The *two* women knew *too* much about each other *to* be friends.

wear **were** **where** **we're**	If you pronounce these words carefully, you won't confuse them. *Wear* rhymes with *pear* and can be a noun or a verb. *Were* rhymes with *purr* and is a verb. ***Where*** is pronounced "hwear," includes the word ***here***, and indicates place. *We're* is a shortened form of *we are* and is pronounced "weer."

After 360 000 km, you shouldn't be surprised that your car is showing signs of *wear* and tear.

What should I *wear* to the wedding?

You *were* joking, *weren't* you?

Where did you want to meet?

We're on our way.

weather **whether**	*Weather* refers to climatic conditions: temperature and humidity, for example. *Whether* means "if" and is used in indirect questions or to introduce two alternatives.

We're determined to go camping this weekend, no matter what the *weather* is like. We'll pack enough gear to be prepared *whether* it rains or it shines.

who's **whose**	*Who's* is a shortened form of *who is* or *who has*. If you can substitute *who is* or *who has* for the *who's* in your sentence, then you have the right spelling. Otherwise, use *whose*.

Who's coming to dinner? (*Who is* coming to dinner?)

Who's been sleeping in my bed? (*Who has* been sleeping in my bed?)

Whose paper is this? ("*Who is* paper is this" makes no sense, so you need *whose*.)

woman
women

Confusing these two is guaranteed to irritate your female readers. *Woman* is the singular form; compare **man**. *Women* is the plural form; compare **men**.

Only one *woman* responded to our ad.

Our company sponsors both a *women's* team and a men's team.

you're
your

You're is a shortened form of *you are*. If you can substitute *you are* for the *you're* in your sentence, then you're using the correct form. If you can't substitute *you are*, use *your*, a possessive.

You're welcome. (*You are* welcome.)

Unfortunately, *your* hamburger got burned. ("You are hamburger got burned" makes no sense, so *your* is the word you want.)

 Go to Workbook Exercises 2.1–2.11

3 | The Apostrophe

What, you may ask, is a chapter on apostrophes doing in a unit on words? Why isn't it in Unit 4 with the other punctuation marks? Here's the reason: while all other punctuation marks show the intended relationship among parts of a sentence, apostrophes show the relationship between two words (in a possessive construction) or two parts of one word (in a contraction). Misused apostrophes change the meaning of words, and that is why we are discussing them here.

Below is a sentence from a letter of application. Can you spot how it reveals the applicant's poor writing skills?

> I would like to contribute to you're companies success as it enters it's second decade of outstanding service to customer's.

Misused apostrophes confuse, amuse, and sometimes annoy readers. Using them correctly is an indication that the writer is competent and careful. The example above contains four apostrophe errors, which irritated the reader so much that the applicant didn't even make it to the interview stage.

- Sometimes you need an apostrophe so your reader can understand what you mean. For example, there's a world of difference between these two sentences:

  > The instructor began class by calling the students' names.

  > The instructor began class by calling the students names.

- In most cases, however, misused apostrophes just amuse or annoy an alert reader:

  > The movie had it's moments.

  > He does a days' work every week.

  > The Green's thank you for your donation.

It isn't difficult to avoid such mistakes. Correctly used, the apostrophe indicates either **contraction** or **possession**. An apostrophe NEVER makes a singular word plural. The following three sentences show you where to use—and not use—apostrophes:

1. The dog's chasing cars again. (Contraction: *dog's = dog is*)

2. The dog's bark is more reliable than the doorbell. (Possessive: the bark belongs to the dog)

3. **The dogs bark incessantly.** (Plural: no apostrophe)

CONTRACTION

Contraction is the combining of two words into one, as in *they're* or *can't*. Contractions are common in conversation and in informal written English. Unless you are quoting someone else's words, however, you should avoid using them in the writing you do for school or work.

When two words are combined into one, and one or more letters are left out, the apostrophe goes in the place of the missing letter(s).

Here are some examples.

I am → I'm	they are → they're
we will → we'll	it is → it's
she is → she's	it has → it's
do not → don't	who has → who's

RGJ Richard Jolley/CartoonStock

Go to Workbook Exercises 3.1–3.4

POSSESSION

The apostrophe is also used to show ownership or **possession**. Here's the rule that applies in most cases:

If the owner word is singular, add *'s* to indicate possession.
If the owner word is plural and ends in *s*, add only an apostrophe.

Here are some examples that illustrate the rule.

singer + 's = singer's voice
band + 's = band's instruments
players + 's = players's uniforms
ships + 's = ships's sails

women + 's = women's voices
James + 's = James's attitude
students + s = students's report cards
colleges + s = colleges's teams

To form a possessive, first find the word in the sentence that identifies the owner. Then decide if the owner is singular or plural. For example, "the managers duties" can have two meanings, depending on where you put the apostrophe:

the manager's duties (the duties belong to one *manager*)

the managers' duties (the duties belong to two or more *managers*)

To solve an apostrophe placement problem, follow this two-step process:

1. Find the owner word.
2. Apply the possession rule.

Problem: Laras hair is a mess.
Solution: 1. The owner word is *Lara* (singular)
                2. Add *'s* to *Lara*

Lara's hair is a mess.

Problem: The technicians strike stopped production.
Solution: 1. The owner word is *technicians* (plural)
         2. Add an apostrophe: *technicians'*

The *technicians'* strike stopped production.

Sometimes the meaning of your sentence is determined by where you put the apostrophe.

Problem: The writer was delighted by the critics response to her book.

You have two possibilities to choose from, depending on your meaning.

Solution A: 1. The owner word is *critic* (singular)
          2. Add *'s* to *critic*

The writer was delighted by the *critic's* response to her book.

Solution B: 1. The owner word is *critics* (plural)
          2. Add an apostrophe to *critics*

The writer was delighted by the *critics'* response to her book.

Both solutions are correct, depending on whether the book was reviewed by one critic (Solution A) or by more than one critic (Solution B).
    Possession does not have to be literal. It can be used to express the notion of "belonging to" or "associated with." That is, the owner word need not refer to a person or group of people. Ideas or concepts (abstract nouns) can be "owners" too.

today's news = the news of today

a month's vacation = a vacation of one month

a year's salary = the salary of one year

   Go to Workbook Exercise 3.5

A few words, called **possessive pronouns**, are already possessive in form, so they don't have apostrophes.

yours	ours
hers, his, its	theirs
whose	whose

The decision is *hers*, not *yours*.

Whose story do you believe, *ours* or *his*?

The dog has lost *its* bone.

Four possessive words (*its, theirs, whose,* and *your*) are often confused with the contractions that sound like them. When deciding which spelling to use, expand the contraction into its original two words and try those words in your sentence. If the sentence still makes sense, use the contraction. If it doesn't, use the possessive.

Possessive	Contraction
its = *it* owns something	it's = it is/it has
their = *they* own something	they're = they are
whose = *who* owns something	who's = who is/who has
your = *you* own something	you're = you are

Error: They're (they are) going to sing *they're* (they are) latest song.
Revision: They're going to sing *their* latest song.

Error: It's (it is) *you're* (you are) favourite song.
Revision: It's *your* favourite song.

Error: Who's (Who is) CD are you listening to?
Revision: *Whose* CD are you listening to?

Error: My car has a hole in it's (it is) muffler.
Revision: My car has a hole in *its* muffler.

 Go to Workbook Exercises 3.6–3.8

PLURALS

The third apostrophe rule is very simple. Memorize it, apply it, and you will instantly correct many of your apostrophe errors.

NEVER use an apostrophe to make a word plural.

The plural of most English words is formed by adding *s* to the root word, not *'s*. The *s* alone tells the reader that the word is plural. For example, *memos, letters, files, broadcasts, tweets, newspapers*. If you add an apostrophe + *s*, you are telling your reader that the word is either a contraction or a possessive.

Incorrect: Never use apostrophe's to make word's plural.
Correct: Never use apostrophes to make words plural.

Go to Workbook Exercises 3.9–3.12

**I'm sorry, but shouldn't there be
an apostrophe in that?**

Nigel Sutherland/CartoonStock

Jim Naylor/CartoonStock

"More might have turned up, Sir, if you had put

the apostrophe in the correct place..."

Before you do the mastery test for this chapter, carefully review the information in the Summary box below.

SUMMARY

APOSTROPHE RULES

- When contracting two words into one, put an apostrophe in the place of the missing letter(s).
- Watch for owner words: they need apostrophes.
- To indicate possession, add *'s* to the owner word. (If the owner word is plural and already ends in *s*, add just the apostrophe.)
- Possessive pronouns (e.g., *yours*, *its*, *ours*) do not take apostrophes.
- Never use an apostrophe to form the plural of a word.

Go to Workbook Exercise 3.13

Capital Letters | 4

Capital letters belong in a few specific places and nowhere else. Some writers suffer from "capitalitis." They put capital letters on words without thinking about their position, function, or meaning in a sentence. Other writers seem too lazy to use the shift key; their sentences ignore the sense or purpose of specific words.

WHEN TO USE CAPITALS

Capitalize the first letter of any word that fits into one of the six categories highlighted below.

1. Capitalize the first word of a sentence, a direct quotation, or a sentence from a quoted source.

Are you illiterate? Write to us today for free help.

"It was a dark and stormy night," typed Snoopy.

Lister Sinclair stated, "The only thing Canadians have in common is that we all hate Toronto."

 Go to Workbook Exercise 4.1

2. Capitalize the names of specific people, places, and things.

Names of people (and their titles):

Feist, Governor General David Johnston, the Reverend Henry Jones, Professor Ursula Franklin, Senator Serge Joyal, Sergeant Preston, Ms. Akila Hashemi

Names of places, regions, and astronomical bodies (but not general geographical directions):

> Stanley Park, Lake Superior, Cape Breton Island; Nunavut, the Prairies, the Badlands; Saturn, Earth, the planet Mercury, the Asteroid Belt; south, north, east, west

Official names of buildings, institutions, organizations, companies, departments, and products:

> the National Art Gallery; McGill University, Camosun College; the Liberal Party, the Kiwanis Club; Petro-Canada, Rogers; the Department of English, the Human Resources Department; Kleenex, Volvo, Labatt Blue

Go to Workbook Exercise 4.2

3. Capitalize the names of major historical events, historical periods, religions, holy texts, and holy days.

> World War I, the Depression; the Renaissance, the Industrial Age; Judaism, Islam, Christianity, Buddhism, Hinduism; the Torah, the Koran, the Bible, the Upanishads; Easter, Ramadan, Yom Kippur

Go to Workbook Exercise 4.3

4. Capitalize the days of the week, months of the year, and specific holidays—but not the seasons.

> Monday; June; Remembrance Day, Canada Day; spring, autumn, winter

Go to Workbook Exercise 4.4

5. Capitalize major words in titles (books, magazines, films, essays, poems, songs, works of art, names of websites). Do not capitalize minor words (articles, prepositions, coordinating conjunctions) unless the word is the first or last word in the title. *Note:* Not all documentation styles follow this rule.

Eats, Shoots, and Leaves (book)   The Thinker (sculpture)
Of Mice and Men (book, film)   "The Case against Quickspeak" (essay)
Maclean's (magazine)   "In Flanders Fields" (poem)
Harry Potter and the Goblet of   Facebook (website)
  of Fire (book, film)

Go to Workbook Exercise 4.5

Pay special attention to this next category. It is one that causes every writer trouble.

6. Capitalize the names of specific school courses

Marketing 101, Psychology 100, Mathematics 220, English 110

but not the names of subject areas

marketing, sociology, mathematics, history, literature, poetry

unless the subjects are languages or pertain to specific geographical areas.

English, Greek; the study of Chinese history, modern Caribbean literature, Latin American poetry

Note: Names of languages, countries, and geographical regions are *always* capitalized: Spanish, Chinese, English; Spain, China, Canada; the Basque Region, Hong Kong, the Maritimes.

Go to Workbook Exercises 4.6–4.9

Sentences

Before you start this unit, complete the Quick Quiz. Once you have finished this unit, complete the Rapid Review.

5 | Cracking the Sentence Code

A baby's first word is a big step, one that all parents mark as a significant stage of development. Not all parents recognize that an even more significant step in a baby's progress is the first time she or he puts together the two elements of a complete sentence: a subject and a verb. *Words* enable us to communicate images; *sentences* are the tools with which we communicate ideas.

There is nothing mysterious or difficult about sentences. You've been speaking them successfully since you were a toddler. The difficulty occurs when you try to write—not sentences, oddly enough, but paragraphs. Most college students, if asked to write 10 sentences on 10 different topics, could do so without error. But when those same students write paragraphs, errors such as fragments and run-ons appear. Sometimes these errors cause a communication failure; at other times, they cause the reader to think poorly of the writer.

The solution to sentence-structure problems has two parts.

Be sure every sentence you write
• has both a subject and a verb and
• expresses a complete thought

If English is your first language, test your sentences by reading them aloud. You should be able to tell from their sound whether they are complete and clear. Sometimes, however, your ear may mislead you, so this chapter will show you, step by step, how to decode your sentences to find their subjects and verbs. If English is not your first language, you need to learn how to find the subject and verb in every sentence you write. When you know how to decode sentences, you can make sure that every sentence is complete.

Read the following sentences aloud:

Video gaming is the world's newest spectator sport.

Although video gaming is still a young spectator sport.

The second "sentence" doesn't sound right, does it? It does not make sense on its own and is, in fact, a sentence fragment.

Testing your sentences by reading them aloud won't work if you read your paragraphs straight through from beginning to end. The trick is to read from the end to the beginning. That is, read your last sentence aloud and *listen* to it. If it sounds all right, then read aloud the next-to-last sentence, and so on, until you have worked your way back to the first sentence you wrote.

Now, what do you do with the ones that don't sound right? Before you can fix them, you need to decode each sentence to find out if it has both a subject and a verb. The subject and the verb are the bare essentials of a sentence. Every sentence you write must contain both. There is one exception:

In a **command**, the subject is suggested rather than stated.

Consider these examples:

Sign here. = [You] sign here. (The subject you is implied or understood.)

Charge it. = [You] charge it.

Play ball! = [You] play ball!

S. Harris/CartoonStock

"MY INVENTION IS EVEN MORE REMARKABLE THAN YOURS. IT IS THE SIMPLE DECLARATIVE SENTENCE."

FINDING SUBJECTS AND VERBS

A sentence is about *someone* or *something*. That someone or something is the **subject**.[1] The word (or words) that tells what the subject *is* or *does* is the **verb**. In the following sentences, the subject is underlined once and the verb twice.

Snow falls.

Lily dislikes winter.

We love snowboarding.

Mt. Washington offers excellent opportunities for winter sports.

In Canada, winter is six months long.

Some people feel the cold severely.

The subject of a sentence is always a **noun** (the name of a person, place, thing, or concept) or a **pronoun** (a word such as *I, you, he, they, all,* or *everyone* used in place of a noun). In the examples above, the subjects include persons (*Lily, we, people*); a place (*Mt. Washington*); a thing (*snow*); and a concept (*winter*). In one sentence, a pronoun (*we*) is the subject.

Find the verb first.

One way to find the verb in a sentence is to ask what the sentence says about the subject. There are two kinds of verbs:

- **Action verbs** tell you what the subject is doing. In the examples above, *falls, dislikes, love,* and *offers* are action verbs.
- **Linking verbs** link or connect a subject to a noun or adjective describing that subject. In the examples above, *is* and *feel* are linking verbs. Linking verbs tell you the subject's condition or state of being. (e.g., "Tadpoles *become* frogs," "Frogs *feel* slimy.") The most common linking verbs are forms of *to be* (*am, is, are, was, were, have been,* etc.) and verbs such as *look, taste, feel, sound, appear, remain, seem,* and *become.*

Another way to find the verb in a sentence is to put a pronoun (*I, you, he, she, it, we,* or *they*) in front of the word you think is the verb. If the result makes sense, it is a verb. For example, you could put *it* in front of *falls* in the first

---

[1] If you have forgotten (or have never learned) the parts of speech and the basic sentence patterns, you will find this information in Appendix A (pages 287–294).

sentence listed above: "It falls" makes sense, so you know *falls* is the verb in this sentence. Try this test with the other five sample sentences.

Keep these guidelines in mind as you work through the exercises:

To find the subject, ask who or what the sentence is about.
To find the verb, ask what the subject is or is doing.

Go to Workbook Exercises 5.1–5.2

Usually, but not always, the subject comes before the verb in a sentence.

Occasionally, we find the subject after the verb:

- In sentences beginning with *Here* + a form of *to be* or *there* + a form of *to be* (*here* and *there* are never the subject of a sentence):

  Here are the test results. (Who or what are? Results.)

  There is a fly in my soup. (Who or what is? A fly.)

- In sentences that are deliberately inverted for emphasis or variety:

  Finally, at the end of the long, boring joke came the pathetic punch line.

  Out of the stadium and into the rain marched the demonstrators.

- In questions:

  Are we there yet?

  Is she the one?

But notice that in questions beginning with *Who, Whose, What,* or *Which,* the subject and verb are in normal order: subject followed by verb.

Who ate my sandwich?   Whose horse came first?

What caused the accident?   Which car uses less gas?

Go to Workbook Exercise 5.3

MORE ABOUT VERBS

The verb in a sentence may be a single word, as in the exercises you've just done, or it may be a group of words. When you are considering whether or not a word group is a verb, there are two points you should remember:

1. No verb form preceded by *to* is ever the verb of a sentence.[2]
2. **Helping verbs**[3] are often added to main verbs.

The list below contains the most common helping verbs.

be (all forms, including *am, are, is, was, were, will be, have/had been*)	can	could/could have
	do/did	have/had
	may/may have	might/might have
	must/must have	ought/ought to have
	shall/shall have	should/should have
	will/will have	would/would have

The complete verb in a sentence consists of any **helping verbs** + the **main verb**.

Below are a few of the forms of the verb *to take*. Study this list carefully, and note that when the sentence is in question form, the subject comes between the helping verb and the main verb.

We <u>are taking</u> a required English course.

You <u>must take</u> the prerequisite course.

We <u>should have taken</u> your advice.

---

[2] The form *to* + verb (e.g., *to speak, to write, to help*) is an **infinitive**. Infinitives can act as subjects or objects, but they are never verbs.

[3] If you are familiar with technical grammatical terms, you will know these verbs as **auxiliary verbs**. They also include modal auxiliaries and conditional forms (see Chapter 29).

You <u>can take</u> it with you.

You <u>may take</u> a break now.

We <u>might take</u> the championship.

Alice <u>ought to take</u> a course in stress management.

Shall we <u>take</u> the offer?

<u>Could</u> we <u>have taken</u> a wrong turn?

One verb form ALWAYS requires a helping verb. Here's the rule:

A verb ending in *-ing* must have a helping verb (or verbs) before it.

Here are a few of the forms a verb ending in *-ing* can take:

Mira <u>is taking</u> the test.

<u>Am</u> I <u>taking</u> your place?

You <u>are taking</u> an awfully long time.

<u>Have</u> you <u>been taking</u> French lessons?

Go to Workbook Exercise 5.4

Beware of certain words that are often confused with helping verbs:

Words such as *always, ever, just, never, not, often, only,* and *sometimes* are NOT part of the verb.

These words usually appear in the middle of a verb phrase, but they are modifiers, not verbs. Do not underline them.

Sofia <u>is</u> always <u>chosen</u> first.

<u>Will</u> you never <u>learn</u>?

<u>Do</u> you ever <u>have</u> doubts about your ability?

I <u>have</u> often <u>wondered</u> about that.

They <u>have</u> just <u>been married</u>.

That question <u>has</u> never before <u>been asked</u>.

Go to Workbook Exercises 5.5–5.6

MORE ABOUT SUBJECTS

Groups of words called **prepositional phrases** often come before the subject in a sentence or between the subject and the verb. When you're looking for the subject, prepositional phrases can trip you up unless you know the following rule:

The subject of a sentence is NEVER in a prepositional phrase.

You must be able to identify prepositional phrases so that you will know where *not* to look for the subject.

A prepositional phrase is a group of words that begins with a **preposition** and ends with a noun or pronoun.[4]

This noun or pronoun is called the **object** of the preposition. It is this word that, if you're not careful, you may think is the subject of the sentence.

Below is a list of prepositional phrases. The highlighted words are prepositions; the words in regular type are their objects.

about your message	around the office	concerning your request
above the door	at the meeting	despite the shortfall
according to the book	before lunch	down the corridor
after the meeting	behind my back	except the contract workers
against the wall	below the window	for the manager
along the hall	beside my computer	from the office
among the staff	between them	
	by the way	

---

[4] If you are studying English as an additional language, you will find useful information about prepositions in Chapter 32.

in the filing cabinet	on the desk	under the table
inside the office	onto the floor	until the meeting
into the elevator	over the page	up the corridor
near the wall	through the window	with permission
of the memo	to the staff	without the software

Before you look for the subject in a sentence, lightly cross out all prepositional phrases.

A bird in the hand is messy.	What is messy? The bird, not the hand.
Walking under a ladder is bad luck.	What is bad luck? Walking, not the ladder.
Many houses in our neighbourhood need painting.	What needs painting? The houses, not the neighbourhood.

Go to Workbook Exercises 5.7–5.9

MULTIPLE SUBJECTS AND VERBS

So far, you have been decoding sentences containing a single subject and a single verb, even though the verb may have consisted of more than one word. Sentences can, however, have more than one subject and one verb. Multiple subjects are called **compound subjects**; multiple verbs are **compound verbs**.

Here is a sentence with a multiple subject:

Coffee and a doughnut are Brian's idea of a balanced breakfast.

This sentence has a multiple verb:

Aysha walks and dresses like a supermodel.

And this sentence contains both a multiple subject and a multiple verb.

Kevin and Jaden drove to the mall and shopped for hours.

The parts of a multiple subject are usually joined by *and* or *or*, sometimes by *but* or *nor*. Compound subjects and verbs may contain more than two elements. Look at the following examples.

Clarity, brevity, and simplicity are the basic qualities of good writing.

Dev deleted his work, shut down his computer, unplugged it, and dropped it out the window.

Go to Workbook Exercises 5.10–5.12

Here's a summary of what you've learned in this chapter. Keep it in front of you as you write the Mastery Test.

SUMMARY

SUBJECTS AND VERBS

- The subject is *who* or *what* the sentence is about.
- The verb tells what the subject *is* or *does*.
- The subject normally comes before the verb. (Exceptions are questions, sentences that begin with *here* or *there*, and some sentences that begin with prepositional phrases.)
- An infinitive (a phrase consisting of *to* + verb) is never the verb of a sentence.
- The complete verb consists of a main verb + any helping verbs.
- A word ending in *-ing* is not, by itself, a verb.
- The subject of a sentence is never in a prepositional phrase.
- A sentence can have more than one subject and verb.

Go to Workbook Exercise 5.13

Solving Sentence-Fragment Problems

Every complete sentence has two characteristics: It contains a subject and a verb, and it expresses a complete thought. Any group of words that is punctuated as a sentence but lacks one of these characteristics is a **sentence fragment**. Fragments are appropriate in conversation and in some kinds of writing, but normally they are not acceptable in college, business, or technical writing.

The two kinds of fragments you should watch out for are
• the "missing piece" fragment and
• the dependent clause fragment

"MISSING PIECE" FRAGMENTS

Sometimes a group of words is punctuated as a sentence but is missing one or both of its essential parts: a subject and a verb. Consider the following examples:

1. Won the award for creativity.
   (Who or what won the award? The sentence doesn't tell you. The subject is missing.)

2. Their arguments about politics.
   (The sentence doesn't tell you what the arguments were or did. The verb is missing.)

3. The team missing two of its best players.
   (Part of the verb is missing. Remember that a verb ending in -*ing* needs a helping verb to be complete.)

4. During the mid-term break.
   (Who or what was or did what during the mid-term break? Both the subject and the verb are missing.)

Finding fragments like these in your work is the hard part. Fixing them is easy. There are two ways to correct sentence fragments. Here's the first one:

> To change a "missing piece" fragment into a complete sentence, add whatever is missing: a subject, a verb, or both.

1. You may need to add a subject:

   Meiling's design won the award for creativity.

2. You may need to add a verb:

   Their arguments were about politics. (linking verb)

   Their arguments about politics destroyed their relationship. (action verb)

3. You may need to add a helping verb:

   The team was missing two of its best players.

4. Or you may need to add both a subject and a verb:

   During the mid-term break, Arbi completed a draft of his major paper.

Don't let the length of a fragment fool you. Students sometimes think that if a string of words is long, it must be a sentence. Not so. No matter how long the string of words, if it doesn't contain both a subject and a verb, it is not a sentence. For example, here's a description of a woman paddling a canoe on a lake in summertime:

> The paddle dipping into the lake, sliding beneath the surface, and emerging at the end of the stroke, the face of the paddle glistening in the sun and droplets from its edge making a trail in the water as she reaches forward to dip again just as before, repeating the movement hundreds of times, thousands of times, in a hypnotic rhythm that becomes as natural as breathing, as calming as meditation.

At 71 words, this "sentence" is long, but it is a fragment. It lacks both a subject and a verb. If you add "She watches" at the beginning of the fragment, you would have a complete sentence.

THE FIRST SENTENCE FRAGMENT

Baloo Rex-May/CartoonStock

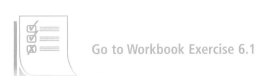

Go to Workbook Exercise 6.1

Most of us can identify a fragment when it stands alone. But when we write, of course, we write in paragraphs, not in single sentences. Fragments are harder to identify when they occur in a context.

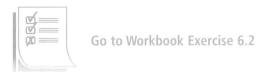

Go to Workbook Exercise 6.2

Once you have learned to identify fragments that occur within a paragraph, it's time to consider the best way to correct them. You could fix all of them the way you did in Exercise 6.1, by adding the missing piece or pieces to each fragment, and in some cases, that is your only choice. However, there is another, shorter, way that can often be used to correct fragments in a paragraph.

You can sometimes correct a "missing piece" fragment by attaching it to a complete sentence that comes before or after it—whichever makes better sense.

Sometimes you need to put a comma between a "missing piece" fragment and the complete sentence to which you attach it. (See Chapter 17, "The Comma," Rules 3 and 4.)

Go to Workbook Exercises 6.3–6.5

DEPENDENT CLAUSE FRAGMENTS

Any group of words containing a subject and a verb is a **clause**. There are two kinds of clauses. An **independent clause** is one that makes complete sense. It can stand alone as a sentence. A **dependent clause**, as its name suggests, cannot stand alone as a sentence. It depends on (and must be attached to) another clause to make sense.

Dependent clauses (also known as subordinate clauses) begin with dependent clause cues (technically known as **subordinating conjunctions**):

Dependent Clause Cues

after	that
although	though
as, as if	unless
as long as	until
as soon as	what, whatever
because	when, whenever
before	where, wherever
even if, even though	whether
if	which, whichever
just as	while
since	who, whose
so (that)	

Whenever a clause begins with one of these words or phrases, it is dependent.

A dependent clause must be attached to an independent clause. If it stands alone, it is a sentence fragment.

Here is an independent clause:

Mildred writes a daily blog.

If we put one of the dependent clause cues in front of it, it can no longer stand alone:

Although Mildred writes a daily blog

We can correct this kind of fragment by attaching it to an independent clause:

Although Mildred writes a daily blog, she has almost nothing to say.

 Go to Workbook Exercise 6.6

Most sentence fragments are dependent clauses punctuated as sentences. Fortunately, these are the easiest fragments to fix.

To correct a dependent clause fragment, join it either to the sentence that comes before it or to the one that comes after it—whichever link makes the most sense.

Problem: We want to move into our new apartment. As soon as the current tenants leave. It's perfect for our family.

The second "sentence" is incomplete. The dependent clause cue *as soon as* is the clue you need to identify it as a sentence fragment. You could join the fragment to the sentence that follows it, but then you would get "As soon as the new tenants leave, it's perfect for our family," which doesn't make sense. This fragment should be linked to the sentence before it.

Revision: We want to move into our new apartment as soon as the current tenants leave. It's perfect for our family.

If, as in the example above, your revised sentence *ends* with the dependent clause, you do not need to use a comma before it. If, however, your revised sentence *begins* with the dependent clause, put a comma between it and the independent clause that follows.

As soon as the current tenants leave, we want to move into our new apartment. It's perfect for our family. (See Chapter 17, "The Comma," Rule 3.)

Go to Workbook Exercises 6.7–6.12

Solving Run-On Sentence Problems

Some sentences lack essential elements and thus are fragments. Other sentences contain two or more independent clauses that are incorrectly linked together. A sentence with inadequate punctuation between clauses is a **run-on**. Run-ons tend to occur when you write in a hurry and don't take time to revise your work. If you remember the essential components of a sentence and punctuate carefully, you should have few problems with run-ons.

There are two kinds of run-on sentence to watch out for: comma splices and fused sentences.

COMMA SPLICES

As its name suggests, the **comma splice** occurs when two complete sentences (independent clauses) are joined (or spliced) by a comma. Consider these examples:

Yogurt is good for you, poutine is not.

This film is boring, it has no plot.

FUSED SENTENCES

A **fused sentence** occurs when two complete sentences are joined together with no punctuation between them. For example:

Yogurt is good for you poutine is not.

This film is boring it has no plot.

There are four ways you can fix comma splices or fused sentences.

1. Make the independent clauses separate sentences.

Yogurt is good for you. Poutine is not.

This film is boring. It has no plot.

This solution works well if you do not use it too often. Writing that consists of nothing but single-clause sentences lacks smoothness and sounds immature. (See Chapter 10.)

2. Separate the independent clauses with a comma and one of the FANBOYS words: *for, and, but, or, yet,* and *so.*[1]

Yogurt is good for you, but poutine is not.

This film is boring, for it has no plot.

3. Make one clause dependent on the other by adding one of the dependent clause cues listed on page 54.

Yogurt is good for you although poutine is not.

This film is boring because it has no plot. (*Or:* Because it has no plot, this film is boring.)

4. Use a semicolon, either by itself or with a transitional expression, to separate the independent clauses.[2]

Yogurt is good for you; poutine is not.

This film is boring; for one thing, it has no plot.

Note: All four solutions to comma splices and fused sentences require you to use a word or punctuation mark strong enough to come between two independent clauses. A comma by itself is too weak, and so is a dash.

Go to Workbook Exercises 7.1–7.7

---

[1] These words are called **coordinating conjunctions** because they are used to join equal (or coordinating) clauses. See Appendix A for an explanation and illustration of the different kinds of conjunctions and how to use them.

[2] If you are not sure when or why to use a semicolon, see Chapter 18.

Solving Modifier Problems | 8

Having been underwater for more than 150 years, Dr. Philbrick found the warship in excellent condition.

Both students were expelled as a result of cheating by the college registrar.

For sale: A set of first-year medical textbooks by a needy student in almost perfect condition.

How could Dr. Philbrick stay underwater for 150 years? Was the college registrar cheating? Did the needy student write the medical textbooks, and is this student in almost perfect condition? As you can see, the meaning in these examples is not clear. The confusion comes from incorrect placement of modifiers.

A **modifier** is a word or phrase that adds information about another word in a sentence. In the examples above, the highlighted words are modifiers. Used correctly, modifiers describe, explain, or limit another word, making its meaning more precise. Used carelessly, modifiers confuse or—even worse— amuse your reader.

You need to be able to recognize and solve two kinds of modifier problems: **misplaced modifiers** and **dangling modifiers**.

MISPLACED MODIFIERS

Modifiers must be as close as possible to the words they apply to. Readers usually assume that a modifier modifies whatever it's next to. It's important to remember this because, as the following examples show, changing the position of a modifier can change the meaning of your sentence.

Only I love you. (No one else loves you.)

I only love you. (I have no other feelings for you.)

I love only you. (You are the only one I love.)

To make sure a modifier is in the right place, ask yourself "What does it apply to?" and put it beside that word or phrase.

When a modifier is not close enough to the word it refers to, it is said to be misplaced.

• A misplaced modifier can be a single word in the wrong place.

My supervisor told me that the payroll department needs someone who can use accounting software badly .

Is some company really hiring people to do poor work? Or does the company urgently need someone familiar with accounting software? The modifier *badly* belongs next to the word it applies to, *needs*:

My supervisor told me that the payroll department badly needs someone who can use accounting software.

Be especially careful with these words: *almost, nearly, just, only, even, hardly, merely, scarcely*. Put them right before the words they modify.

Misplaced: I nearly passed every course I took.

Correct: I passed nearly every course I took.

Misplaced: The candidate was almost elected by 56 per cent of her riding's voters.

Correct: The candidate was elected by almost 56 per cent of her riding's voters.

Misplaced: Emilia only writes with her left hand.

Correct: Emilia writes only with her left hand .

• A misplaced modifier can also be a group of words in the wrong place.

Playing happily , the new mother watched her baby.

The modifier, *playing happily,* is too far away from the word it applies to: *baby.* It seems to modify *mother,* making the sentence ridiculous. We need to revise the sentence.

The new mother watched her baby playing happily .

Now look at this example:

I worked for my aunt, who owns a variety store during the summer .

During the summer applies to *worked* and should be closer to it:

During the summer , I worked for my aunt, who owns a variety store.[1]

Occasionally, as in the examples above, the modifier is obviously out of place. The writer's intention is often clear, and the sentence is easy to correct. Sometimes, however, modifiers are misplaced in such a way that the intended meaning is not clear, as in this example:

My supervisor told me on Friday I was being let go .

Did she speak to the employee on Friday? Or did she tell the employee that Friday would be his last day? To avoid confusion, we must move the modifier and, depending on the meaning we want, we might write

On Friday , my supervisor told me I was being let go.

or

My supervisor told me I was being let go on Friday .

Go to Workbook Exercises 8.1–8.2

---

[1] Notice that a modifier cannot always go right next to the word it modifies. It should, however, be placed as close as possible to it.

DANGLING MODIFIERS

A dangling modifier occurs when there is no specific word or phrase in the sentence to which the modifier can sensibly refer. With no appropriate word to refer to, the modifier seems to apply to whatever it's next to, often with ridiculous results:

After a good night's sleep , my teachers were impressed by my alertness.

(This sentence seems to say that the teachers had a good night's sleep.)

While paying for our purchases , a security guard watched closely.

(The security guard paid for our purchases?)

Torn by the storm from the old maple , our front window was shattered by a huge branch.

(The front window was torn from the maple tree?)

Dangling modifiers are harder to fix than misplaced ones. You can't simply move danglers to another spot in the sentence. There are two ways to correct them. One way requires that you remember the following guideline:

When a modifier begins a sentence, it modifies the subject of the sentence.

There are two ways to avoid dangling modifiers:

1. Make sure that the subject is an appropriate one for the modifier to apply to.

To determine whether a subject is appropriate, ask yourself *who* or *what* the modifying phrase refers to. For example:

Who had a good night's sleep? *I* did. (not my teachers)

Who paid for our purchases? *We* did. (not the security guard)

What was torn from the old maple? *A huge branch* (not our front window)

Using this method, we can correct our three examples by changing the subjects.

After a good night's sleep , I impressed my teachers with my alertness.

While paying for our purchases , we were closely watched by a security guard.

Torn by the storm from the old maple , a huge branch shattered our front window.

2. Change the dangling modifier into a dependent clause.

After I had a good night's sleep, my teachers were impressed by my alertness.

While we paid for our purchases, a security guard watched us closely.

When the storm tore a huge branch from the old maple, our front window was shattered.

Sometimes a dangling modifier comes at the end of a sentence.

A Smart is the car for me, looking for efficiency and affordability.

Can you correct this sentence? Try it, then look at the suggestions at the bottom of the page.[2]

SUMMARY

AVOIDING MODIFIER PROBLEMS

1. Ask "What does the modifier refer to?"
2. Be sure there is a word or phrase in the sentence for the modifier to apply to.
3. Put the modifier as close as possible to the word or phrase it refers to.

---

[2] Here are two possible corrections for the Smart car sentence:

a. **Add an appropriate subject:** Looking for efficiency and affordability , I decided a Smart was the car for me.
b. **Change the dangler to a dependent clause:** A Smart is the car for me since I am looking for efficiency and affordability.

Go to Workbook Exercises 8.3–8.4

By now, you will have figured out at least one way to fix modifier problems, so it's time for you to experiment with other "fixes." The more you experiment with moving sentence pieces around, the closer you will get to mastering sentence structure. Writing English sentences is like constructing jigsaw puzzles: the pieces (words, phrases, clauses) fit in some places but not in others. Only experimentation and practice can teach you how to put the pieces into places where they work to clarify rather than cloud your message.

Go to Workbook Exercises 8.5–8.6

The Parallelism Principle

Brevity, clarity, and force: these are three characteristics of good writing style. **Parallelism** will reinforce these characteristics in everything you write.

PARALLEL CONSTRUCTION

When your sentence contains a series of two or more items, they must be grammatically parallel. That is, they must be written in the same grammatical form. Consider this example:

> College requires us to manage our time, to work independently, and critical thinking.

The three items in this series are not parallel. Two are infinitive phrases (*to manage, to work*), but the third ends in *-ing* and is a noun phrase. To correct the sentence, you must put all items in the same grammatical form. You have two choices. You can write

> College requires us *to manage* our time, [*to*] *work* independently, and [*to*] *think* critically. (all infinitive phrases)

Or you can write

> College requires time management, independent work, and

> critical thinking. (all noun phrases)

Now look at an example with two non-parallel elements:

> Most of us seek happiness in long-term relationships and work that provides us with satisfaction.

Again, you could correct this sentence in two ways. You could write "Most of us seek happiness *in relationships that are long term* and *in work that provides us with satisfaction*," but that solution produces a long and clumsy sentence. The shorter version works better: "Most of us seek happiness *in long-term relationships* and *satisfying work*." This version is concise, clear, and forceful.

Correct faulty parallelism by writing all items in a series in the same grammatical form: all words, all phrases, or all clauses.

One way to tell whether the items in a series are parallel is to write them out in list form, one below the other. That way, you can see at a glance if all the elements "match," that is, are in the same grammatical form.

Not parallel	Parallel
My supervisor is *demanding, short-tempered,* and *an obnoxious person.*	My supervisor is *demanding, short-tempered,* and *obnoxious.*
(This list has two adjectives and a noun phrase.)	(This list has three adjectives.)
I support myself by *delivering pizza, poker,* and *shooting pool.*	I support myself by *delivering pizza, playing poker,* and *shooting pool.*
(This list has two phrases and a single word as objects of the preposition *by*.)	(This list has three phrases as objects of the preposition *by*.)
Jules wants a job that will interest him, will challenge him, and pays well.	Jules wants a job that *will interest him, challenge him,* and *pay him well.*
(This series of clauses contains two future tense verbs and one present tense verb.)	(All three subordinate clauses contain future tense verbs.)

As you can see, achieving parallelism is partly a matter of developing an ear for the sound of a correct list. A parallel sentence has a smooth, unbroken rhythm. Practice and the exercises in this chapter will help you recognize and fix nonparallel structures. Once you have mastered parallelism in your sentences, you will be ready to develop ideas in parallel sequence—in thesis statements, for example—and thus to write clear, well-organized prose. Far from being a frill, parallelism is a fundamental characteristic of good writing.

Go to Workbook Exercises 9.1–1.7

10 Refining by Combining

SENTENCE COMBINING

If you have worked carefully through Unit 2 to this chapter, you should now be writing complete sentences—a solid achievement, but one that does not yet meet the requirements of academic and professional writing. Your paragraphs may consist of sentences that are short, choppy, and monotonous; that is, your writing may be lacking in style. Now is the time to try your hand at **sentence combining**, a technique that enables you to produce correct and pleasing sentences. Sentence combining accomplishes three things: it reinforces your meaning; it refines and polishes your writing; and it results in a style that will keep your reader alert and interested in what you have to say.

Let's look at two short, technically correct sentences that could be combined:

Our office manager is highly efficient.

She will be promoted soon.

There are four ways of combining these two statements into a single sentence. Note that the meanings of the resulting sentences are slightly different. These differences are important when you're deciding which method to use in a particular situation.

1. You can connect sentences with an appropriate linking word, such as *and, but, or, nor, for, so,* or *yet.*

Our office manager is highly efficient, so she will be promoted soon.

Our office manager will be promoted soon, for she is highly efficient.

2. You can change one of the sentences into a subordinate clause.

Our office manager, who is highly efficient, will be promoted soon.

Because our office manager is highly efficient, she will be promoted soon.

3. You can change one of the sentences into a modifying phrase.

Being highly efficient, our office manager will be promoted soon.

Our office manager, a highly efficient woman, will be promoted soon.

4. Sometimes you can reduce one of your sentences to a single-word modifier.

Our efficient office manager will be promoted soon.

In sentence combining, you are free to move parts of the sentence around, change words, add or delete words, or make whatever other changes you want. Anything goes, as long as you don't drastically alter the meaning of the base sentences. Remember that your aim in combining sentences is to create effective sentences, not long ones.

COORDINATION OR SUBORDINATION?

When you join two or more short independent clauses, you need to think about their logical relationship. Are the ideas equally significant? If so, link them with an appropriate coordinating construction: a linking word such as *and, but, so, for, or, nor,* or *yet.* Is one idea more significant than the other? Put it in the main clause and put the less important idea in a subordinate construction: a clause, phrase, or word.

The most common way of linking ideas is with **conjunctions**. Every conjunction has a distinct meaning and purpose. If you choose your conjunctions carefully, you will reinforce the meaning you wish to convey. If you choose them carelessly, you will not say what you mean and may baffle your reader.

COORDINATION

To join two ideas that are equal in content or importance, use either
- a **coordinating conjunction** (*and, but, so, for, or, nor, yet*) or
- **correlative conjunctions**: *either ... or, neither ... nor, not only ... but also, both ... and*

Consider these examples:

1. Illogical relation:

   Water is vital to life, for it must be protected.

   Logical relation:

   Water is vital to life, so it must be protected. (coordinating conjunction)

Logical relation:

Water must be protected, for it is vital to life. (coordinating conjunction)

2. Illogical relation:

I reread the text and reviewed my notes, so I failed the test anyway.

Logical relation:

I reread the text and reviewed my notes, but I failed the test anyway.
(coordinating conjunction)

3. Poor logical relation:

Ms. Benson teaches school, and she is a writer too.

Logical relation:

Ms. Benson is both a teacher and a writer. (correlative conjunctions)

4. Poor logical relation:

I am not young, and I am not inexperienced either.

Logical relation:

I am neither young nor inexperienced. (correlative conjunctions)

 Go to Workbook Exercise 10.1

SUBORDINATION

To connect ideas of unequal importance, put the dominant idea in a main clause and the less significant idea in a subordinate clause beginning with either
• a **relative pronoun** (*who, whom, whose, which,* or *that*) or
• a **subordinating conjunction** such as *although, because, if, when, where,* or *after* (see list on page 54)

Consider these examples:

1. Illogical relation:

   Karim did well on all his tests, and he began working with a tutor.

   Logical relation:

   After he began working with a tutor, Karim did well on all his tests.
   (subordinating conjunction)

   Logical relation:

   Karim did well on all his tests after he began working with a tutor.
   (subordinating conjunction)

2. Illogical relation:

   No day is depressing to my English teacher, and he is an incurable optimist.

   Logical relation:

   No day is depressing to my English teacher, who is an incurable optimist.
   (relative pronoun)

   Logical relation:

   Because he is an incurable optimist, no day is depressing to my English
   teacher. (subordinating conjunction)

Go to Workbook Exercise 10.2

S. Harris/CartoonStock

"GOT IDEA. TALK BETTER. COMBINE
WORDS. MAKE SENTENCES."

The box below contains information that students studying English as an additional language may find helpful. If you are a native speaker of English, go to Exercise 10.5.

TIPS ON USING CONJUNCTIONS AND RELATIVE PRONOUNS

A. Using Conjunctions to Combine Clauses

Use only one connecting word to join two clauses.

This rule applies whether you intend to create a sentence consisting of two coordinating independent clauses or a sentence consisting of a main clause and a subordinate clause. For example, let's suppose you want to combine "I enjoy school" with "I also like my part-time job."

Incorrect:	*Although* I enjoy school, *and* I also like my part-time job.
Correct:	I enjoy school, *and* I also like my part-time job.
Also correct:	*Although* I enjoy school, I also like my part-time job.

Go to Workbook Exercise 10.3

B. Using Relative Pronouns to Combine Clauses

You can often combine two clauses by using a relative pronoun (*who, whom, whose, that, which*) to join them. (If you are not sure when to use *that/which* or *who/whom*, see Chapter 15, pages 106–108). On the next page are some examples of the different ways you can use a relative pronoun to join two clauses.

Separate Sentences	Combined Sentence
The man is waiting in the car. He is my father.	The man *who* is waiting in the car is my father. (NOT "The man who is waiting in the car he is my father.")
Yesterday Gina met Raffi. His family lives in Beirut.	Yesterday Gina met Raffi, *whose* family lives in Beirut.
I need a copy of *Frankenstein*. Ms. Lee assigned this book last week.	I need a copy of *Frankenstein*, *which* Ms. Lee assigned last week.
Frankenstein is a novel. It was written in 1818 by Mary Shelley.	*Frankenstein* is a novel *that* was written in 1818 by Mary Shelley.

Go to Workbook Exercise 10.4

Go to Workbook Exercise 10.5–10.10

After you have practised sentence combining, you can evaluate your work. Read your exercise sentences out loud. How they *sound* is important. Test your work against these six characteristics of successful sentences.

SUMMARY

CHARACTERISTICS OF SUCCESSFUL SENTENCES

1. **Meaning:** Have you said what you mean?
2. **Clarity:** Is each sentence clear? Can it be understood on the first reading?
3. **Coherence:** Do the parts of your sentences fit together logically and smoothly?
4. **Emphasis:** Is the most important idea in a main clause? Does it appear either at the beginning or at the end of the sentence?
5. **Conciseness:** Is every sentence direct and to the point? Have you cut out all redundant or repetitious words?
6. **Rhythm:** Do your sentences flow smoothly? Are there any interruptions in the development of the key idea(s)? If so, do the interruptions help to emphasize important points, or do they distract the reader?

If your sentences pass all six tests of successful sentence style, you can be confident that they are both technically correct and pleasing to the ear. No reader could ask for more.

Grammar

Grammar

Before you start this unit, complete the Quick Quiz.
Once you have finished this unit, complete the Rapid
Review.

Choosing the Correct Verb Form

Errors in grammar are like flies in soup. Most of the time, they don't affect meaning any more than flies affect flavour, but they are distracting and off-putting. You must eliminate grammar errors from your writing if you want your readers to pay attention to what you say rather than to how you say it.

The **verb** is the most complex and essential part of a sentence. In fact, a verb is to a sentence what an engine is to a car: the source of power and a frequent cause of trouble.[1]

This chapter looks at two verb problems that occur in many people's writing: incorrect use of irregular verbs and difficulties with the passive voice.

THE PRINCIPAL PARTS OF VERBS

All verb formations are based on a verb's **principal parts**. Technically, the principal parts are the elements that are used to construct the various **tenses** (time indicators) of verbs.

> Every verb has four forms, called its *principal parts*:
> 1. the base or **infinitive** form—the form used with *to*
> 2. the **simple past** (also called the **past tense**)
> 3. the **present participle**—the *-ing* form
> 4. the **past participle**—the form used with *has, have,* or *had*

Here are some examples:

Infinitive	Simple past	Present participle	Past participle
A. (to) call	called	calling	(has) called
(to) dance	danced	dancing	(has) danced
(to) work	worked	working	(has) worked

---

[1] Verb tenses are reviewed in Chapter 28. Negatives, modals, conditionals, and participial adjectives (e.g., *confused* and *confusing*) are reviewed in Chapter 29.

Infinitive	Simple past	Present participle	Past participle
B. (to) do	did	doing	(has) done
(to) eat	ate	eating	(has) eaten
(to) say	said	saying	(has) said

If you study the list above, you will notice an important feature of principal parts. In the first group of three verbs (A), the simple past and the past participle are identical: they are both formed by adding -ed (or simply -d if the verb ends in -e, as *dance* does). When both the simple past and the past participle of a verb are formed with -ed, the verb is called a **regular verb**. Fortunately, most of the many thousands of English verbs are regular.

In the second group (B), the simple past and past participle are not formed by adding -ed; these verbs are called **irregular verbs**. With *do* and *eat*, the simple past and the past participle are different words: *did/done, ate/eaten*. The simple past and past participle of *say* are the same, *said*, but they are not formed with the regular -ed ending.

GRAMMARIAN

S. Harris/CartoonStock

Unfortunately, although there are only a few hundred irregular verbs in English, these verbs are among the most common in the language; for example, *begin, come, do, go, see,* and *write* are all irregular. Their simple past tenses and past participles are formed in unpredictable ways. Consider the following sentences, all of which are grammatically incorrect:

I begun classes yesterday.

He come to see me last week.

I done it before.

She has went away on vacation.

He seen his girlfriend with another man.

I have wrote you an email answering your questions.

Depending on your experience with English, these sentences may or may not sound wrong to you, but if you look at the irregular verbs listed on pages 79–82, you will understand why they are incorrect.

If you are not sure of the principal parts of a verb, check your dictionary. If the verb is irregular, you will find the principal parts listed after the entry for the infinitive (base) form. For instance, if you look up *sing* in your dictionary, you will find *sang* (simple past), *sung* (past participle), and *singing* (present participle). If no principal parts are listed after the verb you are checking, it is regular; you form its simple past and past participle by adding *-ed.*

The verbs listed on pages 79 to 82 are used so frequently you should take the time to learn their principal parts. We have not included the present participle (the *-ing* form) because it rarely causes difficulty. The good news is that not every verb on this list will cause you trouble.

To identify the verbs that cause you problems, take a blank piece of paper and use it to cover the middle and right-hand columns of the list. Begin with the infinitive form of the first verb, *be.* Say the past tense and past participle of *be,* and then move the paper down one line to check your responses. If your answers are correct, go to the next verb in the left-hand column, *bear.* Again, say the past tense and the past participle, check your responses, and move on to the next verb, *beat.* Continue this exercise until you reach the end of the list.

Whenever you come to a verb whose past tense or past participle you aren't sure of or get wrong, highlight that verb across all three columns (infinitive, simple past, past participle). After you've gone through the list once, you'll have a quick and easy reference to the correct forms of verbs you need to watch out for in your writing.

Rupert Besley/CartoonStock

THE PRINCIPAL PARTS OF IRREGULAR VERBS

Infinitive	Simple Past	Past Participle
(Use with *to* and with helping/auxiliary verbs)		(Use with *has, have, had*)
be (am, is)	was/were	been
bear	bore	borne
beat	beat	beaten
become	became	become
begin	began	begun
bend	bent	bent
bind	bound	bound
bite	bit	bitten
blow	blew	blown
break	broke	broken
bring	brought (*not* brang)	brought (*not* brung)
broadcast	broadcast	broadcast

Infinitive	Simple Past	Past Participle
(Use with *to* and with helping/auxiliary verbs)		(Use with *has, have, had*)
build	built	built
burst	burst	burst
buy	bought	bought
catch	caught	caught
choose	chose	chosen
cling	clung	clung
come	came	come
cost	cost	cost
cut	cut	cut
deal	dealt	dealt
dig	dug	dug
dive	dived/dove	dived
do	did (*not* done)	done
draw	drew	drawn
dream	dreamed/dreamt	dreamed/dreamt
drink	drank (*not* drunk)	drunk
eat	ate	eaten
fall	fell	fallen
feed	fed	fed
feel	felt	felt
fight	fought	fought
find	found	found
fly	flew	flown
forbid	forbade	forbidden
forget	forgot	forgotten/forgot
forgive	forgave	forgiven
freeze	froze	frozen
get	got	got/gotten
give	gave	given
go	went	gone (*not* went)

Infinitive	Simple Past	Past Participle
(Use with *to* and with helping/auxiliary verbs)		(Use with *has, have, had*)
grow	grew	grown
have	had	had
hide	hid	hidden
hold	held	held
hurt	hurt	hurt
keep	kept	kept
know	knew	known
lay (to put or place)	laid	laid
lead	led	led
leave	left	left
lie (to recline)	lay	lain (*not* layed *or* laid)
lose	lost	lost
make	made	made
mean	meant	meant
meet	met	met
mistake	mistook	mistaken
pay	paid	paid
raise	raised	raised
ride	rode	ridden
ring	rang	rung
rise	rose	risen
say	said	said
see	saw (*not* seen)	seen
seek	sought	sought
sell	sold	sold
shake	shook	shaken (*not* shook)
shoot	shot	shot
show	showed	shown
shrink	shrank	shrunk

Grammar

Infinitive	Simple Past	Past Participle
(Use with *to* and with helping/auxiliary verbs)		(Use with *has, have, had*)
sing	sang	sung
sink	sank	sunk
sit	sat	sat
sleep	slept	slept
slide	slid	slid
speak	spoke	spoken
speed	sped	sped
spend	spent	spent
stand	stood	stood
steal	stole	stolen
strike (hit)	struck	struck
strike (affect)	struck	stricken
swear	swore	sworn
swim	swam	swum
swing	swung (*not* swang)	swung
take	took	taken
teach	taught	taught
tear	tore	torn
tell	told	told
think	thought	thought
throw	threw	thrown
understand	understood	understood
wear	wore	worn
win	won	won
withdraw	withdrew	withdrawn
write	wrote	written

Go to Workbook Exercises 11.1–11.4

CHOOSING BETWEEN ACTIVE AND PASSIVE VOICE

Verbs have another quality besides tense (or time). Verbs also have **voice**, which is the quality of being either active or passive. In sentences with **active-voice** verbs, the "doer" of the action is the grammatical subject of the sentence.

Active voice:	Helmets protect cyclists.
	My dog ate my homework.
	Someone will show a movie in class.

In sentences with **passive-voice** verbs, the grammatical subject of the sentence is the "receiver" of the action (i.e., the subject is "passively" acted upon), and the "doer" becomes an object of the preposition *by* or is absent from the sentence entirely, as in the third example below.

Passive voice:	Cyclists are protected by helmets.
	My homework was eaten by my dog.
	A movie will be shown in class.

Notice that active and passive verbs can occur in any tense. Present, past, and future tense verbs are used in both sets of examples above.

Passive-voice verbs are formed by using a form of *be* + a past participle. To use the passive voice correctly, you must know the past participle form of irregular verbs; for instance, in the third example above, the correct passive construction is *will be shown*, not *will be showed*. In the examples below, note the different tenses and pay special attention to the passive-voice verb forms.

	Active	Passive
Present	The clerk signs the invoice.	The invoice is signed by the clerk.
Past	The clerk signed the invoice.	The invoice was signed by the clerk.
Future	The clerk will sign the invoice.	The invoice will be signed by the clerk.
Present progressive	The clerk is signing the invoice.	The invoice is being signed by the clerk.
Past progressive	The clerk was signing the invoice.	The invoice was being signed by the clerk.

Go to Workbook Exercises 11.5–11.6

Active-voice verbs are more direct and emphatic than passive verbs. Good writers use the active voice unless there is a specific reason to use the passive. There are three situations in which the passive voice is preferable.

1. The person or agent that performed the action is not known.

The computer had been left unplugged for two days.

The name of our street has been changed from Primate Road to Primrose Circle.

This workstation is ergonomically designed.

2. You want to place the emphasis on the person, place, or thing that was affected by an action rather than on the subject that performed the action.

The president's office was occupied by a group of angry students.

This sentence focuses the reader's attention on the office rather than on the students. If we reconstruct the sentence in the active voice, we produce a different effect.

A group of angry students occupied the president's office.

3. You are writing a technical or scientific report or a legal document.

Passive verbs are the appropriate choice when the focus is on the facts, methods, or procedures involved in an experiment, situation, or event rather than on the person(s) who discovered or performed them. Passive verbs establish an impersonal tone that is appropriate to these kinds of writing. Contrast the emphasis and tone of these sentence pairs:

Passive:	The heat was increased to 150°C and was maintained at that temperature.
Active:	My lab partner and I increased the heat to 150°C and maintained it at that temperature.
Passive:	Our annual report was approved by the board in April.
Active:	The board approved our annual report in April.

In general, because active verbs are more concise and forceful than passive verbs, they add focus and strength to your writing. When you find a passive verb in your writing, think about *who* is doing *what* to *whom*. Ask yourself why the *who* is not the subject of your sentence. If there is a good reason, then use the passive voice. Otherwise, change the verb.

 Go to Workbook Exercises 11.7–11.9

Grammar

Mastering Subject–Verb Agreement

SINGULAR AND PLURAL

One of the most common writing errors is lack of **agreement** between subject and verb. Both must be singular, or both must be plural. If one is singular and the other plural, you have an agreement problem. You have another kind of agreement problem if your subject and verb are not both in the same "person" (see Chapter 16).

Let's clarify some terms. First, it's important to distinguish between **singular** and **plural**.

- *Singular* means one person or thing
- *Plural* means two or more persons or things

Second, it's important to know what is meant by the concept of **person**:

- *First person* is the person(s) speaking or writing: *I, me; we, us.*
- *Second person* is the person(s) being addressed: *you.*
- *Third person* is the person(s) being spoken or written about: *he, him, she, her, it; they, them.*

Here's an example of the singular and plural forms of a regular verb in the present tense:

	Singular	Plural
First person	I win	we win
Second person	you win	you win
Third person	she wins (*or* he, it, the horse wins)	they win (*or* the horses win)

The third-person singular form often causes trouble because the endings of the verb and its subject do not match. Third-person singular present-tense verbs end in *-s*, but their singular subjects do not. Third-person plural verbs never end in *-s*, while their subjects normally do. Look at the following examples:

The fire burns.

The brake fails.

A neighbour cares for our children.

The three singular verbs, all of which end in *-s* (*burns*, *fails*, *cares*), agree with their singular subjects (*fire*, *brake*, *neighbour*), none of which ends in *-s*. When the subjects become plural, the verbs change form too.

> Four fires burn.

> The brakes fail.

> The neighbours care for our children.

Now all of the subjects end in *-s*, and none of the verbs do.

To ensure **subject–verb agreement**, follow this basic rule:

Subjects and verbs must both be either singular or plural.

This rule causes difficulty only when the writer doesn't know which word in the sentence is the subject and so makes the verb agree with the wrong word. As long as you decode the sentence correctly (see Chapter 5), you'll have no problem making every subject agree with its verb.

If you have not already done so, now is the time to memorize this next rule:

The subject of a clause or sentence is NEVER in a prepositional phrase.

Here's an example of how errors can occur:

> Only one of the 20 000 ticket buyers are going to win.

The subject of this sentence is not *buyers*, but *one*. The verb must agree with *one*; it must be singular. The sentence should read

> Only one of the 20 000 ticket buyers is going to win.

If you are careful about identifying the subject of your sentence, even when it is separated from the verb by other words or phrases, you'll have no difficulty with subject–verb agreement. Before you try the exercises in this chapter, reinforce what you've learned by studying the following examples.

Incorrect: One of my sisters speak five languages.
Correct: One of my sisters speaks five languages.

Incorrect:	Alix, one of the few girls on the team, keep trying for a perfect score.
Correct:	Alix, one of the few girls on the team, keeps trying for a perfect score.
Incorrect:	One of the first-year journalism students keep writing graffiti on the walls of the computer lab.
Correct:	One of the first-year journalism students keeps writing graffiti on the walls of the computer lab.

"Yes, grammar rules do evolve over time, but making up your own to 'stay ahead of the curve' won't work in this English class!"

Chris Wildt/CartoonStock

Go to Workbook Exercise 12.1

Pay special attention to words that end in *-one*, *-thing*, or *-body*. They cause problems for nearly every writer.

Words ending in *-one*, *-thing*, or *-body* are always singular.

When used as subjects, these pronouns require singular verbs:

anyone	anything	anybody
everyone	everything	everybody
no one	nothing	nobody
someone	something	somebody

The last part of the pronoun subject is the tip-off here: every*one*, any*thing*, no*body*. If you think of these as the "*-one*, *-thing*, *-body*" words, you'll remember to use a singular verb.

These pronouns tend to cause trouble when modifiers come between them and their verbs. For example, you would never write "Everyone are here." But when you insert a word or phrase between the subject and the verb, you might, if you weren't careful, write this: "Everyone involved in implementing the company's new policies and procedures are here." The meaning is plural: several people are present. But the subject (*everyone*) is singular, so the verb must be *is*.

Most subject–verb agreement errors are caused by violations of this rule. Be sure you understand it. Memorize it, and then test your understanding by doing Exercises 12.2–12.5 before you go any further.

Go to Workbook Exercises 12.2–12.5

So far, so good. You can find the subject, even when it is hiding on the far side of the verb or is separated from the verb by one or more prepositional phrases. You can match up singular subjects with singular verbs and plural subjects with plural verbs. Now let's take a look at a few of the complications that make subject–verb agreement such a disagreeable problem.

FOUR SPECIAL CASES

Some subjects are tricky. They look singular but are plural, or they look plural when they're really singular. There are four kinds of these slippery subjects, all of them common and all of them likely to trip up an unwary writer:

1. Multiple subjects joined by *or, either … or, neither … nor,* or *not … but*

Most compound subjects we've dealt with so far have been joined by *and* and have required plural verbs, so agreement hasn't been a problem. But watch out when the elements of a multiple subject are joined by *or, either … or, neither … nor,* or *not … but*. In these cases, the verb agrees with the nearest subject. That is, if the subject closest to the verb is singular, the verb will be singular; if the subject closest to the verb is plural, the verb must be plural too.

> Neither the federal government nor the provinces effectively control pollution.

> Neither the provinces nor the federal government effectively controls pollution.

 Go to Workbook Exercise 12.6

2. Subjects that look plural but aren't

Don't be fooled by phrases beginning with words such as *with, like, as well as, together with, in addition to,* and *including*. These prepositional phrases are not part of the subject of a sentence. You can mentally cross them out since they do not affect the verb.

> My math professor, as well as my counsellor, has advised me to change my major.

Two people were involved in the advising; nevertheless, the subject (math professor) is singular, so the verb must be singular (<u>has advised</u>).

All my courses, including English, seem easier this term.

If you mentally cross out the phrase "including English," you can see that the verb (<u>seem</u>) must be plural to agree with the plural subject (<u>courses</u>).

Go to Workbook Exercise 12.7

3. Collective nouns

A **collective noun** is a word naming a group. Some examples are *audience, band, class, committee, company, crowd, family, gang, group, majority,* and *public.* When you are referring to the group acting all together, as a unit, use a singular verb. When you are referring to the members of the group acting individually, use a plural verb.

The <u>team is</u> sure to win tomorrow's game.	(Here *team* refers to the group acting as one unit.)
The <u>team are</u> getting into their uniforms now.	(The members of the team are acting individually.)

Go to Workbook Exercise 12.8

4. Units of money, time, mass, length, and distance

These expressions require singular verbs.

Fifteen dollars is too much to pay for a hamburger.

Two hours seems like four in our sociology class.

Eighty kilograms is the mass of an average man.

Five kilometres is too far to walk to the beach.

Go to Workbook Exercises 12.9–12.14

The box that follows contains a summary of the rules governing subject–verb agreement. Review these rules carefully before you do the Mastery Test for this chapter.

SUMMARY

RULES GOVERNING SUBJECT–VERB AGREEMENT

- Subjects and verbs must agree: both must be singular, or both must be plural.
- The subject of a sentence is never in a prepositional phrase.
- Pronouns ending in *-one, -thing,* or *-body* are singular and require singular verbs.
- Subjects joined by *and* are always plural.
- When subjects are joined by *or, either … or, neither … nor,* or *not … but,* the verb agrees with the subject that is closest to it.
- When looking for the subject in a sentence, ignore phrases beginning with *as well as, including, in addition to, like, together with,* and so on. They are prepositional phrases.
- Collective nouns are usually singular.
- Units of money, time, mass, length, and distance are always singular.

Go to Workbook Exercise 12.15

Keeping Your Tenses Consistent

Verbs are time markers. Changes in tense express changes in time: past, present, or future.

I (was) hired yesterday; I (hope) this job (will last) longer than my last one.

past   present   future

Sometimes, as in the sentence above, it is necessary to use several different tenses in a single sentence to convey your meaning. But most of the time, whether you're writing a sentence or a paragraph, you use one tense throughout.

AVOIDING VERBAL WHIPLASH

Normally, you choose either the past or the present tense, depending on the nature of your topic. (Few paragraphs are written completely in the future tense.) Here is the rule to follow:

Don't change tense in a sentence or a paragraph unless meaning requires it.

Readers like and expect consistency. If you begin a sentence with "I argued, protested, and even appealed to his masculine pride," the reader will tune in to the past tense verbs and expect any other verbs in the sentence to be in the past tense too. So, if you finish the sentence with "... but he looks at me with those big brown eyes and gets me to pay for the movie," your readers will be yanked out of one time frame into another. Such abrupt jolts are uncomfortable, and readers don't like them.

Shifting tenses is like shifting gears. It should be done smoothly and when necessary—never abruptly, out of carelessness, or on a whim. Avoid causing verbal whiplash: keep your tenses consistent.

Now consider these examples, both of which mix tenses inappropriately.

Problem: I'm *standing* right behind Sula when she suddenly *screamed*.

Solution 1: I *was standing* right behind Sula when she suddenly *screamed*.

Solution 2: I'm *standing* right behind Sula when she suddenly *screams*.

Problem: Kevin *procrastinated* until the last minute and then *begins* to write his paper. When he *gets* halfway through, he *decided* to change his topic.

Solution 1: Kevin *procrastinated* until the last minute and then *began* to write his paper. When he *got* halfway through, he *decided* to change his topic.

Solution 2: Kevin *procrastinates* until the last minute and then *begins* to write his paper. When he *gets* halfway through, he *decides* to change his topic.

Now look at the following example, which expresses a more complex idea.

Problem: I *handed* my paper in just before the deadline, but when I *see* the professor the next day, she *says* it was late, so I *will lose* marks.

This sentence is a hopeless muddle. It begins with the past tense, shifts to the present for no reason, and ends with the future.

Solution: I *handed* my paper in just before the deadline, but when I *saw* the professor the next day, she *said* it was late, so I *will lose* marks.

Here the past tense is used consistently until the last clause, where the shift to future tense is appropriate to the meaning.

Mike Flanagan/CartoonStock

Grammar

Go to Workbook Exercises 13.1–13.4

14 | Choosing the Correct Pronoun Form

Pronouns are not generally well understood. In this chapter and the two following, we will look at the three aspects of pronoun usage that can trip you up if you're not careful: **pronoun form**, **agreement**, and **consistency**. We will also present a solution to the problem of pronoun use creating sexist language.

Three kinds of pronouns can cause difficulty for writers:

Personal pronouns	Examples: I, we, she, they
Relative pronouns	Examples: who, which, that
Indefinite pronouns	Examples: any, somebody, none, each

(See Appendix A for a complete list of these pronouns.)

The first thing you need to do is be sure you are using the correct pronoun form. Look at the following examples of incorrect pronoun usage:

Her and me offered to pick up the car.

Between you and I, I think Tina's mother does her homework.

How do you know which form of a pronoun to use? The answer depends on the pronoun's place and function in your sentence.

SUBJECT AND OBJECT PRONOUNS

There are two forms of personal pronouns. One is used for subjects, and one is used for objects. Pronoun errors occur when you confuse the two. In Chapter 5, you learned to identify the subject of a sentence. Keep that information in mind as you learn the following basic rule.

When the subject of a sentence is (or is referred to by) a pronoun, that pronoun must be in **subject** form; otherwise, use the **object** form.

Subject Pronouns

Singular	Plural
I	we
you	you
he, she, it, one	they

She and *I* offered to pick up the car.
(The pronouns are the subject of the sentence.)

The lucky winners of the tickets to the Circus Monkeys concert are *they*.
(The pronoun refers to the subject of the sentence, *winners*.)

The only person who got an A in the course was *she*.
(The pronoun refers to the subject of the sentence, *person*.)

We serious bikers prefer Harleys to Hondas.
(The pronoun refers to the subject of the sentence, *bikers*.)

Object Pronouns

Singular	Plural
me	us
you	you
him, her, it, one	them

Sasha saw *him* and *me* having coffee at Tim Hortons.
(*Him* and *me* are not the subject of the verb *saw*; *Sasha* is, so the pronouns must be in the object form.)

Between you and *me*, I think Tina's mother does her homework.
(*Me* is not the subject of the sentence; it is one of the objects of the preposition *between*.)

The police are always suspicious of *us* bikers.
(*Us* does not refer to the subject of the sentence, *police*; it refers to *bikers*, the object of the preposition *of*.)

Be especially careful with pronouns that occur in compound subjects or after prepositions. If you remember the following two rules, you'll be able to eliminate most errors in pronoun form.

1. All pronouns in a compound (multiple) subject are *always* in subject form.
2. Pronouns that follow a preposition are *always* in object form.

Corollary: A grammatical sentence can never begin with "Him (Her) and me," or "Us and them."

We and *they* have season's tickets.
(The pronouns are used as a compound subject.)

I am delighted for *you* and *her*.
(The pronouns follow the preposition *for*.)

When you're dealing with a pair of pronouns and can't decide which form to use, try this test.[1] Mentally cross out one pronoun at a time, and then read aloud the sentence you've created. Applying this test to the first example above, you get "*We* have season's tickets" and "*They* have season's tickets." Both sound right and are correct. In the second sentence, if you try the pronouns separately, you get "I am delighted for *you*" and "I am delighted for *her*." These are the correct forms. You would never say "*Us* have tickets" or "*Them* have tickets," or "I am delighted for *she*." If you deal with paired pronouns one at a time, you are unlikely to choose the wrong form.

Note, too, that when a pair of pronouns includes *I* or *me*, that pronoun comes last. For example, we write "between *you* and *me*" (not "between *me* and *you*"; we write "*she* and *I*," not "*I* and *she*"). There is no grammatical reason for this rule. It's based on courtesy. In English, good manners require that you speak of others first and yourself last.

Go to Workbook Exercises 14.1–14.2

---

[1] This test is reliable only for those who are fluent in English. Until they become fluent, unfortunately, English language learners must rely on memorizing the rules.

USING PRONOUNS IN CONTRAST CONSTRUCTIONS

Choosing the correct pronoun form is more than a matter of not wanting to appear ignorant or careless. Sometimes the form determines the meaning of your sentence. Consider the following two sentences:

James treats his dog better than *I*.

James treats his dog better than *me*.

There's a world of difference between the meaning of the subject form ("James treats his dog better than *I* [do]") and the object form ("James treats his dog better than [he treats] *me*").

> When using a pronoun after *than*, *as well as*, or *as*, decide whether or not you mean to contrast the pronoun with the subject of the sentence. If you do, use the subject form of the pronoun. If not, use the object form.

David would rather listen to Feist than *I*.
(*I* is contrasted with *David*.)

David would rather listen to Feist than *me*.
(*Me* is contrasted with *Feist*.)

Here's a quick way to check that you've used the correct pronoun form. If you've used a subject form, mentally insert a verb after it. If you've used an object form, mentally insert a preposition before it. If your sentences make sense, you have chosen correctly. For example,

David would rather listen to Feist than I [would].

David would rather listen to Feist than [to] me.

Some writers prefer to leave the clarifying verb or preposition in place, a practice that eliminates any possibility of confusion.

 Go to Workbook Exercises 14.3–14.5

Mastering Pronoun–Antecedent Agreement

"I am writing in response to your ad for a server and bartender, male or female. Being both, I am applying for the position."

Pronoun confusion can take several forms, and some of the resulting sentences can be unintentionally hilarious. In this chapter, we'll look at how to use pronouns consistently throughout a sentence or paragraph to avoid confusing (and embarrassing) mistakes.

PRONOUN–ANTECEDENT AGREEMENT

The name of this pronoun problem may sound difficult, but the idea is simple. Pronouns are words that substitute for or refer to a person, place, or thing mentioned elsewhere in your sentence or paragraph. The word(s) that a pronoun substitutes for or refers to is called the **antecedent**.

Hannibal had his own way of doing things. (*His* refers to *Hannibal*.)

Chantal respects her boss. (*Her* refers to *Chantal*.)

The computer is processing as fast as it can. (*It* substitutes for *the computer*.)

Usually, as in these three examples, the antecedent comes before the pronoun[1] that refers to it. Here is the rule to remember:

A pronoun must agree with its antecedent in
- number (singular or plural)
- person (first, second, or third)
- gender (masculine, feminine, or neuter)

---

[1] Strictly speaking, possessive words such as *my*, *his*, *her*, *our*, and *their* are adjectives formed from pronouns rather than pronouns themselves. We are dealing with them in this chapter, however, because they follow the same agreement rule that governs pronouns.

You normally follow this rule without even realizing that you know it. For example, you would never write

> Hannibal had *your* own way of doing things.

> Chantal respects *its* boss.

> The computer is processing as fast as *she* can.

You know these sentences are incorrect even if you may not know exactly why.

There are three kinds of pronoun–antecedent agreement that you need to learn. Unlike the examples above, they are not obvious, and you need to know them so you can watch out for them. The rules you need to learn involve **indefinite pronouns** ending in *-one, -body,* or *-thing*; **vague references**; and **relative pronouns**.

1. PRONOUNS ENDING IN *-ONE, -BODY, -THING*

The most common pronoun–antecedent agreement problem involves the following **indefinite pronouns**:

anyone	anybody	anything
everyone	everybody	everything
no one	nobody	nothing
someone	somebody	something
each (one)		

In Chapter 12, you learned that when these words are used as subjects, they are singular and require singular verbs. So it makes sense that the pronouns that stand for or refer to them must also be singular.

> Antecedents ending in *-one, -body,* and *-thing* are singular.
> They must be referred to by singular pronouns: *he, she, it; his, her, its.*

> Everything has *its* place and should be in it.

> Everyone deserves a break from *her* children now and then.

> Everybody is expected to do *his* share of the work.

> No one had the courage to express *his* frustration with the decision.

Now take another look at the last three sentences. Until about 50 years ago, the pronouns *he*, *him*, and *his* were used with singular antecedents to refer to both men and women. Modern readers are sensitive to gender bias in writing, and most think it inappropriate to use the masculine pronoun to refer to both sexes. As a writer, you should be aware of this sensitivity. If you want to appeal to the broadest possible audience, you should avoid what readers may consider sexist language.

In casual communications, we often see or hear plural pronouns used with *-one*, *-body*, and *-thing* antecedents. Although these pronouns are grammatically singular, they are often plural in meaning, so in conversation we tend to say

> Everybody is expected to do *their* share of the work.

> No one had the courage to express *their* frustration with the workload.

This usage is acceptable in speech, but it is not acceptable in academic or professional writing.

Writers sometimes make errors in pronoun–antecedent agreement because they are trying to avoid identifying the gender of the person(s) referred to. "Everybody is expected to do *their* share of the work" is grammatically incorrect, as we have seen; however, it does avoid making "everybody" male or "everybody" female. The writer could replace the plural *their* with the singular and non-sexist *his or her*—"Everybody is expected to do *his or her* share of the work"—but *his or her* sounds clumsy if it is used frequently. There are two better ways to solve the problem:

1. Revise the sentence to leave out the pronoun.

> Everybody is expected to share the work.

> No one had the courage to express frustration with the workload.

Such creative avoidance of gender-specific language or incorrect constructions can be an interesting intellectual challenge. The resulting sentence sometimes sound a little artificial, however. The second solution is easier to accomplish.

2. Revise the sentence to make both the antecedent and the pronoun plural.

> *We* are all expected to do *our* share of the work.

> *The staff* did not have the courage to express *their* frustration with the workload.

Here are some examples for you to study:

Problem:	Everyone has submitted *their* assignment.
Solution 1:	*Everybody* has submitted *an* assignment.
Solution 2:	*All* of the students have submitted *their* assignments.

Problem:	*No one* likes to have *their* writing corrected.
Solution 1:	*No one* likes to have written work corrected.
Solution 2:	Most *people* dislike having *their* writing corrected.

If you are writing on a word processor, you can use it to help ensure agreement between indefinite pronouns and their antecedents. Do a search for the word *their*. Then check to be sure the antecedent of every *their* is plural. If it isn't, use one of the solutions given above to revise the error. This step takes less time than you might think and is well worth it, especially if your instructor has asked for a formal paper or report.

Go to Workbook Exercises 15.1–15.2

2. VAGUE REFERENCES

Avoiding the second potential difficulty with pronoun–antecedent agreement requires common sense and the ability to put yourself in your reader's place. If you read your writing from your reader's point of view, it is unlikely that you will break the following rule.

Every pronoun must have a clearly identifiable antecedent.

The mistake that occurs when you fail to follow this rule is called **vague reference**.

Jon pointed to his brother and said that he had saved his life.

Who saved whom? Here's another:

Emily wrote a song about her sister when she was five years old.

Is the song about a five-year-old sister, or was Emily a musically talented child?

In sentences like these, you can only guess the meaning because you don't know who the pronouns refer to. The antecedents are not clear. You can make such sentences less confusing either by using proper names (Jon, Emily) more frequently or by reconstructing the sentences. These solutions aren't difficult; they just take a little time and some imagination. Try them on our examples above.

Another type of vague reference occurs when there is no antecedent for the pronoun to refer to.

> Yuri loves off-road rallies and would like to try *it* himself. (Try what?)

> Snowboarding is Olivia's favourite sport, and she's hoping to get *one* for her birthday. (One what?)

> My roommate smokes constantly, *which* I hate. (There is no noun or pronoun for *which* to refer to.)

> My sister's work schedule overlaps with her husband's. *This* creates child-care problems. (There is no noun or pronoun for *this* to refer to.)

How would you revise these sentences? Try it, and then see our suggestions below.

Suggestions: Yuri loves off-road rallies and would like to try *the sport* himself.

Snowboarding is Olivia's favourite sport, and she's hoping to get *a board* for her birthday.

My roommate is an incurable chain-smoker, *which* I hate.

My sister's work schedule overlaps with her husband's. *This* conflict creates child-care problems.

Make sure that every pronoun has a clear antecedent and that every pronoun agrees with its antecedent. Both must be singular, or both must be plural. Once you have mastered this principle, you'll have no trouble with pronoun–antecedent agreement.

Go to Workbook Exercise 15.3

Grammar

Roy Delgado/CartoonStock

3. RELATIVE PRONOUNS

The third potential difficulty with pronoun–antecedent agreement is using relative pronouns—*who, whom, whose, which,* and *that*—correctly. Relative pronouns must refer to someone or something already mentioned in the sentence. Here is the guideline to follow:

Use *who* and *whom* to refer to people.
Use *that* and *which* to refer to everything else.

The chef *who* prepared this meal deserves a thumbs-up on Yelp.

The servers *who* presented it deserve to be fired.

The appetizer *that* I ordered was covered with limp, brown cilantro.

My soup, *which* was cold, arrived at the same time as my main course.

My father's meal, *which* was delicious, demonstrated the talent *that* the chef is famous for.

Whether you need *who* or *whom*[2] depends on the pronoun's place and function in your sentence. Apply the basic pronoun rule:

> If the pronoun is, or refers to, the subject of the sentence, use *who*. Otherwise, use *whom*. Or you can revise the sentence to eliminate the pronoun.

Jessa is the lucky contestant *who* won tickets to the Brite Futures concert. (The pronoun refers to the subject of the sentence, *Jessa*.)

Your tour guide will be Bhawani, *whom* you met last week. (The pronoun does not refer to the subject, *guide*; it is the object of the verb *met*.)

A better solution is to solve the problem by rewriting the sentence so you don't need either *who* or *whom*.

Jessa won tickets to the Brite Futures concert.

You met Bhawani, your tour guide, last week.

That is required more often than *which*. You should use *which* only in a clause that is separated from the rest of the sentence by commas. (See Comma Rule 4 in Chapter 17.)

The moose *that* I met looked hostile.

The moose, *which* was standing in front of my car, looked hostile.

---

[2] The distinction between *who* and *whom* has all but disappeared in spoken English and is becoming rarer in written English. Ask your instructor for guidance.

Go to Workbook Exercises 15.4–15.5

SUMMARY

PRONOUNS AND ANTECEDENTS

- Every pronoun must agree with its antecedent (a word or phrase mentioned, usually earlier, in the sentence or paragraph). Both must be singular, or both must be plural.
- Antecedents ending in *-one*, *-body*, and *-thing* are singular and must be referred to by singular pronouns: *he, she, it; his, her, its*.
- A pronoun must clearly refer to a specific antecedent.
- Use *who* and *whom* to refer to people; use *that* and *which* to refer to animals, objects, and ideas.
- As a courtesy to your reader, try to make your writing gender neutral.

Go to Workbook Exercise 15.6

Maintaining Person Agreement

So far, we have focused on using pronouns correctly and clearly within a sentence. Now let's turn to the problem of **person agreement**, which means using pronouns consistently within a sentence or throughout a paragraph or essay.

CATEGORIES OF PERSON

There are three categories of **person** that we use when we write or speak:

	Singular	Plural
First person	I; me	we; us
Second person	you	you
Third person	she, he, it, one; her, him *and all pronouns ending in* -one, -body, -thing	they; them

Here is the rule for person agreement:

> Do not mix "persons" unless meaning requires it.

In other words, be consistent. If you begin a sentence using a second-person pronoun, you should use the second person all the way through. Look at this sentence:

If *you* want to succeed, *one* must work hard.

Mixing second-person *you* with third-person *one* is a common error. Sometimes mixed pronouns can puzzle or mislead the reader, as in the following sentence:

Everyone must shower before you go into the pool. (Why should everyone shower if you are the only person swimming?)

Most of the time, however, lack of agreement among pronouns is just poor style, as this example illustrates:

> *One* can live happily in Vancouver if *you* have a sturdy umbrella.

We can correct this error by using the second person throughout:

> (1) *You* can live happily in Vancouver if *you* have a sturdy umbrella.

We can also correct it by using the third person throughout:

> (2) *One* can live happily in Vancouver if *one* has a sturdy umbrella.

or

> (3) *One* can live happily in Vancouver if *he or she* has a sturdy umbrella.

These last three examples raise two points of style that you should remember:

1. Don't overuse *one*.

All three revised sentences are grammatically correct, but they make different impressions on the reader, and impressions are an important part of communication.

- The first sentence, in the second person, is the most informal—it sounds like something you would say. It's a bit casual for general writing purposes.
- The second sentence, which uses *one* twice, sounds the most formal—even a little stuffy.
- The third sentence falls between the other two in formality. It is the one you'd be most likely to use in writing for school or business.

Although it is grammatically correct and non-sexist, this third sentence raises another problem. Frequent use of the *he or she* construction in a continuous prose passage, whether that passage is as short as a sentence or as long as an essay, is guaranteed to irritate your reader.

2. Don't overuse *he or she*.

He or she is inclusive, but it is a wordy construction. If used too frequently, the reader cannot help shifting focus from what you're saying to how you're saying it. The best writing is transparent—that is, it doesn't call attention to itself. If your reader becomes distracted by your style, your meaning is lost. Consider this sentence:

> A student can easily pass this course if he or she applies himself or herself to his or her studies.

Readers deserve better. There are two solutions to this problem, and they are already familiar to you because they are the same as those for making pronouns ending in *-one*, *-body*, or *-thing* agree with their antecedents:

- You can rewrite the sentence without using pronouns.

  > A student can easily pass this course by applying good study habits.

- You can change the whole sentence to the plural.

  > Students can easily pass this course if they apply themselves to their studies.

 Go to Workbook Exercises 16.1–16.5

Punctuation

Punctuation

Before you start this unit, complete the Quick Quiz. Once you have finished this unit, complete the Rapid Review.

17 The Comma

Many writers-in-training tend to sprinkle punctuation like pepper over their prose. Please do not use punctuation to spice up or decorate your writing. Punctuation marks are functional: they indicate to the reader how the various parts of a sentence relate to one another. By changing the punctuation, you can change the meaning of a sentence. Here are two examples to prove the point:

1. An instructor wrote the following sentence on the board and asked the class to punctuate it appropriately: "woman without her man is nothing."

   The men wrote, "Woman, without her man, is nothing."

   The women wrote, "Woman: without her, man is nothing."

2. Now it's your turn. Punctuate this sentence: "I think there's only one person to blame myself."
   If you wrote, "I think there's only one person to blame, myself" the reader will understand that you believe only one person—who may or may not be known to you—is to blame.
   If you wrote, "I think there's only one person to blame: myself" the reader will understand that you are personally accepting the blame.

The comma is the most frequently used—and misused—punctuation mark in English. Perhaps nothing is so sure a sign of a competent writer as the correct use of commas. This chapter presents five comma rules that cover most situations in which commas are required. If you apply these five rules faithfully, your reader will not be confused by missing or misplaced commas in your writing. And if, as occasionally happens, the sentence you are writing is not covered by one of our five rules, remember the first commandment of comma usage: WHEN IN DOUBT, LEAVE IT OUT.

FIVE COMMA RULES

RULE 1

Use commas to separate three or more items in a series. The items may be expressed in words, phrases, or clauses.

Words
: The required subjects in this program are math, physics, and English.

Phrases
: Punctuation marks are the traffic signals of prose: they tell us to slow down, notice this, take a detour, and stop. (Lynne Truss)

Clauses
: The wedding was delayed an hour because the groom was hung over, the best man had forgotten the ring, and the bride was in tears.

The comma before the *and* at the end of the list is optional, but we suggest you use it. Misunderstandings can occur if it is left out.[1]

Go to Workbook Exercise 17.1

The second comma rule is already familiar to you. You encountered it in Chapter 7, "Solving Run-On Sentence Problems."

---

[1] Here is an example: I love my children, Harry Styles and Leonard Cohen.

This sentence seems to say that Harry Styles and Leonard Cohen are the writer's children. If you insert a comma before the final *and*, however, the meaning is clear: I love my children, Harry Styles, and Leonard Cohen.

Punctuation

I hope I do well in the interview, for I really want this job.

I like Feist, but I prefer Norah Jones.

We shape our tools, and our tools shape us. (Marshall McLuhan)

I knew I was going to be late, so I went back to sleep.

Be sure that the sentence you are punctuating contains two independent clauses rather than one clause with a single subject and a multiple verb.

We loved the book but hated the movie.
(*We* is the subject, and there are two verbs, *loved* and *hated*. Do not put a comma between two or more verbs that share a single subject.)

We both loved the book, but Harry *hated* the movie.
(This sentence contains two independent clauses—*We loved* and *Harry hated*—joined by *but*. The comma is required here.)

Go to Workbook Exercise 17.2

Word	Dillon, you aren't paying attention.
Phrase	Exhausted and cranky from staying up all night, I staggered into class.
Clause	If that's their idea of a large pizza, we'd better order two.
Clause	Until she got her promotion, she was quite friendly.

But note that if a subordinate clause FOLLOWS a main clause, no comma is needed (e.g., She was quite friendly until she got her promotion).

Go to Workbook Exercise 17.3

RULE 4

Use commas to set off any word, phrase, or dependent clause that is NOT ESSENTIAL to the main idea of the sentence.

Following this rule can make the difference between your readers' understanding and misunderstanding what you write. For example, the following two sentences are identical, except for a pair of commas. But notice what a difference those two tiny marks make to meaning:

The students who haven't done their homework will lose one full grade.
(Only the students who failed to do their homework will be penalized.)

The students, who haven't done their homework, will lose one full grade.
(All the students failed to do their homework, and all will be penalized.)

To test whether a word, phrase, or clause is essential to the meaning of your sentence, mentally put parentheses around it. If the sentence still makes complete sense (i.e., the main idea is unchanged; the sentence just delivers less information), the material in parentheses is *not essential* and should be set off from the rest of the sentence by a comma or pair of commas.

Non-essential information can appear at the beginning,[2] in the middle, or at the end of a sentence. Study the following examples.

Atom Egoyan whose parents are both painters made his first film at the age of 19.

Without punctuation, this sentence leads readers to believe that all of the information is equally important. In fact, the material between the subject and the verb is extra information—a supplementary detail. It can be deleted

---

[2] Rule 3 covers non-essential information at the beginning of a sentence.

without changing the sentence's meaning, and so it should be separated from the rest of the sentence by commas:

> Atom Egoyan, whose parents are both painters, made his first film at the age of 19.

Here's another example:

> The Queen who has twice as many birthdays as anyone else officially celebrates her birthday on May 24.

Again, the sentence is hard to grasp. You can't expect your readers to go back and reread every sentence they don't understand at first glance. As a writer, you are responsible for giving readers the clues they need as to what is crucial information and what isn't. In the example above, the information between the subject and the verb is not essential to the meaning of the sentence, so it should be set off by commas:

> The Queen, who has twice as many birthdays as anyone else, officially celebrates her birthday on May 24.

In this next sentence, the non-essential information comes at the end.

> The Queen officially celebrates her birthday on May 24 the anniversary of Queen Victoria's birth.

The phrase "the anniversary of Queen Victoria's birth" is not essential to the main idea, so it should be separated from the rest of the sentence by a comma:

> The Queen officially celebrates her birthday on May 24, the anniversary of Queen Victoria's birth.

And finally, consider this sentence:

> Writing a letter of application that is clear, complete, and concise is a challenge.

If you take out "that is clear, complete, and concise," you change the meaning of the sentence. Not all letters of application are a challenge to write. Writing vague and wordy letters is easy; anyone can do it. The words "that is clear, complete, and concise" are essential to the meaning of the sentence, and so they are *not* set off by commas.

Jorodo/CartoonStock

Go to Workbook Exercise 17.4

RULE 5
Use commas to separate coordinate adjectives but not cumulative adjectives.

Coordinate adjectives are adjectives that
- can be arranged in any order and
- can be separated by the word *and*

without changing the meaning of the sentence.

> Our company is looking for energetic, courteous salespeople.

The adjectives *energetic* and *courteous* could appear in reverse order, and you could put *and* between them:

Our company is looking for courteous and energetic salespeople.

In a series of **cumulative adjectives**, however, each adjective modifies the word that follows it. You cannot change their order, nor can you insert *and* between them.

The bride wore a pale pink silk dress, and the groom wore a navy wool suit.

You wouldn't say "The bride wore a silk pink pale dress" or "The groom wore a navy and wool suit." Commas are not used between cumulative adjectives.

Go to Workbook Exercise 17.5

The rest of the exercises in this chapter require you to apply all five comma rules. Refer to the rules in the Summary box below frequently as you punctuate the sentences. After you've finished each exercise, check your answers and make sure you understand any mistakes you've made.

"I typed it that way because I thought that punctuation would just slow it down."

SUMMARY

THE FIVE COMMA RULES

1. Use commas to separate three or more items in a series. The items may be expressed as words, phrases, or clauses.
2. Put a comma between independent clauses when they are joined by *for*, *and*, *nor*, *but*, *or*, *yet*, or *so*.
3. Put a comma after an introductory word, phrase, or dependent clause that comes BEFORE an independent clause.
4. Use commas to set off any word, phrase, or dependent clause that is NOT ESSENTIAL to the main idea of the sentence.
5. Use commas to separate coordinate adjectives but not cumulative adjectives.

 Go to Workbook Exercises 17.6–17.8

Punctuation

18 The Semicolon

The semicolon and the colon are often confused and used as if they were interchangeable. They have distinct purposes, however, and their correct use can dramatically improve a reader's understanding of your writing.

THREE USES FOR THE SEMICOLON

The semicolon has three functions.

1. A semicolon can replace a period; that is, it can appear between two independent clauses.

You should use a semicolon when the two clauses (sentences) you are joining are closely connected in meaning or when there is a cause-and-effect relationship between them.

> I'm exhausted; I can't stay awake any longer.

> Montréal is not the city's original name; it was once called Ville-Marie.

A period could have been used instead of a semicolon in either of these sentences, but the close connection between the clauses makes a semicolon more effective in communicating the writer's meaning.

2. Certain transitional words or phrases can be put between independent clauses to show a cause-and-effect relationship or the continuation of an idea.

"Yes, a winky face is correct... But in ancient times, the semicolon was actually used to separate archaic written devices known as 'complete sentences.'"

Loren Fishman/CartoonStock

Words or phrases used in this way are usually preceded by a semicolon and followed by a comma:

; accordingly,	; furthermore,	; nevertheless,
; also,	; however,	; on the other hand,
; as a result,	; in addition,	; otherwise,
; besides,	; in fact,	; then,
; consequently,	; indeed,	; therefore,
; finally,	; instead,	; thus,
; for example,	; moreover,	; unfortunately,

The forecast called for sun; instead, we got snow.

My screen went blank; nevertheless, I kept on typing.

I'm not offended by all the dumb blond jokes because I know I'm not dumb; besides, I also know I'm not blond. (Dolly Parton)

In other words, A SEMICOLON + A TRANSITIONAL WORD/PHRASE + A COMMA = a link strong enough to come between two related independent clauses.

Note, however, that, when transitional words and phrases are used as non-essential expressions rather than as connecting words, they are separated from the rest of the sentence by commas (see Chapter 17, Rule 4).

Your application form, unfortunately, was not completed.

The emissions test, moreover, will ensure that your car is running well.

3. To make a complex list easier to read and understand, use semicolons between the items instead of commas. (A complex list is one in which at least one component part already contains commas.)

Here are two examples:

I grew up in a series of small towns: Cumberland, British Columbia; Red Deer, Alberta; and Timmins, Ontario.

When we opened the refrigerator, we found a limp, brown head of lettuce; two small containers of yogurt, whose "best before" dates had long since passed; and a hard, dried-up piece of cheddar cheese.

 Go to Workbook Exercises 18.1–18.5

The Colon 19

The colon functions as an introducer. When a statement is followed by a list, one or more examples, or a quotation, the colon alerts the reader that some sort of explanatory detail is coming up.

> When I travel, I am never without three things: sturdy shoes, a money belt, and my laptop.

> There is only one enemy we cannot defeat: time.

> We have two choices: to study or to fail.

> Early in his career, Robert Fulford did not think very highly of intellectual life in Canada: "My generation of Canadians grew up believing that, if we were very good or very smart, or both, we would someday *graduate* from Canada."

The statement that precedes the colon must be a complete sentence (independent clause).

A colon should never come immediately after *is, are, was,* or *were.* Here's an example of what *not* to write:

> The three things I am violently allergic to are: cats, ragweed, and country music.

This construction is incorrect because the statement before the colon is not a complete sentence.

WHEN TO USE A COLON

The following are three different situations in which you need to use a colon.

1. Use a colon between an independent clause and a LIST or one or more EXAMPLES that define, explain, summarize, or illustrate the independent clause.

The information after the colon often answers the question "what?" or "who?"

> I am violently allergic to three things: (what?) cats, ragweed, and country music.

> Business and industry face a new challenge: (what?) the unstable Canadian dollar.

> The president has found the ideal candidate for the position: (who?) her husband.

2. Use a colon after a complete sentence introducing a quotation.

> Maude Barlow of the Council of Canadians encouraged young people to vote: "If you want to know who is going to change this country, go home and look in the mirror."

3. Use a colon to separate the title of a book, film, or television show from a subtitle.

> *In Defense of Food: An Eater's Manifesto* (book)

> *Tae Guk Gi: The Brotherhood of War* (film)

> *CSI: Miami* (TV show)

If you remember this summary, you'll have no more trouble with colons:

The colon follows an independent clause and introduces one of three things: an example, a list, or a quotation.

Go to Workbook Exercises 19.1–19.5

Quotation Marks

A quotation is one or more words originally spoken or written by another person that you want to include in your paper. Quotations can enhance meaning and add interest to your writing—as long as they are used sparingly. If you insert quotations into every other sentence, your own ideas will be buried under the weight of other people's words. Your reader wants to hear what *you* think about your topic. Use the words of others to support or illustrate your ideas, not as substitutes for them.

When you quote, you need to provide a signal to your reader that the words are borrowed, not your own. Quotation marks (" ") are used to set off short passages of quoted material and some titles. Long passages of quoted material are treated differently, as you'll see later.

Quotation marks come in pairs. There must be a set to show where the quotation or title begins and a set to show where it ends. The words in between must be *exactly* what you heard or read. If you wish to omit or change a word or words for clarity or for flow within your paragraph and can do so without changing the meaning of the original, you may do so, but again you must alert your reader that you have altered the original. For an example of how to add, delete, or alter an original source so that it fits smoothly into your paragraph, go to the documented essay in Unit 7 on page 271 (formatted in Modern Language Association style) or on page 277 (in American Psychological Association style). Note how the author modifies her source quotation in the last sentence of the third paragraph. She indicates that word(s) have been omitted by using three spaced dots called ellipses (. . .). Words that she has added or changed are enclosed in square brackets: [*younger learners are*].

The only other thing you need to know about quotations is how to introduce and punctuate them.

PUNCTUATING DIALOGUE

When you quote direct speech, start with a double quotation mark (") and use normal sentence punctuation. If you identify the speaker in your sentence, set the identification off with commas. Put a comma or an end punctuation mark—whichever is appropriate—inside the final set of quotation marks (").

"Yes, officer," said the young man, "that's her. That's the lady I stole the purse from."

Put quotation marks around the speaker's exact words. But do not use quotation marks with indirect speech (a paraphrase or summary of someone's words).

The young man confessed that the woman the officer pointed to was the woman from whom he had stolen the purse.

Go to Workbook Exercise 20.1

PUNCTUATING AND FORMATTING QUOTATIONS

Inserting quotations from print and electronic sources into your own writing smoothly and seamlessly is not easy. It takes practice. Quotations cannot simply be dropped (splash!) into your paragraphs. Every quotation must be introduced, usually in a phrase or clause that identifies the source.

When you quote a *short passage* (four lines of print or less in MLA; less than 40 words in APA), you should work it into your own sentence using appropriate punctuation.

1. Normally, you use a short phrase and a comma to mark off a quotation of one or more sentences. Put quotation marks at the beginning and end of the passage you are quoting, enclosing the end punctuation mark.

   According to Margaret Atwood, "If you like men, you can like Americans. Cautiously. Selectively. Beginning with the feet. One at a time."

   "As you grow old," wrote Richard Needham, "you lose your interest in sex, your friends drift away, and your children often ignore you. There are other advantages, of course, but these would seem to me the outstanding ones."

"My idea of long-range planning is lunch," confesses Frank Ogden, one of Canada's foremost futurists.

2. If your own introductory words form a complete sentence, use a colon to introduce the quotation.

Frank Ogden, one of Canada's foremost futurists, confesses that he has little respect for traditional business-planning cycles: "My idea of long-range planning is lunch."

3. If the passage you are quoting is a couple of words, a phrase, or anything less than an independent clause, do not use any punctuation to introduce it.

Woody Allen's one regret in life is that he is "not someone else."

Neil Bissoondath argues that racism is based on "willful ignorance and an acceptance of—and comfort with—stereotype."

4. A quotation *within* a quotation is punctuated by single quotation marks.

According to John Robert Colombo, "The most widely quoted Canadian aphorism of all time is Marshall McLuhan's 'The medium is the message.'"

Go to Workbook Exercises 20.2–20.3

All of the lines of a *long quotation* (more than four lines of print in MLA; 40 words or more in APA) should be indented from the left margin (see documented essays in Unit 7 for indentation measures). Do not use quotation marks around a long quotation that is set off from the text.

A block indentation indicates to the reader that the words set off in this way are not yours but some other writer's. Here is an example:

> In "An Immigrant's Split Personality," Sun-Kyung Yi describes the painful dilemma faced by the children of immigrants, who often feel torn between two worlds. She cites her own case as an example. Neither Korean nor Canadian, she
>
> > remain[s] slightly distant from both cultures, accepted fully by neither. The hyphenated Canadian personifies the ideal of multiculturalism, but unless the host culture and the immigrant cultures can find ways to merge their distinct identities, sharing the best of both, this cultural schizophrenia will continue. (253)

Sun-Kyung Yi, "An Immigrant's Split Personality," *The Globe and Mail*, April 12, 1992.

College writing normally requires that you indicate the source of any material you quote. In the example above, since the author's name and the essay title are included in the introduction to the quotation, the full reference (given underneath the quotation) would appear in a "References" or "Works Cited" list at the end of your paper or, if your instructor prefers, in a footnote or an endnote.

The following examples illustrate the two basic ways to incorporate a short quotation into your own writing and credit your source in MLA style. The first example identifies the author in the sentence introducing the quotation; the second does not. Both examples include the page number where the quotation appears in the publication.

> American humorist Mark Twain once observed, "I never let schooling interfere with my education" (97).

> An American humorist once remarked, "I never let schooling interfere with my education" (Twain 97).

These source identifications are called *parenthetical citations* and refer to entries in the "References" or "Works Cited" list. For examples of "References" and "Works Cited" lists, see the Dahlia Rodriguez essays in Unit 7.

Find out what format your instructor requires and follow it. Some institutions are very particular about documentation, so you would be wise to ask your instructor which style to use.

The information and exercises that follow are based on the MLA format.

PUNCTUATING AND FORMATTING TITLES

- *Italicize* the titles of books, websites, and other works made up of parts.
- Use quotation marks around the titles of parts of books and the titles of parts of other works.

The title of anything that is published or produced as a separate entity (e.g., books, magazines, newspapers, pamphlets, blogs, plays, movies, TV shows, CDs) should be italicized. The title of anything that has been published or produced as *part* of a separate entity (e.g., articles, essays, stories, poems, a single episode of a TV series, songs) should be placed in quotation marks. As you can see from the following examples, this rule is very simple, and it applies to all types of sources, both print and electronic.

Source type	Format
Book:	*The Bare Essentials Plus*
Chapter in a book:	"Quotation Marks"
Magazine:	*Maclean's*
Article in a magazine:	"Uber v. Taxi"
Newspaper:	*Calgary Herald*
Article in a newspaper:	"The Ramallah Miracle"
TV program:	*The Nature of Things*
TV episode:	"The Hobbit Enigma"
Music CD:	*So Beautiful or So What*
Song on CD:	"The Afterlife"
Website sponsor:	*National Film Board of Canada*
Website page:	"The Facebook Challenge"
Blog:	*Snailspace*
Blog entry:	"January: The French Resolution"

Why the difference? The way you format and punctuate a title indicates what sort of document you are quoting from or referring to: it may be a complete work that the reader can find listed by title, author, or subject online or in a library, or it may be an excerpt that the reader can find only by looking up the name of the work in which it was published.

 Go to Workbook Exercises 20.4–20.5

Question Marks, Exclamation Marks, and Punctuation Review

21

THE QUESTION MARK

Everyone knows that a question mark follows an interrogative, or asking, sentence, but we all sometimes forget to include it. Let this chapter serve as a reminder not to forget!

> Put a question mark at the end of every interrogative sentence.

The question mark gives your readers an important clue to the meaning of your sentence. "There's more?" (interrogative) means something quite different from "There's more!" (exclamatory), and both are different from "There's more." (declarative). When you speak, your tone of voice conveys the meaning you intend; when you write, your punctuation tells your reader what you mean.

The only time you don't end a question with a question mark is when the question is part of a statement.

Question	Statement
Are you going?	I asked if you were going.
Do you know about them?	I wonder what you know about them.
Is there enough evidence to convict him?	The jury deliberated whether there was enough evidence to convict him.

 Go to Workbook Exercise 21.1

THE EXCLAMATION MARK

Consider the difference in tone between the following two sentences:

There's someone behind you.

There's someone behind you!

In the first sentence, information is being supplied, perhaps about the line of people waiting their turn at a grocery store checkout counter. The second sentence might be a shouted warning about a mugger.

> Use an exclamation mark as end punctuation only in sentences requiring extreme emphasis or dramatic effect.

Note that the exclamation mark will have "punch" or dramatic effect only if you use it sparingly. If you use an exclamation mark after every other sentence, how will your readers know when you really mean to indicate

Snapshots

"Do you always have to shout?
Well? Do you? Huh?"

Jason Love/CartoonStock

excitement? Overuse of exclamation marks is a technique used by comic book writers to heighten the impact of their characters' words. Ironically, the effect is to neutralize the impact: when all conversation is at top volume, top volume becomes the norm, and the writer is left with no way to indicate emphasis—other than by adding two, three, or more exclamation marks to punctuate each statement. This is why you seldom find exclamation marks in academic or business writing.

Almost any sentence could end with an exclamation mark, but remember that the punctuation changes the emotional force of the sentence. Read the following sentences with and without an exclamation mark, and picture the situation that would call for each reading.

They've moved	Don't touch that button
The file was empty	Listen to that noise
Mom is home	I quit

Go to Workbook Exercises 21.2–21.3

Snapshots

"Yes, I'm very punctual. I always use commas and periods."

Jason Love/CartoonStock

PUNCTUATION REVIEW

The exercises for this section will test your knowledge of the punctuation marks you have studied in Unit 4. All of the sentences contain errors: punctuation or italics are either missing or misused. Work through the sentences slowly and carefully. Check your answers to each set before continuing. If you make a mistake, go back to the chapter that deals with the punctuation mark you missed, and review the explanation and examples.

Go to Workbook Exercises 21.4–21.6

Paragraphs and Essays

Paragraphs and Essays

Finding Something to Write About

Every writer knows that content is important. Not so many seem to know that form is just as important. In fact, you can't really separate the two: *what you say is how you say it*. Writing a paper (or an essay or a report or a letter or anything else) is like doing a chemistry experiment or baking a cake: you need the right amount of the right ingredients put together in the right proportions and in the right order. There are five steps to follow:

1. Choose a satisfactory subject
2. Discover your thesis and main points
3. Write a thesis statement and/or an outline
4. Write the paragraphs
5. Revise the paper

If you follow these steps faithfully, in order, we guarantee that you will write clear, organized papers.

Note that when you get to step 3, you have a choice. You can choose to plan your paper with a thesis statement, with an outline, or with both. The thesis statement approach works well for short papers—about 500 words or less. An outline is necessary for longer papers. Ideally, you should learn to use both methods of organizing your writing. In fact, your teacher may require that you do so.

Steps 1, 2, and 3 make up the planning stage of the writing process. Be warned: done properly, these three steps will take you about as long as steps 4 and 5, which involve the actual writing. The longer you spend on planning, the less time you'll spend on drafting and revising, and the better your paper will be.

CHOOSING A SATISFACTORY SUBJECT

Unless you are assigned a specific subject (or topic) by a teacher or supervisor, choosing your **subject** can be the most difficult part of writing a paper. Apply the following guidelines carefully because no amount of instruction can help you write a good paper on something you know nothing about or on something that is inappropriate for your audience or purpose. Your subject should satisfy the 4-S TEST.

A satisfactory subject is SIGNIFICANT, SINGLE, SPECIFIC, and SUPPORTABLE.

1. Your subject should be SIGNIFICANT. Write about something that your reader needs or might want to know. Consider your audience and choose a subject that they will find significant. This doesn't mean that you can't ever be humorous, but, unless you're another Stephen Leacock, an essay on "How I deposit money in my bank" will not be of much interest to your readers. The subject you choose must be worthy of the time and attention you expect your readers to give to your paper.

2. Your subject should be SINGLE. Don't try to cover too much in your paper. A thorough discussion of one topic is more satisfying to a reader than a superficial treatment of several topics. A subject such as "The challenge of government funding cutbacks to colleges and universities" includes too much to deal with in one paper. Limit yourself to a single topic, such as "How private-sector donations are helping our college meet the challenge of funding cutbacks."

3. Your subject should be SPECIFIC. Given a choice between a broad topic and a narrow one, choose the latter. In a short paper, you can't hope to say anything new or significant about a large topic: "Employment opportunities in Canada," for example. But you could write an interesting, detailed discussion on a more specific topic, such as "Employment opportunities in Alberta's hospitality industry."

   You can narrow a broad subject by applying one or more limiting factors to it. Think of your subject in terms of a specific *kind* or *time* or *place* or *number* or *person* associated with it. To come up with the hospitality topic, for example, we limited the subject of employment opportunities in Canada in terms of both *place* and *kind*.

4. Your subject must be SUPPORTABLE. You must know something about the subject (preferably, more than your reader does), or you must be able to find out about it. Your discussion of your subject will be clear and convincing only if you can include examples, facts, quotations, descriptions,

Andrew Toos/CartoonStock

"Hawaii can wait. These reports cannot."

anecdotes, and other details. Supporting evidence can be taken from your own experience or from the experience of other people. In other words, your topic may require you to do some research.[1]

Go to Workbook Exercises 22.1–22.3

---

[1] Many colleges and most universities require students to write formal research papers in their first year. The five steps to essay writing that we outline in this unit apply to research papers as well as to informal and in-class essays. In addition to finding and incorporating information from sources in your essay, a research paper requires that you format and document your paper according to specific guidelines, such as those of the Modern Language Association (MLA) or the American Psychological Association (APA), the two styles most frequently required in undergraduate courses.

DISCOVERING YOUR THESIS AND MAIN POINTS

Once you've chosen a suitable subject for your paper, you need to decide what you want to say about it (your thesis). There are many possible ways of thinking and writing about any subject. In a short paper, you can deal effectively with only a few aspects of your topic. How do you decide what approach to take?

The approach to your subject that you choose is your thesis: a **thesis** is an idea about a limited subject. It is an opinion or point of view that needs to be explained or proved. A statement of fact is not a thesis. Compare the examples that follow.

Fact	Thesis
Most people experience some anxiety when they begin a first job.	The stress I experienced in my first job was caused by my employer, my co-workers, and—surprisingly—myself. (Needs to be explained.)
For several years, Canada ranked first on the UN list of the world's best countries to live in.	Canadians don't know how lucky they are. (Needs to be explained.)
Some universities do not require students to demonstrate writing competence before graduation.	All universities should require students to demonstrate writing competence before graduation. (Needs to be proved.)

A thesis can be discovered in several ways. Brainstorming, freewriting, listing, and clustering are strategies that many college students are familiar with from high school. You should continue to use any technique you've learned that produces good results. However, if these approaches haven't produced good results in the past, you may need a more structured approach to discovering what it is you can and want to say about a subject.

Try questioning—asking lead-in questions about your subject. A lead-in question is one that guides you into your subject by pointing to an angle or viewpoint—a thesis—that you can explore in your paper. The answers to your lead-in question become the main points your paper will explain.

Paragraphs and Essays

SIX QUESTIONS TO ASK ABOUT YOUR SUBJECT

1. How can my subject be defined or explained? What are its significant features or characteristics? Examples: Generation Y; The Canadian personality

2. How is my subject made or done? How does it work? Examples: How hybrid electric cars work; How to protect yourself from identity theft; How to make a short film

3. What are the main kinds, components, or functions of my subject? Examples: Internet addicts; The perfect workout; The duties of a line manager

4. What are the main similarities and/or differences between my subject and something else like it? Examples: Differences between college and university; A fan's view of professional vs. amateur hockey; Nissan Leaf vs. Ford Focus Electric

5. What are the causes or effects of my subject? Examples: Why parents and teenagers disagree; Effects of single-sex education; Causes of first-year dropouts

6. What are the advantages or disadvantages of my subject? What are the reasons for or against it? Examples: Toll roads; Wind power; Smartphones in classrooms

These questions suggest some common ways of looking at or thinking about a subject. Some questions will yield better results than others, and most subjects will produce answers to more than one of the questions. Choose as your subject the question that produces the answers you can or want to explain.

Here's an example of how the process works. Let's assume you've been asked to write a paper on the topic "A satisfying career."[2] Apply each question to your subject and make notes of the answers.

---

[2] If your instructor has assigned the topic of your essay, don't grumble—be grateful. The way your instructor words the assignment may contain information that will help you decide how to approach it. Assignment instructions usually contain *direction words*, which are reliable clues to the kind of paper your instructor is looking for. For example, *Define* points you to question 1; *Describe* means you should apply questions 1 and 2; *Discuss* and *Explain* tell you to apply questions 3, 4, 5, and possibly 6; and *Evaluate* points you to question 6.

1. "What is a satisfying career?" What are its significant features or characteristics?

   This question produces useful answers. Answers might include a career that is interesting, well paid, respected, and provides opportunities for advancement.

2. "How is a satisfying career made or chosen?"

   This question would also work. Some answers might include career counselling, experience (perhaps through part-time or volunteer work), research, and aptitude tests.

3. "What are the main parts or components of a satisfying career?"

   We could use this question, too. The components of a satisfying career might include challenging work, good pay, compatible co-workers, and respect in the community.

4. "How is a satisfying career different from something else?"

   This question has limited possibilities. You could develop a contrast between a satisfying career and an unsatisfying one, but there isn't much new to say. The main points are obvious.

5. "Does a satisfying career have causes or effects?"

   It has both:

   • "What causes a satisfying career?"

     Self-analysis, planning, preparation

   • "What are the effects of a satisfying career?"

     Confidence, stability, recognition, happiness

6. "What are the advantages or disadvantages of a satisfying career?"

   Unless you can think of some unusual advantages (i.e., ones that are not covered by the answers to question 3), this question doesn't produce answers that are worth spending your or your readers' time on. You've already discovered the advantages by answering question 3, and there aren't many disadvantages to a satisfying career!

Asking these six questions about your subject will help you decide what approach would be best for your paper. The "best" approach is the one that is most original and most convincing: the main points your paper discusses should seem fresh to your readers and sound reasonable to an educated audience.

The questioning strategy we've outlined above will

- help you define your thesis by identifying the opinion you can best explain or defend and
- put you on the path to drafting your paper by providing some solid main points to work with

Don't rush this process. The more time you spend exploring your subject in the planning stage, the easier the actual drafting of the paper will be.

Below you will find eight sample subjects, together with main points that were discovered by applying the questions on page 142. Study these examples carefully. Figure out the logic that leads from subject to question to main points in each case. When you're finished, you should have a good understanding of how the questioning process can work for you.

Subject	Selected question	Main points
A good teacher	(1) What are the characteristics of a good teacher?	• knowledge of subject • ability to communicate • respect for students
A successful party	(2) How do you give a successful party?	• invite the right mix of people • plan the entertainment • prepare the food in advance • provide a relaxed, friendly atmosphere
Ending a relationship	(2) How can one break off a relationship?	• in person • by phone or voice mail • by text or email message • through friends • by "un-friending" on Facebook
Internet users	(3) What are the main categories of Internet users?	• dabblers • regulars • addicts

Subject	Selected question	Main points
Communication	(4) Differences between spoken and written language	• speech is spontaneous; writing isn't • speech is transitory; writing is permanent • speech can't be revised; writing can
Refugees in Canada	(5) What are the main causes of refugees' coming to Canada?	• persecution in homeland • war in homeland • poverty in homeland
Ending a relationship	(5) What are the causes of breakups?	• failure to communicate • unrealistic expectations • financial incompatibility • friendships with others
Minority government	(6) What are the advantages of a minority government?	• forces compromise from extreme positions • is more responsive to and reflective of the wishes of the entire electorate • engages interest in meaningful debate and discussion of issues

As a general rule, you should try to identify *two* (the absolute minimum) to *five* main ideas to support your subject. If you have only one main idea, your subject is suitable for a paragraph or two, not for an essay. If you have discovered more than five main ideas that require discussion, you have too much material for a short paper. Either select the most important aspects of the subject or take another look at it to see how you can focus it more specifically.

Go to Workbook Exercises 22.4–22.5

Paragraphs and Essays

TESTING YOUR MAIN POINTS

Take a close look at the main points you've chosen for each subject in Exercise 22.5. It may be necessary to revise some of them before going any further. Are some points too trivial to bother with? Do any of the points overlap in meaning? Are there any points that are not directly related to your subject?

Main points must be SIGNIFICANT, DISTINCT, and RELEVANT.

To be satisfactory, the main points you have chosen to write about must all be *significant*: they must require a paragraph or more of explanation. If you have any trivial ideas on your list, now is the time to discard them.

Each of the main points you've chosen must also be *distinct*. That is, each must be different from all the others. There must be no overlap in meaning. Check to be sure you haven't given two different labels to what is really one aspect of the subject.

Finally, each point must be *relevant*; it must be clearly *related* to your subject. It must be an aspect of the subject you are writing about, not some other subject. For example, if you're writing about the advantages of a subject, cross out any disadvantages that may have appeared on your list.

Go to Workbook Exercises 22.6–22.7

ORGANIZING YOUR MAIN POINTS

Now that you've decided on three or four main points to discuss, you need to decide on the order in which to present them in your paper. Choose the order that is most appropriate for your subject and audience.

There are four ways to arrange main points in an essay: CHRONOLOGICAL, CLIMACTIC, LOGICALLY LINKED, and RANDOM order.

1. **Chronological order** means in order of time sequence, from first to last. Here's an example:

Subject	Main points
The development of a relationship	• attraction • meeting • discovery • intimacy

2. **Climactic order** means presenting your strongest or most important point last. Generally, you would discuss your second-strongest point first and the others in between like this:

Subject	Main points
Reasons for the federal government to legislate lower carbon emissions	• Airborne pollutants endanger the health of individual Canadians. • Damage to trees hurts the economy. • Our emissions affect other countries as well as Canada. • Global warming caused by carbon emissions threatens our very existence.

3. **Logically linked order** means that the main points are connected in such a way that one point must be explained before the next can be understood. Consider this example:

Subject	Main points
Main causes of gang involvement	• lack of opportunity for work • lack of recreational facilities • boredom • need for an accepting peer group

The logical link here is this because of unemployment, recreational facilities are needed, and because of both unemployment and inadequate recreational facilities, boredom becomes a problem. Bored by having nothing to do and nowhere to go, young people need an accepting peer group to bolster their self-esteem. The first three points must be explained before the reader can fully understand the fourth.

4. **Random order** means the main points of your paper could be satisfactorily explained in any order. A random arrangement of points is acceptable only if the main points are *equally significant* and *not chronologically or causally linked*, as in this example:

Subject	Main points
Reasons to cycle to school	• fitness • economy • enjoyment

These three points are independent and equally important; they can be effectively explained in any order.

Go to Workbook Exercise 22.8

In this chapter, you've learned how to choose a satisfactory subject; how to discover a thesis; and how to find, test, and arrange main points that support your thesis. Now it's time to think about how to plan your paper. Which will work best for you: the thesis statement method? Or the outline method? We think the former generally works best for short papers and the latter for long papers, but this distinction isn't hard and fast. Your wisest choice is to learn both ways to organize and develop a paper. You will often get the best results if you use them together.

The Thesis Statement **23**

In Chapter 22, you chose a topic and selected some aspects of it to discuss. Your next task is to plan your paper. There are several methods to choose from, ranging from a sentence or two (a thesis statement) to a formal outline. For short papers, we recommend that you use the method presented in this chapter. For longer papers, or if your instructor requires a more detailed outline, you will find instructions in Chapter 24, "The Outline."

The key to a well-organized essay is a **thesis statement**—a statement near the beginning of your paper that announces its subject and scope. The thesis statement helps both you and your readers because it previews the plan of your paper. It tells your readers exactly what they are going to read about.

In fiction, telling readers in advance what they are going to find would never do. But for practical, everyday kinds of writing, advance notice works well. Term papers, technical reports, research papers, office memoranda, and business correspondence are no place for suspense or surprises. In these kinds of writing, you're more likely to get and keep your readers' attention if you indicate the subject and scope of your paper at the outset. A thesis statement acts like a table of contents. It's a kind of map of the territory covered in your paper: it keeps your reader (and you) on the right track.

A thesis statement clearly and concisely indicates the SUBJECT of your paper, the MAIN POINTS you will discuss, and the ORDER in which you will discuss them.[1]

WRITING A THESIS STATEMENT

To write a thesis statement, you join your *subject* to your *main points*, which you have arranged in an appropriate order. To join the two parts of a thesis

---

[1] Not all thesis statements retain the preview portion (i.e., the main points in order of discussion) in the final draft. Nevertheless, we recommend that you begin the drafting process with a full thesis statement. You can always omit the preview of main points in your final copy if it seems redundant.

statement, you use a *link*. Your link can be a word or a phrase such as *are, include, consists of, because,* or *since,* or it can be a colon.[2] Here is a simple formula for constructing a thesis statement. (*S* stands for your subject.)

subject	link	main points
S	consists of	1, 2, 3 ... *n*.

Here's an example:

subject	link	main points

Three characteristics of a good report are conciseness, clarity, and courtesy.

Go to Workbook Exercise 23.1

When you combine your subject with your main points to form a thesis statement, there is an important rule to remember:

Main points must be stated in grammatically parallel form (parallelism).

This rule means that if main point 1 is a word, then main points 2 and 3 and so on must be words, too. If main point 1 is a phrase, then the rest must be phrases. If your first main point is a dependent clause, then the rest must be dependent clauses. Study the model thesis statements you analyzed in Exercise 23.1. In every example, the main points are in grammatically parallel form. For each of those thesis statements, decide whether words, phrases, or dependent clauses were used. If you think your understanding of parallelism is a bit wobbly, review Chapter 9.

Go to Workbook Exercises 23.2–23.8

---

[2] Remember that a colon can be used only after an independent clause. See Chapter 19 if you need a review.

We said at the beginning of this chapter that a complete thesis statement provides a broad outline of your paper. Before we turn to the actual writing of the paper, you should have a general idea of what the finished product will look like.

In a short paper, each main point can be explained in a single paragraph. The main points of your subject become the *topics* of the paragraphs, as shown on the next page in the model format for a paper with three main points.[3] Once you've mastered this simple structure, you can modify, expand, and develop it to suit papers of any length or kind.

Please note that the model format on page 152 is a basic guideline for anyone who is learning to write English prose. Not all essays are—or should be—five paragraphs long. As you will see in Unit 7, unified, coherent essays can be shorter or longer, depending on their subject and purpose. As you gain writing experience, you will learn how to adapt the basic format to suit your needs. A competent writer always adapts form to content, never the other way around. But learners must start somewhere, and the five-paragraph format is an excellent structure to begin with.

Notice the proportions of the paragraphs in the model format. This format is for a paper whose main points are approximately equal in significance, so the body paragraphs are approximately equal in length. (In a paper in which the last main point is more important than the other points, however, the last body paragraph will probably be longer than the others.)

Notice, too, that the introductory and concluding paragraphs are shorter than the ones that explain the main points. Your introduction should not ramble on, and your conclusion should not trail off. Get to your main points quickly, and end with a bang, not a whimper. (Apologies to T. S. Eliot.)

 Go to Workbook Exercise 23.9

---

[3]Chapter 25 will show you how to develop your paragraphs fully and convincingly.

Paragraphs and Essays

Title

_____

Paragraph 1:
Contains your
introduction
and thesis
statement

_____
_____
_____

Subject consists of 1, 2, and 3.
   Topic sentence introducing main point 1.

Paragraph 2:
Explains your
first main point

_____
_____
_____
_____
_____
_____.

Topic sentence introducing main point 2.

Paragraph 3:
Explains your
second main
point

_____
_____
_____
_____
_____
_____.

Topic sentence introducing main point 3.

Paragraph 4:
Explains your
third main
point

_____
_____
_____
_____
_____.

Paragraph 5:
States your
conclusion

_____
_____
_____
_____.

Tom Prisk/CartoonStock

The Outline 24

For longer compositions—business and technical reports, research papers, and the like—an outline is often necessary. A good outline maps out your paper from beginning to end. It shows what you have to say about each of your main points before you begin drafting. Outlining spares you the pain of discovering too late that you have too much information about one point and little or nothing to say about another.

Once you've chosen a satisfactory subject and main points, the next step is to expand this material into an organized plan for your paper. At this point, you may need to do some more thinking or reading to gather additional information. *Evidence*, the term used for supporting information, consists of data, facts, and statements that have been tested and validated by scholars through research or by writers through personal experience. (For the kinds of evidence you can choose from, see "Developing Your Paragraphs" in Chapter 25.) After you've assembled the information you need, prepare the outline.[1]

There are as many different approaches to outlining as there are writers. The outline you prepare will vary depending on your approach to the topic, the amount of time before the due date, and your instructor's preference (or requirement). Here are a few of the strategies you can choose from:

1. Some writers like to start with a "scratch" outline, which consists of one- or two-word points that act as a bare-bones guide.
2. Other writers prefer an informal outline that sketches out the parts of the paper in more detail, showing major headings and a few supporting points.
3. Some writers do best with a full, formal outline with main points, subheadings, and various levels of evidence (up to nine if you're using Word), which are identified by changes in indentation and font size.
4. Writers who like to begin with brainstorming, freewriting, or another inductive technique often choose to postpone outlining until after they see what their creative process produces.

---

[1] The four ways to arrange main ideas in a paper, which we explained in Chapter 23, also apply to the arrangement of evidence within a paragraph. Choose whichever order best suits the nature of your topic and the needs of your audience.

Whatever approach is right for you, your topic, and your instructor, the time you spend on outlining is invested, not wasted. Your investment will pay off in time saved during drafting and revising.

SCRATCH OUTLINE

Your thesis and main points form the beginnings of a scratch outline. Key these into your word processor, together with a few of the ideas you will elaborate on as you develop the main points in your first draft. Now you have a bare-bones outline to guide you as you draft the body of your paper. Here's an example:

Thesis: A satisfying career—interesting, rewarding, productive
- interesting
  – enjoyable
  – like hobbies
  – Clive Beddoe
- rewarding
  – financial rewards
  – emotional rewards
- productive
  – need to contribute
  – unproductive jobs

While this outline means little to anyone other than its author, this is the skeleton of a paper. Once the writer puts some meat on the bones, adds an introduction and a conclusion, he or she will have a good first draft.

INFORMAL OUTLINE

An informal outline carries the scratch outline a step further, adding ideas and examples that will form the content of each paragraph. If you are writing a research paper, you can include source information under the main points. If whole sentences occur to you, key them in, but generally the informal outline is in point form.

Introduction
  Definition of "career"
  Thesis: A satisfying career should be interesting, rewarding, and
  productive.

- Interesting
  1. look forward to going to work
  2. leisure activities are stimulating, why not your career?
     - Examples: artists, Clive Beddoe
  3. important not to waste your life doing something you hate
- Rewarding
  1. know yourself: what do you need to be happy?
     - Are you ambitious? Need status? A high salary?
     - Or do you want a relaxed, low-stress environment?
  2. success is what it means to you
     - Examples: technician, news director—which one is "successful?"
- Productive
  1. human nature to want to contribute, to make a difference
  2. some jobs are easy but meaningless
     - Examples: factory job, night shift

Conclusion

Understanding yourself is key.

Don't be swayed by opinions of others.

Strive to improve for your own sake, not your employer's.

FORMAL OUTLINE

A formal outline is more detailed than a scratch or informal outline. It may be drafted in point form, but even if it isn't, the finished outline usually consists of complete sentences. If you have access to a word-processing program with an outline feature, try it out. Most programs have a "document view" called "Outline," which can be invaluable: it will create a formal outline as fast as you can type. In Word, select the View tab and choose Outline. (In Apple's Pages, the "Template Chooser" has a variety of Outline options.)

Here's how to proceed:

1. Key in your main points in the order you chose for your thesis statement, and hit Enter after each one.
2. Move the cursor to the end of your first main point, hit Enter, and select Level 2 from the window at the top of the screen. This will indent and reduce the font size of the next line you type, which should be a supporting point for the first main point.
3. Hit Enter again and select Level 3 to add examples, other evidence, or a reminder of the research source you intend to use to develop this main point.

By repeating this process for each of your main points, you will end up with a clear visual plan of your essay. The outline will look something like the following:

+ Introduction
  – Hook
  – Thesis statement or statement of subject

+ First main point
  + Supporting point
    – Evidence
  + Supporting point
    – Evidence

+ Second main point
  + Supporting point
    – Evidence
  + Supporting point
    – Evidence

+ Third main point
  + Supporting point
    – Evidence
  + Supporting point
    – Evidence
  + Supporting point
    – Evidence

+ Conclusion
  – Summary
  – Clincher

The outline stage is the time to decide how to present the supporting information under each main point and how much time to spend on a particular point. If, for example, you have six subheadings under your first main point and one under your second, you need to rebalance your paper. Main points should be supported by approximately equal amounts of information.

Creating a satisfactory outline takes time. Be prepared to spend time rearranging, adding, deleting your ideas and supporting details until you're completely satisfied with their arrangement and proportions.

Now you are ready to draft your paper. Make the main points into paragraphs, develop the supporting points, and add an introduction and a conclusion. (Chapter 25 explains how.)

To show you the relationship between an outline and an essay, we've re-created the outline that was used to write "Career Consciousness" on pages 248–249.

Introduction

Hook:	Choosing a life's vocation is not a decision to be taken lightly.
Thesis statement:	A satisfying career is one that is stimulating, rewarding, and productive.

I.   A satisfying career is stimulating.
  A. When you get up in the morning, you look forward to your day.
      1. Not the image most people have of work, but it is achievable.
      2. People can enjoy work just as they enjoy leisure activities.
  B. Many successful people have turned their interests into careers.
      1. Career professionals in the arts get paid for what they love to do.
          a. write, compose, paint, sculpt, etc.
          b. act, dance, sing, etc.
      2. Clive Beddoe: turned his love of flying into the development of WestJet.
  C. If you deny yourself the chance to do what you love, you will spend most of your life wishing you were doing something else.

II.   A satisfying career is financially and emotionally rewarding.
  A. To choose the right career, you need to know yourself:
      1. Do you want power and status?
      2. Or do you want a less stressful position?
  B. Success is a state of mind.
      1. Contrast the careers of a small-town TV tech and a big-city news director.
          a. TV tech loves his job, family, community, and volunteer activities.
          b. News director thrives on deadline pressure, big-city life, money, and recognition.
      2. Both feel they are successful.

III.   A satisfying career is productive.
  A. Everyone needs meaningful work.
      1. Everyone feels the need to make a difference.
      2. Friendly co-workers, pleasant routine, and big salary do not make up for lack of appreciation.
  B. Many people go unnoticed in their working lives.
      1. Some boast about reading paperbacks on the job.
      2. Some sleep through the night shift and fish or golf during the day.
  C. Knowing that you are doing something worthwhile is essential to your sense of well-being.

Paragraphs and Essays

Conclusion

Summary: It's not easy to find a career that provides stimulating, enjoyable, and meaningful work.

A. You need first to understand yourself, so you can ...

B. ... make career decisions consistent with your values and goals.

C. Once you have found a satisfying career, keep working at it.

    1. Seek challenges and opportunities that stimulate you.

    2. Enjoy the rewards of doing your job well.

    3. Strive for improvement for your own sake (not just your employer's).

Clincher: Your career will occupy three-quarters of your life, so make the most of it!

Go to Workbook Exercises 24.1–24.3

Paragraphs 25

With your thesis statement and outline in front of you, you are ready to turn your main points into paragraphs. Does that sound like a magician's trick? It isn't. All you need to know is what a paragraph looks like and how to put one together.

THE PARTS OF A PARAGRAPH

A paragraph looks like this:

> <u>A sentence that introduces the topic (or main idea) of the paragraph goes here.</u>
>
> _____
> _____
> _____
> _____
> _____
>
> <u>A sentence that concludes your explanation of the topic goes here.</u>

Three or more sentences that specifically support or explain the topic go here.

Sometimes you can explain a main point satisfactorily in a single paragraph. If the point is complicated and requires lots of support, you will need two or more paragraphs. Nevertheless, whether it is explaining a main point or a supporting point, every paragraph must contain three things: a **topic sentence** (usually the first sentence in the paragraph), several sentences that develop the topic, and a conclusion or a transition to the next paragraph.

A clear statement of your topic—usually a single sentence—is a good way to start a paragraph. The sentences that follow should support or expand on the topic. The key to making the paragraph *unified* (an important quality of paragraphs) is to make sure that each of your supporting sentences relates directly to the main idea introduced in the topic sentence.

 Go to Workbook Exercise 25.1

DEVELOPING YOUR PARAGRAPHS

How do you put a paragraph together? First, write your topic sentence, telling your reader what topic (main point or key idea) you're going to discuss in the paragraph. Next, develop your topic. An adequately developed paragraph gives enough supporting information to make the topic completely clear to the reader. A body paragraph typically runs between 75 and 200 words (except for introductions and conclusions, which are shorter), so you will need lots of supporting information for each point.

Unless you are writing from a detailed outline and have enough supporting ideas listed in front of you, you need to do some more thinking at this point. Put yourself in your reader's place. What does your reader need to know in order to understand your point clearly? Ask yourself the six questions listed between pages 160 and 167 to determine what *kind*(s) *of development* to use to support a particular topic sentence. The kind(s) of development you choose is up to you. Let your topic and your reader be your guides.

1. Is a DEFINITION necessary?

If you're using a term that may be unfamiliar to your reader, you should define it. Use your own words in the definition. Your reader needs to know what *you* mean by the term—and, besides, quoting from the dictionary is a boring way to develop a paragraph. In the following paragraph, Jeffrey Moussaieff Masson, author of "Dear Dad" (see pages 265–269), defines and describes a penguin *tortue*, a term with which few readers would be familiar.[1]

> [As] soon as the bad weather starts, generally in June, the males need some protection from the bitter cold, and nearly all of them find it by forming a *tortue*, which is a throng of very densely packed penguins. When the storms come they move in close to one another, shoulder to shoulder, and form a circle. The middle of the tortue is unusually warm and one would think that every penguin fights to be at the epicentre of warmth. But in fact what looks like an immobile mass is really a very slowly revolving spiral. The constantly shifting formation

---

[1] The page numbers in parentheses at the end of each block quotation in this chapter indicate either the page number in Unit 7, "Readings," where you will find the quotation in its context, or the page number in the book or article from which the quotation was taken.

is such that every penguin, all the while balancing [a] single precious egg on his feet, eventually winds up in the middle of the tortue, only to find himself later at the periphery. (page 267)

Jeffrey Moussaieff Masson, *Dear Dad*. Reprinted by permission of the author.

You should include a definition, too, if you're using a familiar term in a specific or unusual way. In the following paragraph, Brian Green defines what he means by "slow food."

> The term "slow food" is often misunderstood. When I first heard of the Slow Food movement, I assumed it was devoted to taking a long time to cook savoury meals. Instead, the term was coined in reaction to everything "fast food" represents, from poor-quality ingredients of unknown origin to hastily gobbled meals served in a plastic environment. "Slow food" can actually be cooked quite quickly, so long as the ingredients are fresh and locally produced, and the meal is consumed in a relaxed and convivial atmosphere.

Brian Green, "Cooking under Pressure: Slow Food … Fast," *The Green Snail, Voice of Pelham Newspaper*, January 2, 2010. Reprinted by permission of the author.

Go to Workbook Exercise 25.2

Jungle of paragraphs

2. Would EXAMPLES help to clarify the point?

Providing examples is probably the most common method of developing a topic. Readers who encounter unsupported generalizations or statements of opinion are not convinced. They know they've been left dangling, and they will be confused. They may even become suspicious, thinking that the writer is trying to put one over on them. One of the most effective ways of getting your idea across to your readers is to provide clear, relevant examples. In the following paragraph, excerpted from a reading in Unit 7, Sun-Kyung Yi uses examples to explain why her job with a Korean company proved to be a "painful and frustrating experience."

> When the president of the company boasted that he "operated little Korea," he meant it literally. A Canadianized Korean was not tolerated. I looked like a Korean; therefore, I had to talk, act, and think like one, too. Being accepted meant a total surrender to ancient codes of behaviour rooted in Confucian thought, while leaving the "Canadian" part of me out in the parking lot with my '86 Buick. In the first few days at work, I was bombarded with inquiries about my marital status. When I told them I was single, they spent the following days trying to match me up with available bachelors in the company and the community. I was expected to accept my inferior position as a woman and had to behave accordingly. It was not a place to practice my feminist views, or be an individual without being condemned. Little Korea is a place for men (who filled all the senior positions) and women don't dare speak up or disagree with their male counterparts. The president (all employees bow to him and call him Mr. President) asked me to act more like a lady and smile. I was openly scorned by a senior employee because I spoke more fluent English than Korean. The cook in the kitchen shook her head in disbelief upon discovering that my cooking skills were limited to boiling a package of instant noodles. "You want a good husband, learn to cook," she advised me. (page 253)

Sun-Kyung Yi, "An Immigrant's Split Personality," *The Globe and Mail*, April 12, 1992.

Sometimes one or two examples developed in detail are enough to enable the reader to picture what you mean. In the following paragraph, Brian Green first defines what he means by *a rewarding career*, and then he provides two examples to illustrate his definition.

> If your career is stimulating, then chances are good that it can also be rewarding. A good career offers two kinds of rewards: financial and emotional. Rewarding work doesn't just happen; it's something you need to plan

for. The first and most important step is to know yourself. Only if you know who you are and what you need to be happy can you consciously seek out career experiences that will bring you satisfaction and steer clear of those that will annoy or stress you. Are you genuinely ambitious, or is power something you seek because you think it is expected of you? The pursuit of status and a high salary brings some people pure pleasure. Many people, however, find leadership positions excruciatingly stressful. Career enjoyment depends to some extent on whether or not you are successful, and success is a state of mind. Consider two graduates from the same college program. One is a technician in a small-town television station who loves his work, takes pride in keeping the station on the air, and delights in raising his family in a community where he is involved in volunteer activities ranging from sports to firefighting. The other is a news director at one of Canada's major television networks. Her work is highly stressful, full of risks, and continually scrutinized by viewers, competitors, and her supervisors. She thrives on the adrenaline rush of nightly production, and loves the big-city life, the financial rewards of her position, and the national recognition she receives. Which graduate is "successful"? Certainly, both feel their careers are rewarding, according to their individual definitions of the term. (pages 248–249)

Go to Workbook Exercise 25.3

3. Is a series of STEPS or STAGES involved?

Sometimes the most effective way to develop the main idea of your paragraph is by explaining how to do it—that is, by relating the process or series of steps involved. Make sure you break the process down into its component parts and explain the steps logically and precisely. Below, Jeffrey Masson explains the mating process of emperor penguins:

> The emperors usually wait for good weather to copulate, any time between April 10 and June 6. They separate themselves somewhat from the rest of the colony and face each other, remaining still for a time. Then the male bends his head, contracts his abdomen, and shows the female the spot on his belly where he has a flap of skin that serves as a kind of pouch for the egg and baby chick. This stimulates the female to do the same. Their

Paragraphs and Essays

heads touch, and the male bends his head down to touch the female's pouch. Both begin to tremble visibly. Then the female lies face down on the ice, partially spreads her wings and opens her legs. The male climbs onto her back and they mate for 10 to 30 seconds. (pages 265–66)

Jeffrey Moussaieff Masson, *Dear Dad*. Reprinted by permission of the author.

Go to Workbook Exercise 25.4

4. Would SPECIFIC DETAILS be useful?

Providing your reader with concrete, specific, descriptive details can be an effective way of developing your main point. In the following paragraph, highlight the specific details that bring to life Russell Wangersky's description of Newfoundland's outport communities:

> There's life yet in gritty, tightly knit outport communities. In Reefs Harbour on Newfoundland's Northern Peninsula, a handful of fishing sheds, their sides weathered to a uniform silver-grey, stand like forgotten teeth on a half-buried lower jaw. Lobster markers hang from coils of yellow rope inside their dusty windows. A single boat curves in towards the harbour, its engine the only sound in the still air, a solitary fisherman at the stern. Every few seconds, a small wave breaks over the shoals in the harbour, loud enough to drown out the vessel's approach. You can't shake the feeling that Reefs Harbour is asleep, asleep like Rip Van Winkle, breathing slowly through a nap that could last for years. (page 21)

Russell Wangersky, "Clinging to the Rock." Reprinted by permission of the author.

In some paragraphs, numerical facts or statistics can be used to support your point effectively. However, ever since Benjamin Disraeli's immortal remark that the media publish "lies, damned lies, and statistics," critical readers tend to be suspicious of statistics. Be certain that your facts are correct and that your statistics are current.

Canadians are great travellers. We not only travel around our own country, exploring every nook and cranny from Beaver Creek in the Yukon Territory to Bay Bulls in Newfoundland, but we also can be found touring around every other country on Earth. Statistics Canada reports that we take more than 320 million overnight trips a year within our own borders. Abroad, we favour our next-door neighbour by a wide margin above other destinations, averaging around 20 million overnight trips a year to the United States. Mexico is our second-favourite destination, with over 1.3 million visits, followed by Cuba (1 million) and the United Kingdom (880,000). The Dominican Republic (753,000) and France (740,000) round out the top six. China ranks ninth in popularity with 300,000 visits, but Hong Kong, now part of China, attracts an additional 183,000 Canadian visitors, making their combined total ahead of Italy for seventh spot, followed by Germany, the Netherlands, and Spain. The top 15 Canadian destinations are rounded out by Jamaica, the Republic of Ireland, and Switzerland. We can make a rough estimate from these figures that, on average, a Canadian travels within Canada nine times a year and takes a trip abroad twice in three years. (n.p. Statistics)

Sun-Kyung Yi, "An Immigrant's Split Personality," *The Globe and Mail,* April 12, 1992.

 Go to Workbook Exercise 25.5

5. Would a COMPARISON or CONTRAST help to clarify your point?

A **comparison** points out similarities between objects, people, or ideas; it shows how two different things are alike. A **contrast** points out dissimilarities between things; it shows how two similar objects, people, or ideas are different. In the paragraph that follows, Sun-Kyung Yi contrasts the two sides of her "split personality":

When I was younger, toying with the idea of entertaining two separate identities was a real treat, like a secret game for which no one knew the rules but me. I was known as Angela to the outside world, and as Sun-Kyung at home. I ate bologna sandwiches in the school lunchroom and rice and kimchee for dinner. I chatted about teen idols and giggled with my girlfriends during my classes, and ambitiously practiced piano and studied in the evenings, planning to become a doctor when I grew up. I waved hellos and goodbyes to my teachers, but bowed to my parents' friends visiting our home. I could also look straight in the eyes of my teachers and friends and talk frankly with them instead of staring at my feet with my mouth shut when Koreans talked to me. Going outside the home meant I was able to relax from the constraints of my cultural conditioning, until I walked back in the door and had to return to being an obedient and submissive daughter. (page 252)

Sun-Kyung Yi, "An Immigrant's Split Personality," *The Globe and Mail*, April 12, 1992.

Sometimes it's possible to develop a single point of comparison or contrast; that is, instead of providing several examples of likeness (or difference—as we saw in the example above), you can focus on a single comparison (or contrast) and provide your reader with a detailed picture. In the following paragraph, the author develops her topic—how lack of planning can kill a city—by comparing the anatomy of a city to that of the human body.

A poorly planned city dies from the centre out. When an unplanned urban area is growing rapidly, businesses and residential developments spring up wherever it is advantageous for them to locate. In time, they become plaque deposits on the very arteries that they chose to build on, gradually narrowing and choking the city's passageways. New routes cannot be constructed without major surgery, nor can the old ones be widened because of the poorly planned developments that line them. Without sufficient flow along its arteries, an organism begins to experience high pressure—whether from traffic or blood. As the pressure builds, those who live and work in the city core seek to relocate to more convenient, less stressful surroundings, and the centre begins to die. Keeping arteries open and healthy requires advance planning and constant vigilance. In the human organism, a healthy diet and physical exercise will keep the blood flowing; in the urban organism, mass transit and well-planned traffic corridors will do the trick. (page 315)

Sarah Norton, "Our Cities, Ourselves." Reprinted by permission of the author.

 Go to Workbook Exercise 25.6

6. Would a QUOTATION or PARAPHRASE be appropriate?

Use a quotation when you find that someone else—an expert in a particular field, a well-known author, or a respected public figure—has said what you want to say better or more convincingly than you could ever hope to say it. In these cases, quotations—as long as they are kept short and not used too frequently—are useful in developing your topic. In the following paragraph, Brian Green quotes humorist Robert Benchley and a Portuguese proverb to sum up what many of us have often thought but not been able to express so wittily and concisely.

> "Nothing is more responsible for the good old days than a bad memory." Robert Benchley got it right. Those who continually praise the past and decry the present are victims of selective memory. They are people who are dissatisfied with their lives and want to believe that conditions in the past were better. For these pessimists, today's glass is half empty, while yesterday's was half full. But under objective scrutiny, the pessimists' bias seldom stands up. Even when a few conditions from the past may be preferable to conditions in the present, innumerable other factors will have improved. We would do well to learn from the Portuguese about the pitfalls of the pessimists' selective nostalgia: "What was hard to bear is sweet to remember." (page 6)

Brian Green. Reprinted by permission of the author.

A **paraphrase** is a summary of someone else's idea in your own words. It is fair to rewrite the idea, but you must identify your source. In the following paragraph, Dahlia Rodriguez uses a paraphrase and then a quotation from an expert to explain one reason that it is so difficult for adults to learn a second language:

> An adult has intellectual and cognitive skills that a child lacks. An adult can think abstractly and is able to memorize vocabulary and learn grammar (Crystal 373). These skills might seem to make it easier to learn a new language, but in fact the opposite is true. An adult already has a firmly established first language in his or her intellectual repertoire, and the native language interferes with mastering the second language. An academic study entitled "When It Hurts (and Helps) to Try: The Role of Effort in Language Learning" researched adult language learners and concluded that effort and concentration on linguistic details can actually impede learning: "a learner with less attentional capacity . . . would have less interference and better learning outcomes" (Finn). Thus children, who learn grammar by osmosis rather than memorization, are more effective language learners than adults. (page 271)

Paragraphs and Essays

College writing normally requires that you identify the source of any material you quote or paraphrase. The easiest way to do this is to include a parenthetical citation at the end of your quotation and full publication details in the Works Cited or References list at the end of your paper. If you give the author's name in the sentence leading up to the quotation, you need give only the page number(s) of the source in which you found it, if using MLA style, and only the year of publication and page number, if using APA style. If you do not give the author's name in your introduction to the quotation, you need to include it as well in the parentheses at the end of the quotation.

If your quotation is short enough to be included in your own sentence, put the period *after* the source information. For example,

> According to Brian Green, "A career can be defined as the employment you prepare for during the first quarter of your life, engage in during the best years of your life, and reap the rewards from when you are least able to enjoy them" (248).

> One writer takes a fairly cynical view of the typical career cycle: "A career can be defined as the employment you prepare for during the first quarter of your life, engage in during the best years of your life, and reap the rewards from when you are least able to enjoy them" (Green 248).

At the end of your paper, include a Works Cited or References list: a list in alphabetical order by authors' surnames of all the websites, books, articles, and other publications from which you have paraphrased, summarized, or quoted in your paper. Ask your instructor which documentation style is required: the Modern Language Association (MLA) style, the one approved by the American Psychological Association (APA), or some other style.[2]

When you plan the paragraphs of your essay, you will often need to use more than one method of development to explain each point. The six methods outlined in this chapter can be used in any combination. Choose whichever kinds of development will best help your reader understand what you want to say about your topic.

Go to Workbook Exercises 25.7–25.8

---

[2] See pages 270–274 for an example of an essay written in MLA format and pages 275–279 for the same paper in APA format.

WRITING INTRODUCTIONS AND CONCLUSIONS

Two paragraphs in your paper are not developed in the way we've just out-lined: the *introduction* and the *conclusion*. All too often, these paragraphs are dull or clumsy and detract from a paper's effectiveness. But they needn't. Here's how to write good ones.

The introduction is worth special attention because that's where your reader either sits up and takes notice of your paper or sighs and pitches it into the wastebasket. Occasionally, for a short paper, you can begin by simply stating your thesis. More usually, though, a **hook** comes before the thesis statement. A hook is a sentence or two designed to get the reader interested in what you have to say.

There are several kinds of hooks to choose from:

1. A question (see "Learning a New Language: Why Is It So Hard?" page 270)
2. A definition (see "Career Consciousness," page 248)
3. A little-known or striking fact (see "An Immigrant's Split Personality," page 252)
4. A comparison or contrast that will intrigue your reader (see "Dear Dad," page 265)
5. An interesting incident or **anecdote** related to your subject (see "Point, Click, Date: The Online Matchmaking Phenomenon," page 261)

Add your thesis statement to the hook and your introduction is complete.

The closing paragraph, too, usually has two parts: a **summary statement** of the main points of your paper (phrased differently, please—not a word-for-word repetition of your thesis statement or topic sentences) and a **clincher**. Your clincher may take several forms. For example, it may do any of the following:

1. refer to the content of your opening paragraph (see "My Father and the Seal," page 251)
2. include a relevant or thought-provoking quotation, statement, or question (see "Learning a New Language: Why Is It So Hard?" page 273)
3. emphasize the value or significance of your subject (see "Point, Click, Date: The Online Matchmaking Phenomenon," page 264)
4. make a suggestion for change (see "An Immigrant's Split Personality," page 253)
5. offer a solution, make a prediction, or invite the reader to get involved (see "Career Consciousness," page 249)

Go to Workbook Exercise 25.9

KEEPING YOUR READER WITH YOU

As you write your paragraphs, keep in mind that you want to make it as easy as possible for your reader to follow your paper. Clear transitions and an appropriate tone can make the difference between a paper that baffles readers and one that enlightens them.

TRANSITIONS

Transitions are words and phrases that show the relationship between one point and the next, making a paragraph or a paper read smoothly. Like turn signals on a car, they tell the person following you where you're going. Here are some common transitions you can use to keep your reader on track:

1. **To show a time relationship:** first, second, third, next, before, during, after, now, then, finally, last
2. **To add an idea or example:** in addition, also, another, furthermore, similarly, for example, for instance
3. **To show contrast:** although, but, however, instead, nevertheless, on the other hand, in contrast, on the contrary
4. **To show a cause–effect relationship:** as a result, consequently, because, since, therefore, thus

The following paragraph has adequate development but no transitions:

There are several good reasons you should not smoke. Smoking is harmful to your lungs and heart. It is annoying and dangerous to those around you who do not smoke. Smoking is an unattractive and dirty habit. It is difficult to quit. Most worthwhile things in life are hard to achieve.

Not very easy to read, is it? Readers are jerked from point to point until, battered and bruised, they reach the end. This kind of writing is unfair to readers. It makes them do too much of the work—more work than many readers are willing to do. The ideas may all be there, but readers have to figure out for themselves how the points fit together. After a couple of paragraphs like this one, even a patient reader can become frustrated.

Now read the same paragraph with transitions added:

> There are several good reasons you should not smoke. Among them, three stand out as the most persuasive. First, smoking is harmful to your lungs and heart. Second, it is both annoying and dangerous to those around you who do not smoke. In addition to these compelling facts, smoking is an unattractive and dirty habit. Furthermore, once you begin, it is difficult to quit. But then, most worthwhile things in life are hard to achieve.

In the revised paragraph, readers are gently guided from one point to the next. By the time they reach the conclusion, they know not only what ideas the writer had in mind but also how they fit together. Transitions make a reader's job easier and more rewarding.

TONE

One final point: as you write the paragraphs of your paper, be conscious of your **tone**. Your audience, purpose, and subject will all influence the tone you choose, which must be appropriate to all three. The words you use, the examples, quotations, and other supporting materials you choose to explain your main points all contribute to your tone.

When you are trying to explain something to someone, particularly if it's something you feel strongly about, you may be tempted to get highly emotional in your discussion. If you give in to this temptation, chances are you won't be convincing. What will be communicated is the strength of your feelings, not the depth of your understanding or the validity of your opinion. To be clear and credible, you need to restrain your enthusiasm or anger and present your points in a calm, reasonable way.

Here are a few suggestions to help you find and maintain the right tone.

- Be tactful. Avoid phrases such as "Any idiot can see," "No sane person could believe," and "It is obvious that...." What is obvious to you isn't necessarily obvious to someone who has a limited understanding of your topic or who disagrees with your opinion.

- Don't address your readers as though they were children or ignorant. Never use sarcasm, profanity, or slang. (If you do, your readers will neither take you seriously nor respect you.)
- Don't apologize for your interpretation of your topic. Have confidence in yourself. You've thought long and hard about your subject, you've found good supporting material to help explain it, and you believe in its significance. State your thesis positively. If you hang back, using phrases such as "I may be wrong, but ..." or "I tend to feel that ...," your reader won't be inclined to give your points the consideration they deserve. If you present your argument with assurance and courtesy, your writing will be clear and convincing.

The following paragraph is an example of inappropriate tone. The writer is enthusiastic about the topic, but the tone is arrogant, bossy, and tactless rather than persuasive.

> How dumb can people get? Here's this guy with a bumper sticker reading "Out of work yet? Keep buying foreign!" on his "North American" car parked in a Walmart parking lot. What can you buy in Walmart that's made in Canada? Zilch. And besides, the car this idiot is driving wasn't made in Canada or even the United States. The engine was imported from Japan, and the transmission was made by Mexicans working for next to nothing. The plastic body moulding came from that model of capitalism and human rights, China, and the interior finishings were made in Taiwan. Not foreign? Give me a break. About the only part of this car that was made here is the bumper that holds his stupid sticker. Meanwhile, parked right next to him was a "Japanese" car that was manufactured in Canada by Ontario workers. Sticker Guy is obviously too ignorant to get the irony.

Now read the paragraph below, which argues the same point but in a more tactful way.

> As the driver pulled into the parking spot beside me, I could hardly help noticing his bumper sticker: "Out of work yet? Keep buying foreign!" It was attached to a car produced by one of North America's "Big Three" auto-makers, but the message lost much of its force because of where we were: in a Walmart parking lot. There is precious little to buy in Walmart that has been produced in Canada. However, even that fact is beside the point,

given the current internationalization of the auto industry. The car with the sticker on it, while nominally North American in origin, had an engine produced in Japan, a transmission built in Mexico, plastic body moulding made in China, and interior finishings imported from Taiwan. One of the few parts actually made in Canada, ironically, was the bumper to which the sticker was attached. Meanwhile, the car next to it, a "Japanese" mid-size, had been built in Ontario.

Go to Workbook Exercises 25.10–25.11

26 Revising Your Paper

No one can write in a single draft an essay that is perfectly organized and developed, let alone one that is free of grammar, spelling, and punctuation errors. The purpose of the first draft is to get down on paper something you can work with until it meets your reader's needs and expectations. Planning and drafting should take about half the time you devote to writing a paper. The other half should be devoted to revision.

Revision is the process of refining your message until

- it says what you want it to say
- your reader(s) will understand it
- your reader(s) will receive it favourably

These three goals are the essentials of good communication. You can achieve them only if you keep your readers in mind as you revise. Because a first draft reflects the contents of the writer's mind, it usually seems fine to the writer. But in order to transfer an idea clearly from the mind of the writer to the mind of the reader, revision is necessary. The idea needs to be honed and refined until it is as clear to your reader as it is to you. By revising from your reader's point of view, you can avoid misunderstandings before they happen.

WHAT IS REVISION?

Revision means "re-seeing." It does *not* mean "re-copying." The aim of revision is to improve your writing's organization, accuracy, and style. Revising is a three-stage process. Each step requires that you read through your entire paper, painful though this may be. The goal of your first reading is to ensure that you've organized and developed your ideas in a way that your reader can follow. In your second reading, you focus on paragraphs and sentences—the building blocks of prose. Your third reading concentrates on correctness and style. Here are the steps to follow in revising a paper.

1. Improve the whole paper by revising its content and organization.
2. Refine paragraph and sentence structure, and correct any errors in grammar.
3. Edit and proofread to eliminate errors in word choice, spelling, and punctuation.

Inexperienced writers often skip the first two stages and concentrate on the third, thinking they will save time. They are making a mistake. They are wasting time—both theirs and their readers'—because the result is writing that doesn't communicate clearly and won't make a positive impression.

The best way to begin revising is to do nothing to the first draft of your paper for several days. Let as much time as possible pass between completing your draft and rereading it. Ten minutes, or even half a day, is not enough. The danger in rereading too soon is that you're likely to "read" what you *think* you've written—what exists in your head, not on the page.

If you haven't allowed enough time for this cooling-off period, don't despair. There are two other things you can do to help you get some distance from your draft. If your first draft is handwritten, type it out. Reading your essay in a different format helps you to "re-see" its content. If you've drafted your paper on a computer, sometimes printing it in a different size and style of font will help you see with fresh eyes what you've written. Alternatively, read your paper aloud and listen to it from the point of view of your reader. Hear how your explanation unfolds, and mark every place your reader may find something unclear, irrelevant, inadequately developed, or out of order. To succeed as a writer—even if your message consists of a brief clinical record or an outline of a simple task—you must be able to get into the head of your reader and compose your message to complement the knowledge (or lack of knowledge) that resides there.

STEP 1: REVISE CONTENT AND ORGANIZATION

As you read your paper aloud, keep in mind the three possible kinds of changes you can make at this stage:

1. You can *rearrange* information. This is the kind of revision that is most often needed but least often done. Consider the order in which you've arranged your paragraphs. From your reader's point of view, is this the most effective order in which to present your ideas? If you are not already using a word-processing program, now is the time to begin. With a good word processor, moving blocks of text around is as easy as shuffling a deck of cards.

Paragraphs and Essays

2. You can *add* information. Adding new main ideas or further development of the ideas already there is often necessary to make your message clear, interesting, and convincing. It's a good idea to ask a friend to read your draft and identify what you should expand or clarify. (Be sure to return the favour. You can learn a great deal by critiquing other people's writing.)

3. You can *delete* information. Now is the time to cut out anything that is repetitious, insignificant, or irrelevant to your subject and reader.

Use the checklist that follows to guide you as you review your paper's form and content.

CONTENT AND ORGANIZATION CHECKLIST

ACCURACY

Is everything you have said accurate?

- Is your information consistent with your own experience and observations or with what you have discovered through research?
- Are all your facts and evidence up to date?

COMPLETENESS

Have you included enough main ideas and development to explain your subject and convince your reader? (Remember that "enough" is determined from the reader's point of view, not the writer's.)

- If your paper involves research, have you provided an appropriate source citation for every quotation and paraphrase?
- Have you attached a Works Cited or References list, if one is required?

SUBJECT

Is your subject

- significant? Does it avoid the trivial or the obvious?
- single? Does it avoid double or combined subjects?
- specific? Is it focused and precise?
- supportable? Have you provided enough evidence to make your meaning clear and convincing?

MAIN POINTS

Are your main points

- significant? Have you deleted any unimportant ones?
- distinct? Are they all different from one another, or is there an overlap in content?
- relevant? Do all points relate directly to your subject?
- arranged in the most appropriate order? Again, "appropriate" means from the reader's perspective. Choose chronological, climactic, logical, or random order, depending on which is most likely to help the reader make sense of your information.

INTRODUCTION

Does your introduction

- catch attention and make the reader want to read on?
- contain a clearly identifiable thesis statement?
- identify the main points that your paper will explain?

CONCLUSION

Does your conclusion

- contain a summary or reinforcement of your main points, rephrased to avoid word-for-word repetition?
- contain a statement that effectively clinches your argument and leaves the reader with something to think about?

TONE

Is your tone reasonable, courteous, and confident throughout your essay?

Paragraphs and Essays

When you have carefully considered these questions, it's time to move on to the second stage of the revision process.

Go to Workbook Exercise 26.1

STEP 2: REVISE PARAGRAPHS AND SENTENCES

For this step, too, you should allow time—at least a couple of days—between your first revision and your second. Enough time must elapse to allow you to tackle your paper as if you were seeing it for the first time. Once again, read your draft aloud, and use this list of questions to help you improve it.

PARAGRAPH AND SENTENCE CHECKLIST

PARAGRAPHS

Does each paragraph
- begin with a clear, identifiable topic sentence?
- develop one—and only one—main idea?
- present one or more kinds of development appropriate to the main idea?
- contain clear and effective transitions to signal the relationship between sentences? between paragraphs?

SENTENCES

Sentence Structure
1. Is each sentence clear and complete?
   - Are there any fragments or run-ons?
   - Are there any misplaced or dangling modifiers?
   - Are all lists (whether words, phrases, or clauses) expressed in parallel form?
2. Are your sentences varied in length? Could some be combined to improve the clarity and impact of your message?

Grammar

1. Have you used verbs correctly?
   - Are all verbs in the correct form?
   - Do all verbs agree with their subjects?
   - Are all verbs in the correct tense?
   - Are there any unnecessary shifts in verb tense within a paragraph?
2. Have you used pronouns correctly?
   - Are all pronouns in the correct form?
   - Do all pronouns agree with their antecedents?
   - Have vague pronoun references been eliminated?
   - Are there any unnecessary shifts in pronoun person within a paragraph?

When you're sure you've answered these questions satisfactorily, complete Exercise 26.2, and then go to the third and last stage of the revision process.

Go to Workbook Exercise 26.2

John Morris/CartoonStock

"Shall I rephrase this letter so it makes sense?"

STEP 3: EDIT AND PROOFREAD

By now you're probably so tired of refining your paper that you may be tempted to skip **editing** (correcting errors in word choice, spelling, punctuation, and formatting) and **proofreading** (correcting errors that appear in the final draft). But these final tasks are essential if you want your paper to make a positive impression. Misspellings, faulty punctuation, and messiness don't always create misunderstandings, but they do cause the reader to form a lower opinion of you and your work. Not convinced? Go to www.youtube .com/watch?v=p_rwB5_3PQc and see for yourself.

Most word-processing programs include a grammar checker and a spell checker. It is worthwhile running your writing through these checks at the editing stage. The newer programs have some useful features. For example, they will question (but not correct) your use of apostrophes, they will sometimes catch errors in subject–verb agreement, and they will catch obvious misspellings and typos.

But don't make the mistake of assuming these programs will do all of your editing for you. Many errors can't be caught by a computer, no matter how comprehensive the salesperson told you it is. Only you or a knowledgeable and patient friend can find and correct all errors.

If spelling is a particular problem for you, you should begin this third stage of revision by running your paper through a spell checker. After that, you're on your own. Read your paper backward, word-by-word, from the end to the beginning. Reading backward forces you to look at each word by itself and helps you to spot those that look suspicious. Whenever you're in doubt about the spelling of a word, look it up! If you find this task too tedious to bear, ask a good speller to read through your paper for you and identify any errors. (Then take this person out for dinner. If you get an A, add a show.)

Here are the questions to ask yourself when you are editing:

EDITING CHECKLIST
WORDS

Usage

Have you used words to *mean* rather than to impress?
- Have you eliminated any slang, pretentious language, or offensive language?
- Have you cut out any unnecessary words?
- Have you corrected any "abusages"?
- Have you looked up the meanings of words you're not absolutely certain about?

Spelling

Are all words spelled correctly?

- Have you double-checked any homonyms? (See Chapter 2, and double-check any words listed there that you've highlighted.)
- Have you used capital letters where they are needed?
- Have you used apostrophes correctly for possessives and omitted them from plurals?

PUNCTUATION

Within Sentences

- Have you eliminated any unnecessary commas and included commas where needed? (Refer to the five comma rules in Chapter 17 as you consider this question.)
- Have you used colons and semicolons where appropriate?
- Are all short and long quotations appropriately indicated? (See Chapter 20.)

Beginnings and Endings

- Does each sentence begin with a capital letter?
- Do all questions—and only questions—end with a question mark?
- Are all quotation marks correctly placed?

FORMATTING AND DOCUMENTATION (IF REQUIRED)

- Does your paper satisfy all formatting details specified by your instructor?
- Have you provided a reference for the source of every quotation and paraphrase?
- Have you attached a properly formatted Works Cited or References list?

 Go to Workbook Exercise 26.3

Paragraphs and Essays

John Morris/CartoonStock

"Contrary to your belief Miss Tonks, spelling and punctuation is not a fad!"

TIPS FOR EFFECTIVE PROOFREADING

By the time you have finished editing, you will have gone over your paper so many times you may have practically memorized it. When you are very familiar with a piece of writing, it's hard to spot the small mistakes that may have crept in as you produced your final copy. Here are some tips to help you find those tiny, elusive errors:

1. Read through your essay line by line, using a ruler to guide you and keep you focused only on the line you're reviewing.
2. If you've been keeping a list of your most frequent errors in this course, scan your essay for the mistakes you are most likely to make.
3. Use the Quick Revision Guide on the inside front cover of this book to make a final check of all aspects of your paper.
4. Use the Correction Abbreviations and Symbols on the inside back cover as you review errors your instructor has identified in your writing.

Your "last" draft may need further revision after your proofreading review. If so, take the time to revise the paper one last time so that the version you hand in is clean and easy to read. Computers make editing and proofreading almost painless since errors are so easy to correct.

 Go to Workbook Exercise 26.4

At long last, you're ready to submit your paper. If you've conscientiously followed the three steps of revision, you can hand in your paper confidently, knowing that it says what you want it to say, both about your subject and about you. One last word of advice:

SAVE EVERY REVISION UNDER A DIFFERENT FILENAME, AND KEEP A COPY OF THE VERSION YOU SUBMITTED (WITH "FINAL" IN THE FILENAME)!

 Go to Workbook Exercise 26.5

Paragraphs and Essays

27 Using Research Resources Responsibly

PARAPHRASE OR PLAGIARISM?

In our culture, using someone else's words or ideas in your writing without acknowledging the source is considered to be **plagiarism**, and it is a serious offence. Plagiarism is an attempt by a writer to deceive the reader into thinking that he or she wrote the material. In the academic world, even when plagiarism is unintentional, it can lead to consequences ranging from a grade of zero on a paper to a failing grade in the course or even expulsion from the college or university. In the business world and in the media, a writer who plagiarizes can expect to be fired.

Many students think that it is all right to use information they've found if they change the wording of the ideas they want to borrow. This is not so. *Any information or ideas that cannot be considered common knowledge must be acknowledged or credited.* Even if you put someone else's original idea into your own words, you must tell your reader the source of the information. Any material that is taken word for word from another writer must be put in quotation marks and its source given. (See "Crediting Your Sources," below.)

Paraphrasing is including another writer's idea in your essay but expressing it in your own words. The ability to paraphrase well is an immensely useful skill, but it is not easy to learn. You will need much experience before you can produce effective paraphrases. One of the reasons you are assigned research papers in college or university is to give you practice in paraphrasing. Here are the guidelines to follow:

1. A paraphrase must accurately and clearly relate the author's idea.
2. A paraphrase must express the author's idea in your own words.
3. The source of the idea must be included, using the documentation format that has been specified by your instructor or chosen by you.

To see the differences between paraphrase and plagiarism, study the paragraphs that follow. We have taken as our example a paragraph from "Career Consciousness," which you will find on page 249.

Original

It is not easy to find a career that provides stimulating, enjoyable, and meaningful work. Understanding yourself—your interests, needs, values, and goals—is an essential first step. Making long-term decisions consistent with your values and goals is the difficult second step. Too many people spend their lives in careers that make them miserable because they allow themselves to be governed by parents, friends, or simple inertia. Finally, once you have launched your career, never rest. Actively seek challenges and opportunities that stimulate you. Relish the rewards of meeting those challenges, being productive, and doing your job well. Continually strive to improve, not for the sake of your employer, but for your own sake. Your career will occupy three-quarters of your life, so make the most of it!

Unacceptable paraphrase

In "Career Consciousness," Brian Green points out that it is not easy to find a career that is stimulating, enjoyable, and meaningful. The first step is to understand yourself, your interests, needs, values, and goals. The second step is making long-term decisions consistent with your values and goals. Too often, people devote their lives to careers that make them unhappy because they permit themselves to be influenced by family, friends, or plain laziness. Once you have decided on a career, look for challenges and opportunities that are stimulating and keep striving to improve, not for the sake of the employer, but for your own sake. Make the most of your career because it will occupy three-quarters of your life.

Neither a quotation nor a true paraphrase, this paragraph is an example of plagiarism. Its phrasing is too close to that of the original. Even though the paragraph acknowledges the source of the ideas, it presents those ideas in the same order and often in the same words as the original. And when the words are not identical, the sentence structure is. For example, compare the following two sentences and note the similarity between the two sets of high- lighted words:

Original

Too many people spend their lives in careers that make them miserable because they allow themselves to be governed by parents, friends, or simple inertia.

and

Too often, people devote their lives to careers that make them unhappy because they permit themselves to be influenced by family, friends, or plain laziness.

The second sentence is an example of what happens when an inexperienced writer tries to create a paraphrase by relying on a thesaurus to "translate" the original. The identical sentence structure is a dead giveaway—not only of what the writer was trying to do but also of how he or she was trying to do it.

Better paraphrase

Two factors are essential to long-term career satisfaction. In "Career Consciousness," Brian Green says that the first is to know yourself and make a career choice that is consistent with your personal values and goals, rather than allow the decision to be made for you by others. The second, according to Green, is to continue to look for opportunities once you have begun your career. By continually seeking ways to improve your performance and meet new challenges, not only will you please your employer, but you will also make your job stimulating and satisfying.

USING ONLINE SOURCES

When using Internet sources for research, remember that the Internet is largely unregulated. Even seasoned researchers are sometimes fooled into thinking that a particular posting is factual when it is only someone's—and not necessarily an expert's—opinion. One of your responsibilities as a student researcher is to evaluate the sources of information you use to ensure that they are authoritative and creditable. Many websites try to give the appearance of being official and objective when, in fact, they have a distinct point of view that they are trying to promote. Unfortunately, there is no standard test or measure you can apply to distinguish between fact and propaganda.

"Nice essay, Tom, your cut and paste skills are beyond reproach."

One of the most popular sites for research material is *Wikipedia*, which is a gold mine of information. However, researchers must be aware that *Wikipedia* entries are written by members of the public. Anyone can add, edit, or contribute to the entries. Can this information be trusted? Since entries are monitored by professional scholars and expert amateurs, as well as by Wikipedia employees, in many cases, it can. But there is no guarantee that a *Wikipedia* entry is accurate, up to date, or unbiased. If you cannot rely on *Wikipedia* without question, imagine how careful you must be in using information from blogs and discussion forums!

A more reliable source of expert information is Google Scholar. This search engine enables you to search for books, articles, dissertations, and other publications across a broad range of disciplines. You can narrow your search in terms of place, date, even author (if you know the name) to come up with potentially useful material. One caution: often just the abstracts of articles are posted. To read the whole text of an article you're interested in, you'll need to find out if your resource centre subscribes to the journal in which the article was published.

Always check the trustworthiness of an Internet source. One way to confirm the accuracy of information you want to use is by consulting several different sources to see if they agree. If you are unsure about a source, check with your instructor to confirm whether information from that source is reliable for the research project you are doing.

CREDITING YOUR SOURCES: MLA AND APA DOCUMENTATION

When you use material that you have found in your reading, you must tell the reader where that material came from. This process is called *documentation*, and it consists of two parts: parenthetical citations, which you insert into the text of your paper immediately after the quotations or paraphrases that you've used to support a point, and a list at the end of the paper of all the sources you refer to in your paper. (Some teachers require that you list all the sources you consulted during the course of your research.)

There are two reasons you must use source citations: first, they enable your readers to locate your sources if they want to read more about your subject; and, second, they protect you from the charge of plagiarism. Unfortunately, you cannot just name the author and title of the work(s) you have borrowed from. The standard style for papers in the humanities (English, history, art, philosophy, etc.) differs from the standard style required for papers in the social sciences (economics, psychology, sociology, political science, etc.). Your instructors may have specific requirements for acknowledging sources. If so, follow them to the letter. And don't be surprised if different teachers have different requirements. Documentation styles are a kind of shorthand for experienced readers: scholars can look at a References or Works Cited entry and know immediately what kind of source it identifies and whether or not that source is current and reliable.

As a student researcher, you need to be familiar with at least two documentation systems: MLA and APA. The initials stand for the organizations (Modern Language Association and American Psychological Association) that developed these formats for writers submitting papers for publication by these organizations in their respective journals.

In MLA and APA styles, in-text citations (basic information about sources) are given in parentheses immediately following the quoted or referenced material in the body of your paper. In MLA style, in-text citations provide the author's last name and the page number in the document where the material was found. APA style also requires the publication year in the in-text citation. At the end of the essay, a Works Cited (MLA) or References (APA) page gives detailed information about each source, including the author's name; title of the work and, if applicable, the larger work in which it appears; publisher; place of publication; and date of publication—not always in that order. The format of each reference depends on where you found the information: on the Internet; in a book, journal, or magazine; through an interview; and so on. In Unit 7, you will find a research paper in APA format (pages 275–279) and in MLA format (pages 270–274) to provide you with an introduction to using these resources.

Go to Workbook Exercise 27.1

Paragraphs and Essays

For EAL Learners: A Review of the Basics

INTRODUCTION

As a college student, you are preparing for a meaningful and rewarding career. If you are preparing for this career in a language that is not native to you, English, we congratulate you on your achievement. Your hard work and your ability to use two (or more) languages suggest that you are able to achieve a high level of success.

You may, however, feel that weak English communication skills are holding you back. Even if your command of spoken English is good, you may lack fluency with standard written English (SWE), and poor writing skills can hinder your opportunities for academic and career success.

The ability to use SWE fluently helps you in three ways. First, it gives you the power to express your ideas clearly. Second, it helps you win the respect of your readers. Finally, it increases the number of people with whom you can communicate. That's why employers look for people who have good writing skills.

This unit of *The Bare Essentials* is designed specifically to help those who are not native speakers master the conventions of standard written English. It focuses on the most common problem areas for those learning English as an additional language (EAL). These include verb tenses and verb formation, plural forms and quantity expressions, articles, and prepositions. Even highly sophisticated EAL writers occasionally make mistakes in these constructions, mistakes that are evident to native speakers. Working on these problem areas will develop and improve your ability to write in English.

These chapters provide concise explanation—likely less explanation than you have come to expect in advanced grammar texts. But there are many exercises and much opportunity for you to practise specific writing skills. Grammatical explanation can certainly help you to understand what constitutes correct English, but ultimately you must gain confidence in your ability to write correctly without constant reference to grammar rules. This confidence is what will make you a fluent writer of English.

You may also find Unit 6 useful as you work on your English speaking and pronunciation skills. If you are in a class with other EAL students, you can do the exercises out loud in class as speaking practice. Hearing and saying the words will help you to remember the grammatical structures and to improve your pronunciation; the practice will help you become a more fluent speaker of English.

> Before you start this unit, complete the Quick Quiz.
> Once you have finished this unit, complete the Rapid Review.

Choosing the Correct Verb Tense

In English, the tense of a verb signals the time of an action: present, past, or future.

> I *work* hard every day.
>
> I *worked* at the library yesterday.
>
> I *will work* at the library next summer.

Of course, as you know, there is more to the English tense system than these simple examples suggest. English verbs change in complicated and subtle ways to describe complex time relations.

> I *am working* at the library now, but I *have worked* at a number of different jobs in the past. I *will be working* for most of my life, so it *is* important that I *learn* more things than I *have learned* so far.

Trying to sort out the tenses of the verbs in these sentences can be a real headache for English language learners. Another headache results from the fact that some verb tenses have the same meaning or close to the same meaning. Most native speakers will not hear a difference in meaning between "I am working at the library now" and "I work at the library now." However, native speakers will certainly pick up the mistake if you say or write "I am been working at the library now" or "I will work at a number of different jobs in the past." To write clearly, you require a thorough understanding of—and lots of practice with— the English verb tense system. This chapter will provide you with both.

- ▲ indicates now, the present moment.

- ● represents *a completed action* or *state of being.*

- ○ indicates *an event that occurred or will occur sometime after the action represented by* ● *took place.*

~~~~~ represents *a continuing action or condition*, both of which are expressed by the progressive forms of a verb.

--------- indicates that *the action or condition may continue into the future.*

Now that you have an overview of the six basic tenses and the "times" they represent, let's look at how the various tenses are formed. Then we will focus on how to use each one.

VERB TENSE FORMATION

The chart below shows how the different tenses are formed. It provides two examples, *work* (a regular verb) and *grow* (an irregular verb), to illustrate the changes. The principal parts of the verbs are presented first because all tenses are formed from them. As you will see from studying the examples below, most tenses are created by adding **auxiliary** or **helping verbs** formed from the verbs *be* (*am, is, are, was, were*) or *have* (*has, have, had*) or both (*have been, has been*). Study the patterns below. See pages 76–82 for more information about principal parts of verbs.

Principal Parts

Base/ infinitive	Present participle	Past	Past participle
(to) work	working	worked	worked
(to) grow	growing	grew	grown

Tense	Example (*work*)	Example (*grow*)
Present Tenses		
Simple present (base; base + *s* for third-person singular)	work/works	grow/grows
Present progressive (*am/is/are* + present participle)	am/is/are working	am/is/are growing
Present perfect (*has/have* + past participle)	has/have worked	has/have grown
Present perfect progressive (*has/have* + *been* + present participle)	has/have been working	has/have been growing

Tense	Example (*work*)	Example (*grow*)
Past Tenses		
Simple past (past form)	worked	grew
Past progressive (*was/were* + present participle)	was/were working	was/were growing
Past perfect (*had* + past participle)	had worked	had grown
Past perfect progressive (*had* + *been* + present participle)	had been working	had been growing
Future Tenses		
Simple future (*will* + base) OR (*am/is/are going to* + base)	will grow am/is/are going to work	will work am/is/are going to grow
Future progressive (*will be* + present participle)	will be working	will be growing
Future perfect (*will have* + past participle)	will have worked	will have grown
Future perfect progressive (*will have* + *been* + present participle)	will have been working	will have been growing

The chart above shows how to form all the English tenses. However, some tenses are rarely used; for example, in the case of the future perfect progressive, the same meaning can usually be expressed in a less complicated manner. So while this chapter provides an overview of all tenses, we concentrate on those most commonly used to make sure that you understand how to form them correctly and use them appropriately.

Go to Workbook Exercises 28.1–28.2

For EAL Learners: A Review of the Basics

THE PRESENT TENSES

A. THE SIMPLE PRESENT TENSE

The simple present is used to express present time (especially with non-action verbs called **linking verbs**), general truths, and regular or habitual activity.

Gianni *is* a handsome man. (*is* is a linking verb)

I *hope* that you *are* happy now. (*are* is a linking verb)

People *need* food and water to survive.

Sarah *swims* every day.

B. THE PRESENT PROGRESSIVE TENSE

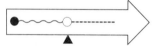

The present progressive is used to express an activity that is in progress now or one that is ongoing. Sometimes the activity takes place over a period of time such as this week, month, or even year.

I *am talking* to you on my cellphone.

They *are driving* home right now.

Everyone *is learning* verb tenses this week.

Some English verbs are rarely used in the progressive tenses. Such verbs describe conditions or states of being rather than actions in progress. Often, these "non-progressive" verbs express mental (cognitive) or emotional states, possession (ownership), or sense perception. Study the following list. (We will come back to the asterisked words later.)

States of being: appear,* be, cost, exist, look,* seem, weigh*

Mental (cognitive) or emotional states: appreciate, believe, care, dislike, doubt, envy, fear, feel,* forget, hate, imagine, know, like, love, mean, mind, need, prefer, realize, recognize, remember, suppose, think, understand, want

Possession: belong, have, own, possess

Sense perception: appear,* be, feel,* hear, see, smell,* taste*

Again, these state-of-being verbs can almost never be used in the progressive tenses. You wouldn't say "I am liking her very much." You would use the simple present: "I like her very much." In the following sentences, replace the incorrect verb forms (in italics) with correct ones.

> I *am hearing* that you *are owning* a laptop computer. I *am needing* to borrow one for today's class. I *am knowing* that you *are hating* to lend your things, but I *am promising* to return it this evening.

(The verbs in italics should be changed to *hear, own, need, know, hate,* and *promise,* all in the simple present tense.)

Note that six of the verbs on the list—the ones marked with an asterisk (*)—can be used to describe actions as well as states of being or conditions.

State of Being	Action
Solaya *weighs* 65 kilograms.	Solaya *is weighing* herself this morning to see how many kilograms she has lost.
Tom *appears* old and tired.	Tom *is appearing* on a reality TV show.
The food *tastes* good.	We *are tasting* the soup to see if it's good.

Often, you have to decide whether the verb is expressing a state of being or an action before you can decide whether or not to use a progressive tense.

Incorrect:	He *is having* a car.
	She *is smelling* of cigarette smoke.
	I *am knowing* you for a long time.

Correct:	He *has* a car.
	She *smells* of cigarette smoke.
	I *have known* you for a long time.

For EAL Learners:
A Review of the
Basics

Go to Workbook Exercise 28.3

C. THE PRESENT PERFECT TENSE

The present perfect tense is used to express three different meanings:

1. events that occurred (or didn't occur) at some unspecified time in the past, the consequences of which persist in the present

The rain *has stopped.*

I *haven't voted yet.*

2. events that were repeated several or many unspecified times in the past and are likely to occur again in the present and future

It *has rained* practically every day this month.

I *have* always *voted* for the best person.

3. events that began at some unspecified time in the past and continue into the present

Yu *has lived* in Canada for a long time.

The children *have been* good today.

Sentences requiring the present perfect tense frequently contain words or phrases that suggest action beginning in the past and persisting into the present, such as *for, since, for a long time, already, so far, always, often, during, recently,* and *this year.*

Note that *for* is used with a period of time and *since* is used with a specific point in time.

I have lived in Canada *for* 15 years.

I have lived in Canada *since* 2002.

Go to Workbook Exercise 28.4

D. THE PRESENT PERFECT PROGRESSIVE TENSE

The present perfect progressive is used
- to express actions that began at some unspecified time in the past and continue in the present or
- to emphasize the duration of a single past-to-present action

Other than the emphasis on the duration of an action, this tense has almost the same meaning as the present perfect tense. Time phrases such as *for*, *since*, *all afternoon*, *all day*, and *all year* are often used with the present perfect progressive tense to emphasize the period of time over which the action has been taking place.

The class *has been working* on verb tenses. (And they are still working on them.)

I *have been sitting* here all day. (And I am still sitting here.)

Your husband *has been waiting* for you for over an hour. (And he is still waiting.)

For EAL Learners: A Review of the Basics

The present perfect progressive and present perfect tenses often express the same meaning, especially when the sentence contains *since* or *for*. There is no difference in meaning in the examples below.

Saed *has been living* here since 1997.   Saed *has lived* here since 1997.

I *have been working* here for 20 years.   I *have worked* here for 20 years.

Go to Workbook Exercises 28.5–28.6

THE PAST TENSES

A. THE SIMPLE PAST TENSE

The simple past tense indicates an action or a state that began and ended in the past. It can be used to refer to an event completed once in the past or to an event completed several times in the past.

I *ate* too much this morning.

The dog *bit* two mail carriers last year.

Binh *lived* in Hong Kong before he *moved* to Montréal.

B. THE PAST PROGRESSIVE TENSE

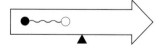

The past progressive tense is used to express an action or condition that began and ended sometime in the past. It emphasizes the duration—or ongoing quality—of an event that is now completed.

The boys *were watching* television all morning.

I *was flying* home from Halifax when the storm struck.

What *were* you *doing* in Halifax?

I *was studying* at Dalhousie University.

The past progressive is also used to indicate an action that was taking place when another occurred. It is often used with time words, such as *for* or *since*, or with a clause that uses *when* or *while* to denote simultaneous occurrences.

Julieta *was driving* to school when the accident happened.

While they *were cooking* dinner, the power went off.

Sometimes there is little difference in meaning between the past and the past progressive: "It snowed last night" and "It was snowing last night" mean the same thing, and both are correct.

 Go to Workbook Exercise 28.7

C. THE PAST PERFECT TENSE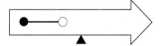

Sometimes two different actions or conditions that occurred in the past are included in the same sentence.

The past perfect tense is used to depict an action that was completed before another event (or time) in the past. It is the "further in the past" tense.

In other words, the action that happened first chronologically is expressed by the past perfect; the action that occurred after it is expressed in the simple past.

For EAL Learners: A Review of the Basics

I *had left* the building before the bomb *exploded*.

Obviously the leaving happened first (and so is in the past perfect tense)—before the explosion (in the simple past tense)—or the speaker wouldn't be around to tell the story.

The past perfect tense is frequently used with time expressions, such as *after*, *before*, and *when*.

Kareem realized his mistake after he *had spoken*.

The class *had left* before the instructor found the room.

To be fair, however, we should acknowledge that if the time sequence is clear from other elements in the sentence, the past perfect is often not necessary. Most native English speakers would not hear an error in the following sentences:

I *left* the building before the bomb *exploded*.

Kareem *realized* his mistake after he *spoke*.

The class *left* before the instructor *found* the room.

However, in sentences with *just, already, scarcely, hardly*, and *no sooner than*, the past perfect is required.

My boyfriend *had* already *gone* home when I *arrived*.

We *had* hardly *unpacked* our suitcases when the fun *began*.

In these sentences, using the simple past (*already went* and *hardly unpacked*) would be incorrect.

 Go to Workbook Exercise 28.8

D. THE PAST PERFECT PROGRESSIVE TENSE

The past perfect progressive tense emphasizes the duration of a past event that took place before another event. Often it is used to refer to a past event that was in progress before being interrupted by another event.

He *had been waiting* in the doctor's office for an hour by the time she arrived.

They *had been talking* about Carol when she walked in.

Exercises 28.9–28.11 will help you with the time sequencing of English verbs by reminding you of the difference between the present perfect progressive (*has/have + been + present participle*) and the past perfect progressive (*had + been + present participle*).

Go to Workbook Exercises 28.9–28.11

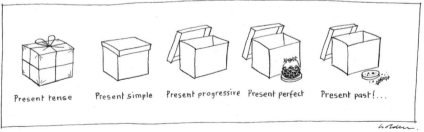

Present tense   Present simple   Present progressive   Present perfect   Present past!...

Caroline Holden/CartoonStock

For EAL Learners: A Review of the Basics

THE FUTURE TENSES

A. THE SIMPLE FUTURE TENSE

There are two ways to express the simple future tense:
1. *will* + base form:

I *will* work hard.

They *will see* you tomorrow.

2. (*be*) + *going to* + base form:

I *am going to work* hard.

They *are going to see* you tomorrow.

Both constructions have the same meaning. In informal English, especially speech, *will* is usually contracted to *'ll* in the future tense:

I'*ll work* hard. They'*ll see* you tomorrow.

You'*ll work* hard. We'*ll see* them tomorrow.

Won't is the contraction for *will not*: I *won't* work hard. You *won't see* me tomorrow.

The (*be*) + *going to* + base form is usually used when the sentence expresses a prior plan or decision. The *will* + base form is used to express willingness or ability. The following examples illustrate the difference.

Prior plan: (*be*) + *going to* + base

Why did you buy these flippers?

I *am going to learn* how to snorkel. (not "I will learn how to snorkel.")

Willingness: *will* + base

Help me! I'm broke, and my rent is due today.

Ask Roderigo. Maybe he'*ll lend* you some money. (not "Ask Roderigo. Maybe he is going to lend you some money.")

Traditional grammar texts often describe different (and very subtle) changes in meanings expressed by the future tense—for example, promise, prediction, permission, volition, supposition, concession—and prescribe using a specific form for each purpose. However, these meanings are often difficult to separate from futurity, and native speakers rarely hear lapses in these distinctions as grammatical errors. Traditional grammar texts also teach that *shall* is used with first-person subjects (*I shall go home*) and *will* is used with second- and third-person subjects (*You/They will go home*). In North American English, this distinction is obsolete. Don't worry about the differences between *will* and *am/is/are going to* or between *shall* and *will*.

Go to Workbook Exercise 28.12

B. THE FUTURE PROGRESSIVE TENSE

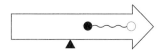

The future progressive tense expresses an action that will be in progress at a time in the future. There is often little difference in meaning between the future progressive and the simple future.

I *will be seeing* him later tonight.

I *will see* him later tonight.

Tomorrow you *will be dining* with us.

Tomorrow *you will dine* with us.

Go to Workbook Exercise 28.13

For EAL Learners: A Review of the Basics

C. THE FUTURE PERFECT TENSE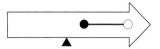

The future perfect expresses an action that will be completed before another time or action in the future.

By next June, we *will have graduated* from college.

Before the end of the semester, we *will have covered* a lot of grammar.
Before we leave Québec City, we *will have seen* all of the tourist attractions.
(Note that the verb in the time clause is in the simple present tense.)

Often, use of the future perfect tense is not absolutely necessary. For instance, the simple future could be used in the above sentences:

By next June, we *will graduate* from college.

Before the end of the semester, we *will cover* a lot of grammar.

Before we leave Québec City, we *will see* all of the tourist attractions.

However, if *already* is used in the sentence, the future perfect is required, as it is in this example:

Incorrect: I *will already go* to bed by the time you arrive.
Correct: I *will already have gone* to bed by the time you arrive.

D. THE FUTURE PERFECT PROGRESSIVE TENSE

The hardly-ever-used future perfect progressive tense stresses the duration of a future action that is to take place before another future action.

Often, the future perfect progressive and the future perfect tenses have the same meaning, as in the examples below:

Our cousins *will have been studying* English for three months before they arrive in Canada.

Our cousins *will have studied* English for three months before they arrive in Canada.

Go to Workbook Exercise 28.14

USING PRESENT TENSES TO INDICATE FUTURE TIME

As if distinguishing among all these tenses is not complicated enough, there is another convention you need to know about. English speakers use the simple present and present progressive tenses to express future time in several circumstances.

1. A few simple present tense verbs—*arrive, begin, close, come, end, finish, leave, open, return, start*—can express that an activity is scheduled in the future.

Usually the sentences contain "future time" words or phrases, like the ones underlined in the three examples below.

Daphne's flight *arrives* at midnight.

School *begins* on September 8 next year.

The stores at the mall *close* at 6 p.m. today.

2. When the sentence contains a time clause (e.g., one beginning with *after* or *before*) or a conditional clause (e.g., one beginning with *if*), the simple present tense is required in that clause even though the verb refers to future or conditional time.

Consider the following examples carefully; the underlined clauses express time or condition, so the verbs must be in the simple present.

Incorrect:	I *will take* a vacation after I *will quit* my job. If the snow *will continue*, the president *will close* the college.
Correct:	I *will take* a vacation after I *quit* my job. If the snow *continues*, the president *will close* the college.

3. The present progressive is often used when a time word or phrase in the sentence indicates the future.

I *am touring* Tuscany next year.

Mara *is having* a baby this spring.

Go to Workbook Exercises 28.15–28.19

In addition to verb formation and tense, there are four related issues with verbs that often present problems for English language learners:

- formation of negatives (*not, n't, never*)
- participial adjectives (*interested* or *interesting*?)
- modal auxiliaries (*can, may, must, ought to*, etc.)
- conditional verbs (*if you only knew* …)

FORMING NEGATIVES

Not expresses a negative idea. In a negative sentence, the word *not* comes immediately after the *be* verb or auxiliary verb.

Auxiliary verbs are verbs used to form different tenses. They include the forms of *be*, *have*, and *do*, and modal auxiliary verbs. (The forms of *be* are *am, is, are, was, were, been*, and *be*. The forms of *have* are *have, has*, and *had*. The forms of *do* are *do, does*, and *did*.) Modal auxiliary verbs are reviewed on page 212.

Yes, the sun *is out*.	No, the sun *is not* out.
I *have learned* my lesson.	I *have not learned* my lesson.
They *will eat* a whole pizza.	They *will not eat* a whole pizza.
She *might visit* her family.	She *might not visit* her family.

If the main verb in the sentence does not have an auxiliary, the *do* verb is added before *not* when forming the negative; the main verb follows *not*. *Not* can be contracted to *n't*:

is not = isn't	does not = doesn't	had not = hadn't
are not = aren't	do not = don't	cannot = can't
was not = wasn't	did not = didn't	could not = couldn't
were not = weren't	has not = hasn't	would not = wouldn't
will not = won't	have not = haven't	

(*Ain't* is not included in the list because using *ain't* is a grammatical error.)

I *love* him.	I *do not love* him.	I *don't love* him
He *loves* me.	He *does not love* me.	He *doesn't love* me.
I *loved* him.	I *did not love* him.	I *didn't love* him.

Remember that the auxiliary verb picks up the number and tense marker when it precedes the main verb, which reverts to the base form, as in the example above with the third-person singular *-s* ending: "He *loves* me" becomes "He *does* (or *doesn't*) *love* me." ("He *doesn't loves* me" is a grammatical error.) Similarly, the past tense *-d* in *loved* becomes *did not* (or *didn't*) *love* (not "He *didn't loved* me," another grammatical error). Here are three more examples to help you recall this important—but difficult—shift in verb forms:

My friend *works* hard.	My friend *does not work* (or *doesn't work*) hard.
We *finished* the job.	We *did not finish* (or *didn't finish*) the job.
He *came* home last night.	He *did not* (or *didn't*) *come* home last night.

Grammatically, the word *not* is a negative adverb; it isn't part of the verb itself. Other negative adverbs that are used to express negative meanings are *never*, *rarely*, *seldom*, *scarcely* (*ever*), *hardly* (*ever*), and *barely* (*ever*), although these words have slightly different meanings. Here are some examples:

I *never* understand what my boyfriend really wants. (I do not ever understand ...)

My wife and I *rarely* go out. (We go out once in a while, but hardly ever.)

The train is *hardly ever* late. (It is usually on time.)

My son *seldom* goes to school. (But rarely he does go.)

The word *no* can be used as an adjective in front of a noun to provide the same meaning as *not*. However, avoid using two negatives, a grammatical error in English known as a "double negative."

Incorrect:	Ali *doesn't have no* problems speaking English. (Double negative)
Correct:	Ali *doesn't have* problems speaking English.
	Ali *has no* problems speaking English.

"Apparently, double negatives are okay in math but not in English."

Baloo Rex-May/CartoonStock

Go to Workbook Exercises 29.1–29.3

PARTICIPIAL ADJECTIVES

Although participial adjectives are not verbs, they are adjectives that are formed from verbs, and that is why we've included them in the "More about Verbs" chapter. These adjectives present problems for most additional-language writers. Am I bored? Or boring? Surprised? Or surprising? Let's try to sort it out with a little story.

Allan and Zeta went out on a date. It didn't go well. The two sentences that follow describe why the evening was not a success, but their meanings are very different.

1. Allan was a *boring* date.
2. Allan was a *bored* date.

Boring and *bored* are adjectives derived from the **participle** forms of the verb *to bore*. *Boring* is the present participle; *bored* is the past participle. Choosing the correct participial adjective is tough. Let's go back to the story.

In sentence 1, Allan is a dull fellow. He is shy and has nothing to talk about. He bored Zeta. She found him *boring*. In sentence 2, Zeta is the dull person with nothing to talk about. Zeta bored Allan, so he was bored and, therefore, a *bored* date.

Are you *confused*? Is the choice *confusing*? Yes. First, we'll explain the principle. Then we'll provide some practice with participial adjectives.

> The **present participle**, the *-ing* form, conveys an active meaning. The noun it describes is or does something.

Allan bores Zeta in sentence 1, so he is *boring*. Participial adjectives often confuse English language learners, so these words are *confusing*.

> The **past participle**, the *-ed* form in regular verbs, conveys a passive meaning. The noun it describes has something done to it.

Zeta bores Allan in sentence 2, so he is *bored*. Participial adjectives confuse English language learners, so these learners are *confused*. Note that the past participles of irregular verbs do not end in *-ed* (e.g., a plant is *grown*, not *growed*). See Chapter 11 for the participial forms of irregular verbs, or check your dictionary.

 Go to Workbook Exercises 29.4–29.5

MODAL AUXILIARIES

As we have seen, any of the verbs *am, is, are, was, were; do, does, did; has, have,* and *had* can stand alone as the only verb in a sentence.

I *am* strong.	You *are* strong.	He *is* strong.	It *was* strong.	They *were* strong.

We *do* things.   She *does* things.   They *did* things.

I *have* money.   George *has*.   All of them *had*
money   money.

These verbs can also work in an auxiliary capacity; that is, they can combine with the main verb in a sentence to change the time of an action (tense) or to form a negative construction.

I *am working* now.	You *are studying* here.	We *were travelling* last year.
I *don't know* her.	*Does* she *work* hard?	They *didn't call* us.
I *haven't seen* you.	He *has checked* your schedule.	They *hadn't told* us.

There is another kind of auxiliary verb called a **modal auxiliary**. These words provide different shades of meaning or mood to the main verb. The modal auxiliaries are

can	might	should
could	must	will
may	shall	would

Some common verb phrases (groups of words) also function as modals (and are sometimes called *phrasal modals*):

(be) able to	(be) supposed to
has/have/had to	used to
ought to	

The examples that follow will show you how modal auxiliary verbs change the meaning of the main verb.

Modal	Interpretation
I *can* work.	I am able and willing to do the job.
I *could* work.	I am able to work if I feel like it.
I *may* work.	I don't know if I will.
I *must* work.	I need to work.
I *should* work.	It is best for me to work.
I *would* work.	I am willing to work if …
I *used to* work.	In the past, I worked but I don't now.

The good news about single-word modals is that they are followed by the base form of the verb (e.g., *work*) with no -*s* added to the third-person singular or -*ed* added to the past tense. Unlike *be*, *have*, and *do*, the modal auxiliaries don't change number, and, except for *can/could*, *will/would*, and *shall/should*, they don't change time.

Verb	Modal + verb
I work	I can work
He works	He must work (*not* He must works)
They worked	They should work (*not* They should worked)

The bad news about modals is that they often suggest subtle changes in meaning that can confuse additional-language writers. Traditional grammar texts use a great deal of ink attempting to distinguish "obligation" versus "advisability" and "polite" versus "impolite" requests. The following chart will help you sort out the meanings of modals. But while you're struggling to learn the differences among various modals, keep in mind that almost no native speakers will hear a difference between your telling them that you *may work tomorrow* and you *might work tomorrow*.

Single-Word Modal Auxiliaries

Auxiliary	Meaning	Example (Present/Future)	Example (Past)
can	1. ability	I *can swim* well.	I could swim when I was two.
	2. informal request	*Can* I *call* you tonight?	
could	1. past tense of *can*		I could swim when I was two.
	2. polite request	*Could* I please *speak* to your wife?	
	3. low level of certainty	It *could rain* tonight, or it *could be* clear.	
may	1. polite request	*May* I please *speak* to your wife?	
	2. low level of certainty	It *may rain* tonight, but it *may* not [*rain*].	
	3. possibility	Harvey says he *may go* with us.	
might	1. low level of certainty	It *might rain* tonight, but it *might* not [*rain*].	
	2. possibility	I *might visit* Paris this summer.	
	3. past tense of *may*		Harvey said he *might go* with us.

Auxiliary	Meaning	Example (Present/Future)	Example (Past)
must	1. strong necessity 2. high level of certainty	You *must drink* water. The teacher isn't here, so she *must be* ill.	
shall	1. polite question 2. future (with *I/we*)	*Shall* I *help* you across the street? I *shall see* you tomorrow. (or *will see* …)	
should	1. advisable 2. high level of certainty 3. obligation	You *should lose* a few pounds. You study hard, so you *should do* well in the course. He *should support* his children.	
will	1. complete certainty 2. willingness 3. polite request	I'm sure you *will succeed.* I*'ll be* happy to help you. *Will* you please *tell* me what you think?	
would	1. preference (with *rather*) 2. polite request 3. repeated action in past	I *would* rather *eat* at a restaurant. *Would* you please *tell* me what you think?	 We *would* always *phone* home on weekends when we lived abroad.

Go to Workbook Exercise 29.6

The chart on pages 216–217 summarizes modal and other auxiliaries that are made up of more than a single word. *Ought to* and *used to* do not require any change in the verb form. Like the single-word modals, they simply precede the base form of the main verb: "I *ought to* see you." "She *used to* love me."

Be able to, be supposed to, and *have to* present some challenge. Because they include the verbs *be* or *have,* they require a change in the auxiliary itself to mark tense and number. Study the following examples:

You *are able to* finish the assignment.

We *were able to* finish the assignment.

I *am supposed to* attend a class at noon today.

She and I *were supposed to* attend a class yesterday.

He *has to* change his clothes.

He *had to* change his clothes.

When you are using past participles such as *supposed to* and *used to,* don't forget to include the *-d* at the end of the word. Omitting the *-d* is a common writing error (for both native and non-native speakers).

Incorrect:	The show was **suppose** to begin an hour ago.
	I **use** to have more money.
Correct:	The show was **supposed** to begin an hour ago.
	I **used** to have more money.

Phrasal Modal Auxiliaries

Auxiliary	Meaning	Example (present/future)	Example (past)
be able to	ability (can)	He *is able to handle* the truck.	He *was able to handle* the truck.
be supposed to	expectation	We *are supposed to meet* them.	We *were supposed to meet* them.
have/has/ had to	necessity (must)	He *has to go* to the bank today.	He *had to go* to the bank on Tuesday.
ought to	1. advisability (should)	We *ought to bring* our raincoats and an umbrella.	
	2. high level of certainty	She studies hard and *ought to do* well in school.	

Auxiliary	Meaning	Example (present/future)	Example (past)
used to	repeated action in the past		She *used to work* hard in school. He *used to weigh* 100 kilograms.

Go to Workbook Exercises 29.7–29.10

CONDITIONAL VERBS

Conditional verb structures are tricky for additional-language learners because they encompass the confusing territory of "real" versus "unreal" (hypothetical) situations. Since these structures are used frequently in English, it's worth reviewing them. Conditionals are usually signalled by the word *if*, although other words, such as *when*, can also be connected to conditionals. Note that *if* and *when/whenever* have different meanings. "*If* I graduate" suggests that you might do so; "*when* I graduate" implies that you will. The explanation and examples below remind you how conditionals work.

Factual conditionals explain what usually happens in a "real" situation. The simple present tense is used in both the independent and dependent clauses. The dependent clause begins with *if* or *when/whenever* and can come either before or after the independent clause.

(See Chapter 6 for a review of clauses and sentence structure.)

Dependent clause	Independent clause
If you *heat* water to 100° Celsius,	it *boils*. (simple present tense)

Independent clause	Dependent clause
I *walk* to work	when (or whenever) I *have* time. (simple present tense)

Present hypothetical conditionals refer to "unreal" situations, those that have not happened and are unlikely to occur. (*Hypothetical* means "not necessarily real or true." A unicorn is a hypothetical animal; your winning a million dollars in the lottery is likely to be a hypothetical occurrence.)

In the present hypothetical mode, the verb in the independent clause is usually in the past tense, and the verb in the dependent clause is a conditional constructed with *would* + the base form. Occasionally, the verb *could* is used in the dependent clause to mean "would be able to."

> If I *lived* in China, I *would speak* Chinese. (I don't.)

> Tommy *would marry* her if she *had* more money. (She doesn't, so he won't.)

> If I *had* wings, I *could* fly. (I don't, so I can't.)

Past hypothetical conditionals refer to "unreal" situations that did not happen or could not have happened in the past. To express this situation, the verb in the independent clause is *would* + *have* + the past participle. The verb in the dependent (*if*) clause is in the past perfect tense.

> I *would have come* to see you if I *had known* you were home. (I didn't know and didn't come.)

> If Morty *had moved* to Canada as a child, he *would have spoken* English better. (He didn't move earlier, so he can't speak English as well as he might have.)

> If you *had worked* harder, you *would have passed* the course. (You didn't work harder, so you didn't pass the course.)

Note that *would* in the conditional structure is often contracted to *'d*: for example, *I'd have come, he'd have spoken, you'd have passed* in the sentences above. The *have* in conditional structures is also frequently shortened: *I would've, I could've, I should've.* (But they aren't "*woulda, coulda, shoulda*," which is actually an idiom referring to a lost chance. Say the actual contractions aloud, and you'll understand why they sound like "*woulda, coulda, shoulda*.") Also remember that the contractions of *could have, would have, should have* are *could've, would've, should've.* Although they sound alike, the constructions *could of, would of,* and *should of* are grammatical mistakes.

> *Future conditionals* predict what may or is likely to happen in the future. The verb in the independent clause is usually *will* + the base form or *be going to* + the base form. The verb in the dependent (*if*) clause is usually in the simple present tense.

My friends *will take* David home if he *asks* them.

If it *rains* tomorrow, we *are going to cancel* the picnic.

If you *find* a four-leaf clover, you*'ll have* good luck.

These examples cover some—but not all—of the permutations in verb form that make up the conditional. Practise using the conditional with the exercises.

Go to Workbook Exercises 29.11–29.17

For EAL Learners: A Review of the Basics

30 Solving Plural Problems

SINGULAR VERSUS PLURAL NOUNS

Nouns in English are words that name people, places, things, or ideas. For example, *Justin Trudeau, Manitoba, alligator,* and *honesty* are all examples of nouns. The first three examples are **concrete** nouns; in other words, they refer to physical objects that we can see, inhabit, or touch. The fourth example, *honesty*, is an **abstract** noun that refers to a concept that exists in our minds; it cannot be seen or touched.

Singular nouns refer to one person, place, thing, or idea: *mother, bedroom, book, justice*. Plural nouns refer to more than one person, place, or thing: *mothers, bedrooms, books*. Abstract nouns are not often found in the plural form, but some of them can be pluralized.

To form the plural of most nouns, you add *-s* to the singular form.

Singular	Plural
classroom	classrooms
cousin	cousins
ocean	oceans
idea	ideas (*plural abstract noun*)
truck	trucks
umbrella	umbrellas

Go to Workbook Exercise 30.1

Plurals can be particularly tricky for English language learners. Because the rules for forming the plural sometimes depend on the pronunciation of the word (see rules 2 and 4 on pages 221–222), you might want to check a pronunciation dictionary or website (e.g., www.forvo.com) to hear how a native speaker would pronounce the word in question. As you probably know, there

Mike Flanagan/CartoonStock

are many exceptions to the "add *-s* for plural" rule. The most common exceptions are listed below. (To be honest, these plurals rely on spelling conventions that most native English speakers find difficult. English is a very tough language to spell.)

1. Some nouns have irregular plural forms that must be memorized.

Most of the following are very common words that are based on an older form of English. You need to become familiar with their irregular plural forms.

Singular	Plural
child	children
foot	feet
goose	geese
man (woman)	men (women)
mouse	mice
tooth	teeth

2. To pluralize nouns ending in "soft" sounds of *-s*, *-x*, *-z*, *-ch*, and *-sh*, add *-es*.

Singular	Plural	Singular	Plural
box	boxes	class	classes
buzz	buzzes	dish	dishes
church	churches	kiss	kisses

If the *-ch* is a "hard" sound—as in *stomach*—add *-s* only: *stomachs*.

For EAL Learners: A Review of the Basics

3. To pluralize nouns ending in *-y* preceded by a consonant, change the *-y* to *-i* and add *-es*.

Singular	Plural	Singular	Plural
country	countries	penny	pennies
lady	ladies	reply	replies

Nouns ending in *-y* preceded by a vowel are regular. Add *-s* to pluralize them.

Singular	Plural	Singular	Plural
boy	boys	key	keys
delay	delays	valley	valleys

4. To pluralize nouns ending in *-f* or *-fe*, add *-ves* if the plural is pronounced with a *-v* sound.

Note that the word *self* is in this category. This rule has important consequences for the *-self* words.

Singular	Plural	Singular	Plural
calf	calves	himself	themselves
knife	knives	herself	themselves
thief	thieves	myself	ourselves
wife	wives	yourself	yourselves

If the plural noun keeps its *-f* sound, add only *-s*.

beliefs	chiefs
chefs	proofs

5. Some nouns ending in *-o* are pluralized by adding *-es*; other nouns ending in *-o* require only *-s*. Use your spell checker or dictionary if you're not sure.

echoes	BUT	pianos
heroes		sopranos
potatoes		studios
tomatoes		zoos

6. Some nouns retain their singular form for the plural.

aircraft	elk	salmon
caribou	mail	sheep
deer	moose	trout

7. Some nouns are used in the plural form only, even though they refer to a single unit.

glasses	pyjamas
jeans	scissors
pants	shorts

8. Some nouns adopted from other languages retain their original plural form.

Singular	Plural	Singular	Plural
analysis	analyses	larva	larvae
criterion	criteria	phenomenon	phenomena
fungus	fungi	stimulus	stimuli
hypothesis	hypotheses	thesis	theses

Go to Workbook Exercises 30.2–30.3

For EAL Learners: A Review of the Basics

"Please, Miss, surely 'trousers' should be singular
at the top and plural at the bottom?"

COUNT VERSUS NON-COUNT NOUNS

Count nouns (also known as *countable nouns*) are words for separate persons, places, or things that can be counted: for example, *college, job, meal, student, toy*.

Count nouns can be made plural in one of the ways explained in the previous pages. (The regular *-s* ending makes each of the previously mentioned count nouns plural: *colleges, jobs, meals, students, toys*.)

Non-count nouns (also known as *uncountable nouns*) identify things that cannot be counted: for example, *water, granite, information, rain*.

Many non-count nouns refer to a "whole" that is made up of different parts. For instance, a room may contain two sofas, three tables, four chairs, and a television. These items can be counted—and the words can be made plural. However, all of these items together can be considered a "whole" and described as *furniture*, which is a non-count noun that is never pluralized.

Incorrect: two chair, all the furnitures
Correct: two chairs, all the furniture

There are several categories of non-count nouns:

- abstract nouns (words for concepts that exist as ideas in our minds): for example, *courage, fun, hatred, health, information* (You acquire *information* as a whole, as you do *knowledge*. You don't say that you have gathered *informations* or *knowledges*. Those abstract nouns cannot be pluralized.)
- words that identify a quantity or mass: for example, *air, food, rice, salt, sugar, water* (These words identify substances that are made up of particles too numerous to count. You can count *bottles of water* or *bowls of rice*, but you cannot count *water* or *rice*.)
- the names of many sports: for example, *golf, hockey, tennis*
- the names of some illnesses: for example, *diabetes, flu, measles*
- subjects of study, whether their form is singular (e.g., *astronomy, biology, chemistry*) or plural (e.g., *economics, mathematics, physics*)
- weather and other natural phenomena: for example, *electricity, fire, lightning, sunshine*

Understanding the difference between count and non-count nouns is essential to determining whether an article (*a, an, the*) should appear before a noun. Chapter 31 deals with articles and modifiers, so make sure that you understand the difference between count and non-count nouns before going on. For now, keep in mind that you do not add plural endings to non-count nouns, although some of them, such as the academic disciplines listed above, already have an *-s* ending.

Incorrect: I should do my homeworks.
Correct: I should do my homework.

Incorrect: We always have funs in good weathers.
Correct: We always have fun in good weather.

Incorrect: My friends and I are concerned about our healths.
Correct: My friends and I are concerned about our health.

Incorrect: The airline lost our baggages.
Correct: The airline lost our baggage.

Go to Workbook Exercise 30.4

So far, so good, but the count/non-count issue has one further complication. Some nouns can be both count and non-count, depending on how they are used. If the noun has a general, as-a-whole kind of meaning, it is non-count and is not pluralized: for example, "We often eat chicken for dinner." If the noun has a specific, count-them-up kind of meaning, it is a count noun and can be pluralized: for example, "Four chickens were running around in the yard." Therefore, some non-count nouns may also be used in a countable sense and have a plural form. Study the four examples below.

1. Non-count (in a general sense): *Exercise* is good for you.
   Count (a specific movement or example): Do all of the *exercises* and check your answers.

2. Non-count (in a general sense): *Food* is an important part of every culture.
   Count (specific cuisines): There were *foods* from all over the world at the party.

3. Non-count (in a general sense): You need *experience* for this job.
   Count (specific happenings): I had some interesting *experiences* in class this semester.

4. Non-count (in a general sense): When did humans learn to use the power of *fire*?
   Count (specific blazes): We could see several different *fires* on the beach.

Check an advanced learner's dictionary if you are unsure whether a noun is count or non-count. Some dictionaries identify non-count nouns as "uncountable" (abbreviated *U*).

Go to Workbook Exercises 30.5–30.7

QUANTITY EXPRESSIONS

The English language contains many words and phrases that tell us the quantity or amount of something. For instance, *one prize, three prizes,* and *fifty prizes* state the exact number of prizes; *many prizes, several prizes,* and *a few prizes* tell us that there is more than one prize, but not exactly how many there are. A noun's status as count or non-count determines the appropriate expression to quantify the noun. Phrases such as *a lot of* and *some of* are also quantity expressions. Study the examples that follow.

Incorrect: We ate a couple of pizza.
Correct: We ate a couple of pizzas.

Incorrect: She grew a lot of vegetable in the garden.
Correct: She grew a lot of vegetables in the garden.

Incorrect: Some of the picture were very ugly.
Correct: Some of the pictures were very ugly.

Note that it is also correct to omit *of the* in this last sentence, but the noun *pictures* remains plural: "Some pictures were very ugly."

Some quantity expressions are used exclusively with count nouns; some are used exclusively with non-count nouns. Other quantity expressions can be used with both. The following chart uses a count noun (*chair*) and a non-count noun (*furniture*) to illustrate how quantity expressions are used with these two noun types.

Quantity Expression	Count Noun	Non-Count Noun
Singular	chair(s)	furniture
one	one chair	—
each	each chair	—
every	every chair	—
Plural		
a couple of	a couple of chairs	—
few/a few	a few chairs	—
a number of	a number of chairs	—
both	both chairs	—
many	many chairs	—
several	several chairs	—
two, three, etc.	two chairs, etc.	—
a great deal of	—	a great deal of furniture
a little/little	—	a little furniture

much	—	much furniture
all	all chairs	all furniture
a lot of/lots of	a lot of chairs	a lot of furniture
hardly any	hardly any chairs	hardly any furniture
lots of	lots of chairs	lots of furniture
not any/no	not any/no chairs	not any/no *furniture*
most	*most chairs*	*most furniture*
plenty of	*plenty of chairs*	*plenty of furniture*
some	*some chairs*	*some furniture*

Go to Workbook Exercise 30.8

Note that *a few* and *few* have different meanings, as do *a little* and *little*. *A few* and *a little* have a positive meaning; for example, "I have a few friends" and "I have a little money" suggest that I have at least some friends and some cash. I'm not completely alone, nor am I completely broke. On the other hand, *few* and *little* have negative connotations. "I have few friends" and "I have little money" suggest that I am a lonely person who has almost no money to spend. It's a strange twist of meaning, but that's how these little phrases work.

Go to Workbook Exercises 30.9–30.12

Using Articles Accurately

People who learn English as their first language never have problems with these three little words, called articles: *a*, *an*, and *the*. But if you have learned English as a second (or third or fourth) language, articles are a potential mine-field of trouble for you. One reason is that the use or non-use of **articles** often depends on meaning that is implied (understood) rather than stated outright. Look at these sentences, for example,

> *A* woman is waiting in your office.

> *The* woman is waiting in your office.

Both sentences are correct, and the sentence most definitely requires an article ("Woman is waiting in your office" is incorrect). But the meanings of the sentences above are quite different. Whether you choose *a* or *the* is determined by what you know about the woman, not by the grammar of the sentence. If she is an unknown, *indefinite* woman, you use the **indefinite article** *a*. But if she is a known, *definite* person whom you perhaps expected, you use the **definite article**, the. Either article *can* be used; which one you *should* use depends on what you mean to say.

There are few specific rules that govern the use of these troublesome little words. You need to take time to practise until you become familiar with them. There are, however, some general guidelines that will help you use articles correctly. In this chapter, we explain the guidelines and give you practice in the workbook applying them.

THE INDEFINITE ARTICLE: *A/AN*

The indefinite article marks a non-specific singular noun. In other words, *a/an* is used to refer to a singular (not plural) common noun in a general way. Here are some examples:

> *A* woman is waiting in your office. (could be any woman)

> I ate *an* apple. (any apple, not a specific apple)

> *A* shark is a dangerous creature. (the whole shark species, not a specific shark)

One rule that always applies (no exceptions) tells you whether to use *a* or *an*: Use *a* if the word that follows begins with a consonant or the sound of a consonant; use *an* if the word that follows begins with a vowel or the sound of a vowel. (If you are unsure about the pronunciation of a sound, check a pronunciation dictionary or a website such as www.forvo.com to learn how a native speaker would say the word.)

Consonant or Consonant Sound	Vowel or Vowel Sound
a party	an event
a sunset	an umbrella
a great evening	an awful evening
a tiny elf	an ugly elf
a university (*university* begins with a vowel, but it sounds like the consonant *-y*)	an honour (*honour* begins with a consonant, but it sounds like the vowel *-o*)

Go to Workbook Exercise 31.1

Now let's look at how to use indefinite articles accurately. Study the five guidelines and examples that follow.

1. Use the indefinite article with singular count nouns. (See Chapter 30 for an explanation of count and non-count nouns.)

- *A/an* is never used with plural nouns.
  Incorrect: A women are waiting in your office.
  Correct: Women are waiting in your office.

- *A/an* is never used with non-count nouns.
  Incorrect: We moved a new furniture into the office.
  Correct: We moved new furniture into the office.
  Also correct: We moved a new desk into the office. (*Desk* is a count noun.)

2. Many nouns have a count meaning as well as a non-count meaning. The indefinite article *a/an* is required if the noun is being used as a singular count noun.

For example, the noun *life* can be used to refer to the general state of being alive. In this sense, *life* is non-count and is never pluralized: for example, "Life is good." The noun *life*, though, also has a count sense and can be pluralized: for example, "Six lives were lost in the earthquake" or "The hurricane did not take a single life." Also, consider the difference between these two sentences:

Incorrect: Life of poverty is very difficult.
Correct: A life of poverty is very difficult. (*Life* is a singular count noun here because it refers to a particular kind of life.)

Again, the meaning—as well as the grammar of your sentence—determines whether or not you need the article.

There are other nouns usually considered to be non-count that are also used as count nouns: for example, beverages that are held in a container (e.g., *coffee* in a cup). Such count nouns can be used with *a* and can also be pluralized.

Coffee is grown in South America. (*Coffee* is used as a non-count noun.)

Please bring me *a* coffee. (*Coffee* is used as a singular count noun.)

Please bring us two coffees. (*Coffee* is used as a plural count noun.)

3. The indefinite article is used with certain quantity expressions such as *a few*, *a little*, and *a couple of* (see page 227).

He has *a few* friends in Mumbai.

We have *a couple of* questions for you.

4. The indefinite article is used in certain time expressions, such as *half an hour* and *a half-hour*. The phrases *once an hour*, *twice a day*, *three times a week*, *several times a month*, and similar expressions use *a/an* to express frequency.

For EAL Learners:
A Review of the
Basics

Can you meet me in *half an hour*?

Take this medication *three times a day*.

5. Many idioms require the indefinite article.

You should become familiar with the common idioms listed below.

as a rule   lend a hand
do a favour   make a living, make a point of, make a
for a long time   difference, make a fool of
give me a break (informal)   once in a while
have a headache   stand a chance
in a hurry   take a trip, take a break, take a look at
keep an eye on   tell a lie

Go to Workbook Exercise 31.2

THE DEFINITE ARTICLE: *THE*

The is a word that makes a noun specific or *definite*. It distinguishes the known from the unknown. In the sentence introduced above, "The woman is waiting in your office," we know the woman isn't a stranger. She is a definite person whose identity the speaker or writer recognizes. Nouns can be particularized—made definite or specific—in several ways. The following guidelines and examples show how nouns are particularized and will help you figure out how to use the definite article.

1. Use the definite article with familiar objects, places, and people in the external environment.

For instance, we speak about *the* North Pole, *the* moon, *the* apartment we live in, *the* school we attend, *the* doctor we consult, and *the* TV shows we watch. All of these things are particularized (made definite) because we are familiar with them. We know who or what we have in mind when we use the word, and the reader or listener is going to understand the same thing.

> *The* equator divides *the* northern hemisphere from *the* southern hemisphere.
>
> Don't leave *the* keys in *the* car.

2. Nouns can be made definite from the context of the sentence. (This principle is called the anaphoric use—or second mention—of *the*.)

Once you refer to an unknown person, place, or thing using the indefinite article, that person, place, or thing becomes a known—or definite—entity the next time you refer to him, her, or it. Consider this example:

> *A* strange woman is waiting in your office. *The* woman is wearing *an* interesting dress. *The* dress is made of blue silk and has red tassels.

The first time we mention the woman, she is unknown and referred to as "*a* woman." This first mention makes her definite, so we refer to her as "*the* woman" in the second sentence. Can you explain the shift in the articles that modify the suit she is wearing?

Go to Workbook Exercise 31.3

3. The definite article can be used with singular and plural nouns and with count and non-count nouns.

> *The* woman is waiting in your office. (singular noun)
>
> *The* women are waiting in your office. (plural noun)
>
> We moved *the* new desk into your office. (count noun)
>
> We moved *the* new furniture into your office. (non-count noun)

4. The definite article can also be used with a singular generic noun; that is, it can be used when you are making a generalization about a class of things.

The violin is a difficult instrument to play.

Usually, the indefinite article is also acceptable in such a sentence. Both of the sentences below have the same meaning, and both are correct.

The grizzly bear is a dangerous animal.

A grizzly bear is a dangerous animal.

Do not place *the* before a plural count noun used in the generic sense. Instead, use the plural form with no article: "Grizzly bears are dangerous." If you are referring to specific animals, though, you can use *the* with the plural count noun: "The grizzly bears in my backyard are dangerous."

Below is another example to illustrate the correct use of articles with generic and specific plural count nouns.

Potentially incorrect:	*The* teenagers are often moody and irritable with their parents.
	This use of *the* is incorrect if you are referring to teenagers as a class of people; it is correct if it refers to a specific group of teenagers.
Correct:	Teenagers are often moody and irritable with their parents.
Also correct:	*The* teenagers in that family are often moody and irritable with their parents. (*The* refers to a specific group of teenagers.)

 Go to Workbook Exercise 31.4

5. The definite article is used in many quantity expressions that contain *of*: for example, *some of the coffee, most of the children, each one of the judges, all of the exams, both of the rings.*

In many of these phrases, it is also correct to omit the *of the* part of the phrase.

> Many of the models in fashion shows are very young.

> Many models in fashion shows are very young.

Both sentences are correct and mean the same thing.

Note that you cannot omit the definite article from a quantity expression without omitting *of* as well.

Incorrect:	Some of people in this building are very wealthy.
Correct:	Some of the people in this building are very wealthy.
Also correct:	Some people in this building are very wealthy.

6. Many idioms use the definite article.

Some common examples are

all the time	play the fool
clear the table	tell the truth
make the beds	wash the dishes

7. Other uses of the definite article are listed below.

- with superlative adjectives: *the* richest man I know
- with number words (ordinals): *the* third child, *the* tenth chapter
- in phrases that specify time or space sequence: *the* next day, *the* beginning, *the* last desk in *the* row, on *the* end
- in phrases that rank things: *the* main reason, *the* only person
- with official titles: *the* prime minister, *the* president (except when the person's name is attached: Prime Minister Trudeau, President Clinton)
- with names of governmental and military bodies, both with common nouns (*the* courthouse, *the* police, *the* army) and with proper nouns (*the* Liberal Party, *the* United Nations, *the* Pentagon)
- with historical periods or events: *the* Renaissance, *the* Ming Dynasty, *the* 1960s
- with legislative bills and acts: *the* Canadian Charter of Rights and Freedoms, *the* Magna Carta

Go to Workbook Exercise 31.5

NO ARTICLE (ZERO ARTICLE)

No article (**zero article**) is used in general statements with non-count and plural nouns unless the noun is particularized or made specific in some way. Study the following guidelines and examples.

1. Do not use an article with non-count nouns:

Water is necessary for life.

Rice is good for you.

Gold is valuable.

No article is required with *water*, *life*, *rice*, or *gold* in these sentences.

2. In general statements, no article is required with plural nouns:

We like bananas.

Bears are dangerous.

People need friends.

To decide whether or not you need an article with a plural noun, you must determine whether the word is being used in a general or a specific sense.

Go to Workbook Exercise 31.6

USING *THE* OR NO ARTICLE IN GEOGRAPHICAL NAMES

Why do we use *the* before the names of oceans (*the* Atlantic Ocean) but not before the names of lakes (Lake Ontario)? Who knows? The conventions around article use in geographical names in English are not really consistent. Unfortunately, you just have to get familiar with them. The list and examples below will help you learn some of the patterns.

No (Zero) Article	Examples
Continents	Asia, Australia, Europe, South America
Countries	Canada, China, Italy, Sudan, Mexico
Cities	London, Paris, Penticton, Rio de Janeiro
Lakes, bays, falls	Lake Simcoe, Hudson Bay, Niagara Falls
Streets and parks	Burrard Street, Portage Avenue, High Park
Colleges and universities with *College* or *University* at end of name	Humber College, Red Deer College, Oxford University, Simon Fraser University
Halls	Carnegie Hall, Convocation Hall, Massey Hall

Definite Article (*the*)	Examples
Plural place names	the Americas, the Balkans, the Maritimes
Countries (or other bodies) that refer to a political union or association	the United Kingdom, the United States
Mountain ranges	the Himalayas, the Rocky Mountains
Groups of islands, *but* not individual islands	the British Isles, the Thousand Islands, the West Indies, *but* Long Island, Manitoulin Island, Vancouver Island
Oceans	the Arctic Ocean, the Atlantic Ocean, the Indian Ocean
Groups of lakes	the Muskokas, the Great Lakes

Definite Article (*the*)	Examples
Rivers, seas, straits	the St. Lawrence River, the Caribbean, the Georgia Strait, the Strait of Juan de Fuca
Colleges and universities that have *of* in the name	the University of Toronto, the University of British Columbia, the University of Saskatchewan
Buildings, towers, bridges, hotels, libraries, museums	the Chrysler Building, the CN Tower, the Granville Street Bridge, the Banff Springs Hotel, the Library of Parliament, the Royal Ontario Museum
Deserts, forests, peninsulas	the Sahara Desert, the Black Forest, the Gaspé Peninsula
Points of the globe or compass	the equator, the Tropic of Capricorn, the Middle East, the North Pole, the southern hemisphere

Go to Workbook Exercises 31.7–31.12

Practising with Prepositions 32

Prepositions are small words that often cause big problems for additional-language learners. People who speak English as a first language don't get confused by the distinction between *in* and *on* or *from* and *for*. But these little words often puzzle and frustrate those learning English.

Prepositions have no special endings or inflections that make them easy to identify. (e.g., *-ous* endings usually indicate adjectives, such as *prosperous*, and *-ity* endings suggest nouns, such as *prosperity*.) The only characteristic that prepositions have in common is that *most* of them are short words. Sometimes two prepositions are joined to make a one-word compound (e.g., *into, without, upon*). English language learners work hard to learn these words and their sometimes multiple meanings.

A **preposition** is a word that usually provides information about a relationship of time, place, or direction. A preposition comes at the beginning of a group of words known as a **prepositional phrase** (preposition + object).

after lunch	*to* school
during the week	*under* the volcano
in the closet	*inside* the house

In each of these phrases, the italicized word is a preposition. Every prepositional phrase requires an **object** (a noun or pronoun); *lunch, week, closet, school, volcano*, and *house* are the objects in the prepositional phrases above.

Below is a list of common prepositions used in English.

about	around	between	from
above	at	beyond	in
across	before	by	inside
after	behind	despite	into
against	below	down	like
along	beneath	during	near
among	beside	for	of

off	past	to	up
on	since	toward	upon
out	through	under	with
outside	throughout	underneath	within
over	till	until	without

We'll divide this long list into four categories to make it easier for you to learn the various uses of prepositions. Each of the four charts on the following pages is organized according to the relationship to which the preposition points. The charts also provide brief definitions and examples of prepositions used correctly.

One of the reasons that prepositions are confusing is that one word can have more than one meaning, so you'll see that some appear in more than one chart (e.g., *at*, *by*, and *from*) or more than once in a single chart. Please note that these charts include only the most common prepositions and their meanings. Your dictionary provides more extensive definitions and examples.

Check your understanding of prepositions by doing the exercises that follow each chart. Occasionally, more than one preposition could be used correctly. If you make any mistakes, study the chart again, and do the exercises provided.

PREPOSITIONS THAT INDICATE TIME RELATIONSHIPS

Preposition	Uses/Meaning	Examples
after	one event follows another event	We will have dinner *after* the concert.
at	used with a specific time of the day	The bell rang *at* midnight. We have dinner *at* 7:00 p.m.
before	one event precedes another	I graduated from college *before* my brother did.
by	no later than	You must finish your assignment *by* Friday.
during	indicating a period of time, usually undivided	I usually sleep *during* a long flight.
for	indicating a quantity of time	Could I talk to you *for* a few minutes?
from	indicating the time in the future when something starts	The tournament is three days *from* now.

Preposition	Uses/Meaning	Examples
in	used with a part of the day, month, year, or season	I'll see you *in* the morning. My birthday is *in* March. Emile was born *in* 2013. Birds fly south *in* the fall.
in	identifying a period of time by which something will happen; also means *during*	I'll see you *in* an hour. Traffic congestion has gotten much worse *in* recent years.
of	used with a date and month	Dennis was born on the third *of* January.
on	used with a day of the week or a specific date	I work *on* Saturday. Passover begins *on* April 7 next year.
since	from one time until now	I have not eaten *since* breakfast.
until, till	as far as the time when another event will occur	I won't have anything to eat *until* dinner.
within	not more than the specified period of time	You will hear from the boss *within* a week.

Mark Heath/CartoonStock

Go to Workbook Exercises 32.1–32.2

PREPOSITIONS THAT INDICATE PLACE OR POSITION

Preposition	Uses/Meaning	Examples
above	directly higher	His apartment is *above* ours.
across	on the other side	She lives *across* the street.
among	included in a group (of more than two)	She sat *among* her 12 grandchildren.
at	indicating a specific location; also used with specific addresses	Maya is *at* school. We live *at* 1500 Bathurst Street.
behind	in back of	Watch out! The grizzly bear is *behind* you!
below	under; directly lower	Her apartment is *below* ours.
beneath	under	Your coat is *beneath* mine in the pile.
beside	next to	Please sit *beside* me so we can talk.
between	in the middle of two	She sat *between* her two grandchildren.
by	near, beside	He has a house *by* the river.
in	within an area or space	Dahlia was born *in* New York City.
near	close to; within a short distance	I live *near* the train station.
on	covering or forming part of a surface	Please write *on* the blackboard.
over	higher than something else	The helicopter flew *over* the highway.
under	lower than something else	The subway runs *under* this theatre.

Preposition	Uses/Meaning	Examples
underneath	beneath, close under	Her purse was *underneath* the bed.
within	not farther than the distance from	The school is *within* a kilometre of her apartment.

Go to Workbook Exercise 32.3

PREPOSITIONS THAT INDICATE DIRECTION OR MOVEMENT

Preposition	Uses/Meaning	Examples
across	from one side to the other	She walked *across* the room.
around	indicating movement within a larger area; moving past something in a circle	The sprinters ran *around* the track. Omar sailed *around* the world.
by	moving past someone or something	Michel walked right *by* his ex-wife without speaking. The car drove *by* the restaurant.
down	from a higher to a lower level	I walked quickly *down* the stairs to the basement.
from	indicating place where movement away began	Our flight to Vancouver left *from* Hong Kong.
into	moving to a point inside	Igor dived *into* the cold water.
out of	moving away from	She jumped *out of* bed happily.

For EAL Learners:
A Review of the
Basics

Preposition	Uses/Meaning	Examples
past	moving by someone or something	Michel walked right *past* his ex-wife without speaking. The car drove *past* the restaurant.
through	passing from one side to another	The Don River flows *through* Toronto.
to	movement in the direction of a specific place	She walks *to* school every day.
toward	in the general direction of something	Walk *toward* the ocean and enjoy the beautiful sunset.
up	from a lower to a higher point	I walked quickly *up* the stairs to the attic.

Go to Workbook Exercise 32.4

OTHER PREPOSITIONAL RELATIONSHIPS

Relation, Source, Manner, Possession, Quantity		
Preposition	Uses/Meaning	Examples
about	on the subject of someone or something	This book is *about* love. We know all *about* your past.
about	concerning something	We can do something *about* the problem.
for	indicating the person receiving something	The message is *for* you. What can I do *for* you?
for	with regard to purpose or function	Tara received roses *for* her birthday. He works *for* a car dealership.
from	indicating the source of some-one or something; indicating the product or raw material with which something is made	Réne comes *from* the Gaspé. Wine is made *from* grapes.

Relation, Source, Manner, Possession, Quantity		
Preposition	Uses/Meaning	Examples
from	indicating the reason for something	The woman cried *from* frustration.
from	used to make a distinction between two things	English is very different *from* French.
of	belonging to somebody or something	He is a friend *of* mine. Please close the lid *of* the box.
of	concerning, relating to, or showing something	This is a photograph *of* my boyfriend. Do you have a map *of* Mexico?
of	indicating what is measured, counted, or contained	We drank a litre *of* wine.
of	used with *some, many, a few,* etc.	Some *of* the students failed the exam. A few *of* us are coming.
with	in the company of someone or something	I took a vacation *with* my husband. Please leave the keys *with* the parking attendant.
with	having or carrying something	The child *with* the red hair is Myer. Take the coffee *with* you.
with	indicating the manner or condition	She did her homework *with* care. He was trembling *with* rage.
with	indicating the tool or instrument used	You can see the stars *with* a telescope.
without	not having, not using	No one can live *without* water. Can you see *without* your glasses?

Go to Workbook Exercises 32.5–32.11

For EAL Learners: A Review of the Basics

UNIT 7

Readings

CAREER CONSCIOUSNESS
Brian Green

1   A career can be defined as the employment you prepare for during the first quarter of your life, engage in during the best years of your life, and reap the rewards from when you are least able to enjoy them. Behind the cynicism of this observation lies an important truth: choosing a life's vocation is not a decision to be taken lightly. To justify the time and effort you will invest in your career, it should be stimulating, rewarding, and productive. The better you know yourself, the more likely you are to choose a career you can live with happily.

2   What would a stimulating career be like? Picture yourself getting up in the morning and looking forward to your day with eager anticipation. This may not be the popular image of most jobs, but it is one that can be achieved. Most people participate in leisure activities that they find interesting, even energizing. There is no rule that says you cannot be as enthusiastic about your work as you are about your play. Many successful people have turned their interests into careers, thus getting paid for what they like to do. Many career professionals in the arts, for example, make their living by doing what they feel they were born to do: write, act, paint, dance, play or compose music, sing, design, or sculpt. Clive Beddoe loved to fly, and from that passion grew his career as a bush pilot and, later, his founding of one of Canada's most successful airlines, WestJet. Of course, it is not always possible to turn a passion into a career, but to deny what excites you, to relegate it to after-hours activities without trying to incorporate it into your working life, means you will spend most of your life wishing you were doing something else.

3   If your career is stimulating, then chances are good that it can also be rewarding. A good career offers two kinds of rewards: financial and emotional. Rewarding work does not just happen; it is something you need to plan for. The first and most important step is to know yourself. Only if you know who you are and what you need to be happy can you consciously seek out career experiences that will bring you satisfaction and steer clear of those that will annoy or stress you. Are you genuinely ambitious, or is power something you seek because you think it is expected of you? The pursuit of status and a high salary brings some people pure pleasure. Many people, however, find leadership positions excruciatingly stressful. Career enjoyment depends to some extent on whether or not you are successful, and success is a state of mind. Consider two graduates from the same college program. One is a technician in a small-town television station who loves his work, takes pride in keeping the station on the air, and delights in raising his family in a community where he is involved in volunteer activities ranging from sports to firefighting. The other is a news director at one of Canada's major television networks. Her work is highly stressful, full of risks, and continually scrutinized by viewers, competitors, and

her supervisors. She thrives on the adrenaline rush of nightly production and loves the big-city life, the financial rewards of her position, and the national recognition she receives. Which graduate is "successful"? Certainly, both feel their careers are rewarding, according to their individual definitions of the term.

4   A job at which you do not feel useful cannot be either rewarding or stimulating for very long. It is human nature to want to contribute, to feel that your efforts make a difference. Camaraderie with fellow workers, a pleasant daily routine, even a good salary cannot compensate in the long run for a sense that your work is meaningless or unappreciated. Sadly, some people spend their entire working lives at jobs in which their contribution is so insignificant that their absence would scarcely be noticed. Everyone knows people who boast about reading paperback novels on the job and others who sleep through their night shift so they can spend their days fishing or golfing. Is this the way you want to spend 45 years of your life? All the paperbacks and the rounds of golf do not add up to much without a sense that you are doing something worthwhile. It may take a few years, but when it comes, the realization that your work lacks meaning is soul-destroying.

5   It is not easy to find a career that provides stimulating, enjoyable, and meaningful work. Understanding yourself—your interests, needs, values, and goals—is an essential first step. Making long-term decisions consistent with your values and goals is the difficult second step. Too many people spend their lives in careers that make them miserable because they allow themselves to be governed by parents, friends, or simple inertia. Finally, once you have launched your career, never rest. Actively seek challenges and opportunities that stimulate you. Relish the rewards of meeting those challenges, being productive, and doing your job well. Continually strive to improve, not for the sake of your employer, but for your own sake. Your career will occupy three-quarters of your life, so make the most of it!

QUESTIONS FOR DISCUSSION

1. What kind of hook does the writer use to open his essay? (See "Writing Introductions and Conclusions" in Chapter 25 for an introduction to the different kinds of hooks.)

2. In paragraph 5, identify the two main parts of the author's conclusion: the summary of the essay's main points and the clincher. What kind of clincher has he used? Is it appropriate for this essay? Why?

3. In what order has Green arranged his points: chronological, logically linked, climactic, or random? (See "Organizing Your Main Points" in Chapter 22 for a discussion of essay organization.) Can you rearrange the points without diminishing the effectiveness of the piece?

4. How do the topic sentences of paragraphs 2, 3, and 4 contribute to the coherence of this essay? Identify three or four transitional words or phrases the author has used within his paragraphs to make them read smoothly.

SUGGESTIONS FOR WRITING

1. How would you define a satisfying career?
2. Who is the most satisfied (dissatisfied) worker you know? What makes him or her happy (unhappy) with the job?
3. If you had enough money invested so that you could live comfortably without paid employment, would you be happy? Why or why not?

MY FATHER AND THE BABY SEAL

Tommy Akulukjuk

1   My father is in Ottawa for surgery. He's been down there for weeks now. It's hard for me to think of him like this. When I was growing up in Pangnirtung, Nunavut, he knew what to do all the time. Only when I was older did I start seeing him as being weaker, as having doubts.

2   When I was a child, he was good to me and my six siblings. He would take us hunting and always made sure we caught something—any animal, any food. When it came time for me to catch my first seal, he consulted my brothers and talked to my mother and then came to me. He said, "Angakuluk, this is the trail of a seal that's strayed away from its hole. The seal will have no place to go, so you can easily kill it." And that's what I did, killing the seal with my father at my side.

3   I went with him and his cousin on a seal hunt once. The sea-ice that year was not formed evenly, so instead of heading out onto the ocean, we went overland. The weather turned bad and we were stuck on the land for a whole week, with not much more to eat than tea and bannock. We were hungry. Finally the weather cleared and we headed for the hunting grounds. On the way, my father said he felt we had to stop. His cousin suggested we make tea, so my father went to get snow for water.

4   That's when he heard a whimpering sound. He listened closer and it was a baby seal, right by his side, hidden under a foot of snow. He grabbed it with his hands and killed it. It had a snow-white coat and dark eyes. It was the first real food we'd had in a week. My father told me he knew that this seal was a gift from God. He knew he needed to stop there and it was for a reason that the baby seal whimpered loud enough for my father to hear. In that way, I feel I can say my father heard the voice of God.

5   On that same trip, on our way back home, we decided to take a risk and travel on the sea-ice that my father had earlier deemed unsafe. Inuit hunters

Tommy Akulukjuk, "My Father and the Baby Seal."

are always careful, checking what they think is dangerous. Along the way we tested the thickness of the ice with a harpoon. At one point, when my father got off the snowmobile to do this, he said to me, "Don't follow. Stay here." I felt apprehension in his voice, an uncertainty I'd never heard before.

6   Walking away from the snowmobile, he fell through the ice up to his waist. I stood up to run to where he was, but his cousin stopped me and told me not to risk it. I was shaking all over. I had adrenaline running through me like it was being pumped from a hose. I was almost in tears. Just a couple days before, he had heard the voice of God, and now his life was in danger.

7   But like any good Inuk hunter, my father didn't panic. He got out of the hole by himself. Still dripping wet from the frigid seawater, he led us down a different, safer trail.

8   That night we slept at an outpost camp, and the strange thing is, we laughed about the ordeals of that week—about how different it had been from our day-to-day life, and how refreshing it was to have a little bit of a scare. To my father, especially, this was part of life: The good can often turn out not-so-good, even at the best of times.

9   And now he's in hospital in Ottawa. It's not the best of times. My father says he's amazed by the doctors and what they're planning to do. He says they have a lot of confidence. But all I can think about is [that] I want to be as humble and compassionate as he is.

QUESTIONS FOR DISCUSSION

1. As a child, how does the author feel about his father? How does he feel about him as a grown man?
2. Where do the introduction and conclusion of this narrative take place? How does this framing device contribute to the effect of the story?
3. How do we learn that killing his first seal is an important rite of passage for a boy in this community?
4. What is the converse (the opposite) of the father's outlook on life expressed in paragraph 8? How does it apply to the situation described in paragraph 9?

SUGGESTIONS FOR WRITING

1. Have you ever gone hunting? Write an essay about the experience.
2. Most young children believe their parents know everything and are all-powerful. (Of course, most teenagers think the opposite.) Write a narrative essay about the time you discovered that one of your parents was mistaken, fearful, or otherwise less than perfect—in other words, human.
3. Write an essay that focuses on the illness and/or hospitalization of one of your family members. How did the family cope with this crisis? How did it make you feel?

AN IMMIGRANT'S SPLIT PERSONALITY
Sun-Kyung Yi

1   I am Korean-Canadian. But the hyphen often snaps in two, obliging me to choose to act as either a Korean or a Canadian, depending on where I am and who I'm with.

2   When I was younger, toying with the idea of entertaining two separate identities was a real treat, like a secret game for which no one knew the rules but me. I was known as Angela to the outside world, and as Sun-Kyung at home. I ate bologna sandwiches in the school lunchroom and rice and kimchee for dinner. I chatted about teen idols and giggled with my girlfriends during my classes, and ambitiously practiced piano and studied in the evenings, planning to become a doctor when I grew up. I waved hellos and goodbyes to my teachers, but bowed to my parents' friends visiting our home. I could also look straight in the eyes of my teachers and friends and talk frankly with them instead of staring at my feet with my mouth shut when Koreans talked to me. Going outside the home meant I was able to relax from the constraints of my cultural conditioning, until I walked back in the door and had to return to being an obedient and submissive daughter.

3   The game soon ended when I realized that it had become a way of life, that I couldn't change the rules without disappointing my parents and questioning all the cultural implications and consequences that came with being a hyphenated Canadian.

4   Many have tried to convince me that I am a Canadian, like all other immigrants in the country, but those same people also ask me which country I came from with great curiosity, following with questions about the type of food I ate and the language I spoke. It's difficult to feel a sense of belonging and acceptance when you are regarded as "one of them." "Those Koreans, they work hard…. You must be fantastic at math and science." (No.) "Do your parents own a corner store?" (No.)

5   Koreans and Canadians just can't seem to merge into "us" and "we."

6   Some people advised me that I should just take the best of both worlds and disregard the rest. That's ideal, but unrealistic when my old culture demands a complete conformity with very little room to manoeuvre for new and different ideas.

7   After a lifetime of practice, I thought I could change faces and become Korean on demand with grace and perfection. But working with a small Korean company in Toronto proved me wrong. I quickly became estranged from my

Sun-Kyung Yi, "An Immigrant's Split Personality," *The Globe and Mail,* April 12, 1992.

own people. My parents were ecstatic at the thought of their daughter finally finding her roots and having a working opportunity to speak my native tongue and absorb the culture. For me, it was the most painful and frustrating two and one-half months of my life.

8   When the president of the company boasted that he "operated little Korea," he meant it literally. A Canadianized Korean was not tolerated. I looked like a Korean; therefore, I had to talk, act, and think like one, too. Being accepted meant a total surrender to ancient codes of behaviour rooted in Confucian thought, while leaving the "Canadian" part of me out in the parking lot with my '86 Buick. In the first few days at work, I was bombarded with inquiries about my marital status. When I told them I was single, they spent the following days trying to match me up with available bachelors in the company and the community. I was expected to accept my inferior position as a woman and had to behave accordingly. It was not a place to practice my feminist views, or be an individual without being condemned. Little Korea is a place for men (who filled all the senior positions) and women don't dare speak up or disagree with their male counterparts. The president (all employees bow to him and call him Mr. President) asked me to act more like a lady and smile. I was openly scorned by a senior employee because I spoke more fluent English than Korean. The cook in the kitchen shook her head in disbelief upon discovering that my cooking skills were limited to boiling a package of instant noodles. "You want a good husband, learn to cook," she advised me.

9   In less than a week I became an outsider because I refused to conform and blindly nod my head in agreement to what my elders (which happened to be everybody else in the company) said. A month later, I was demoted because "members of the workplace and the Korean community" had complained that I just wasn't "Korean enough," and I had "too much power for a single woman." My father suggested that "when in Rome do as the Romans." But that's exactly what I was doing. I am in Canada so I was freely acting like a Canadian, and it cost me my job.

10   My father also said, "It doesn't matter how Canadian you think you are, just look in the mirror and it'll tell you who you *really* are." But what he didn't realize is that an immigrant has to embrace the new culture to enjoy and benefit from what it has to offer. Of course, I will always be Korean by virtue of my appearance and early conditioning, but I am also happily Canadian and want to take full advantage of all that such citizenship confers. But for now I remain slightly distant from both cultures, accepted fully by neither. The hyphenated Canadian personifies the ideal of multiculturalism, but unless the host culture and the immigrant cultures can find ways to merge their distinct identities, sharing the best of both, this cultural schizophrenia will continue.

QUESTIONS FOR DISCUSSION

1. Create a table (chart) in which you summarize the main characteristics of the Korean and the Canadian halves of the author's personality.
2. What method of paragraph development does the author use in paragraph 8? (See pages 160–168 for a discussion of paragraph development methods.)
3. Identify five examples of parallel structure in paragraph 2. How does the author's use of parallelism serve to reinforce her thesis?
4. Identify the summary of main points and the clincher in paragraph 10.

SUGGESTIONS FOR WRITING

1. Do you sometimes feel that you are two people trapped inside a single body? Write an essay in which you contrast the two sides of your personality.
2. Contrast three or four significant values of your generation with those of your parents' (or grandparents') generation.

THE CASE AGAINST QUICKSPEAK
Brian Green

"Thx fr yr rply. no prob. ill call mtg fr tues @ 8 ok?:-)"

1   If you are not familiar with email jargon, this message may look like something in military code or from outer space. Those who use email regularly, however, will recognize it as an example of a form of communication that I call "quickspeak." Many people these days are in such a hurry that they do not take time to spell, punctuate, or write complete sentences in their electronic correspondence. Of course, these folks would not dream of writing messages like this on paper, but there is something about communicating electronically that makes them think it is acceptable, even fashionable, to ignore everything they ever learned about writing in order to "save time." Call me a dinosaur, an antique from the days of the inkwell and quill pen, but I will not succumb to quickspeak. I will continue to ensure that my email is as structured and correct as any other item I write. Why? Because I want my message to be clearly understood, I want to send messages that are thoughtful and complete, and I want to present a positive image to my readers.

2   "But you know what I mean!" protests an email correspondent (written as "bt u no wht i meen:-]"). And it's true that, with some effort, I can make out what I think she means, but I would also understand if she said, "Duh—gonna eat soon?" while scratching her stomach. Any message, whether stored in ink or electrons, communicates more than the meaning of its words. It tells the

reader something about the importance of the message, the intelligence of the writer, and the writer's consideration for the reader.

3   Quickspeak tells the reader that the writer does not care much about the message or the reader. It also implies that the writer may not be capable of writing correctly. At the very least, quickspeak betrays a writer as careless. My father used to describe this approach to communication as "slap-dash," and that's as good a term as any. A slap-dash writer is unlikely to make it into the executive suite.

4   Although I am usually able to decipher the gist of quickspeak, I am seldom sure that I have translated the message accurately. In many cases, this failure stems from the fact that the writer did not provide complete or accurate information. Take the example that introduces this essay. I know there will be a meeting (about what?) on Tuesday (which week?) at 8:00 (a.m. or p.m.?). Where is this meeting? Who will be present? What documents am I expected to bring? Without the answers to these questions, how can I prepare? Far from saving time, quickspeak actually wastes it. Now I have to respond to the email sender to find out the answers to these questions. At least three messages will be needed where one would have done. If only the writer had recognized this basic rule of writing: to be brief takes time!

5   Email is no different from any other business correspondence: it must be clear and concise. Achieving clarity and conciseness is not difficult, but it does require planning. Begin with an introduction that briefly explains the purpose of your message. Next, outline how you are going to develop that message. Use numbered or bulleted points to guide the reader from your position statement through your reasoning to your conclusion. Reinforce your message with a conclusion that states any follow-up actions you require and that confirms the time, place, and responsibilities of those who are contributing to the project. Next, reread your message as if you were reading it for the first time. Revise to be sure that you have included all the necessary details: dates, reference numbers, times and places of meetings, and whatever other information is needed to get the right people together in the right places, on the right days, at the right times, with the right information at hand. Use a spell-checker, but don't rely on it to catch all your errors and typos. Remember: A clear message, clearly delivered, is the essence of effective communication.

6   People who write in quickspeak ignore the reason that rules for correct writing evolved in the first place. Writing that communicates accurately depends upon precise thinking. A message with a statement of purpose, logically arranged points, and a confirming summary is the work of a writer whose message has been thought through and can be trusted. In contrast, quickspeak, which can be bashed out in no time, reflects no planning, little coherent thought, and no sense of order or priority. The message, the reader, and, ultimately, the writer all suffer as a result.

7   My co-worker who wrote the email message that introduces this argument is "slap-dash" and may be semi-literate. That, at least, is the impression she gives. She has wasted not only my time but also her own. And, by using quickspeak, she hasn't taken advantage of the power of precise, structured language to produce clear, complete messages. Her trendy message communicates more about her than it does about the subject of her email, and what it says is far from flattering.

QUESTIONS FOR DISCUSSION

1. In your own words, write a one-sentence summary of the thesis and main points of this essay.
2. What is the main kind of development used by the author in paragraph 5?
3. What is the effect of the questions included in the body of paragraph 4? How do they draw the reader onside?
4. The concluding paragraph does contain a summary of the essay's main points, but they are subtly rather than obviously stated. Find and underline them.

SUGGESTIONS FOR WRITING

1. Is email a time-saver or a time-waster in an office environment? Support your opinion with at least two reasons.
2. Write a short essay in which you contrast email with text messaging.

HELLO, DOLLIES

Stephen Marche

1   The faces of the dolls are as lovely as moulded vinyl can be. The shock of their price—Maplelea Girls sell for $100—wears off when you hold one of their eighteen-inch bodies in your hands. The quality is so apparent. The hair is thick, the hands lock, the eyes are sharp and vibrant, opening and shutting without that opiated, half-lidded look cheaper dolls sometimes endure in repose. The clothes and furnishings are equally beautiful. The doll named Saila Qilavvaq, an Inuit girl from Iqaluit, can be outfitted in a traditional hooded winter garment—an amautik—handmade in Nunavut and worth every nickel of $56.

2   Maplelea Girls are luxury toys, but also markers of consumer identity. Since 2003, Maplelea has sold about 100,000 dolls, along with half a million accessories, making it one of the most successful toy companies in Canada and among the fastest growing. Its success, given the limited market, is a surprise. "The

Stephen Marche, "Hello, Dollies," *The Walrus*, March 2015, pp. 63–65.

goal of most Canadian toy companies is to sell into the United States because it's ten times larger," says Maplelea owner Kathryn Gallagher Morton from her office in Newmarket, Ontario. "To [design a toy] for just the Canadian market is a huge risk."

3   The dolls have emerged amid deep confusion about what Canadian content represents. It's a great time to scream, "I am Canadian," but not a great time to ask what the adjective might mean. If you want to sell beer, you wave the flag. If you want to sell coffee, you explain that your coffee is really about hockey, even if Burger King owns you. Pride runs high. We howl through the streets, celebrating our victories, yet with a few notable exceptions Canadian cultural nationalism is dead. International conglomerates have bought nearly all the major publishers. Our music and film are mere addenda to the Hollywood entertainment machine. The CBC is being stripped for parts.

4   The question of identity is beset by piety and wishful thinking and institutional inertia and plain nostalgia, but Maplelea Girls are free of all that nonsense for the simple reason that they are a product. They represent the Canadianness that parents want to buy for their children, and the Canadianness that children want to be bought for them. They sell the Canadian identity that the market can bear.

5   There are many differences between Canada and the United States. July 1 and July 4. Maple syrup and corn syrup. The West, which America conquered, and the North, which is unconquerable. After a bear attack in the United States, the sympathy lies mostly with the human attacked; after a bear attack in Canada, the sympathy lies mostly with the bear. To this list of differences, we may add American Girl and Maplelea.

6   The American franchise has been in business for nearly thirty years and amounts to a craze, both here and in the US. American Girl has sold more than 25 million dolls and 147 million books since 1986; sales hit $633 million in 2013. Its website attracts 72 million visits a year. Its magazine's circulation has surpassed 450,000. Barbie sales have dropped steadily since 2011: at five times the price, expensive dolls with stories are replacing the down-market plastic toys. (Mattel owns both Barbie and American Girl.)

7   In 2014, American Girl established retail spaces within Indigo stores in Toronto, Vancouver, and Ottawa. The boutique at the Yorkdale mall in Toronto was swarmed by 2,000 girls on opening day. Among market analysts, the rule of thumb is that Canada represents 10 percent of North American sales, which would translate to a staggering $60 million annually. (Maplelea sales are just under $5 million a year.)

8   There are forty combinations of eye, hair, and skin colour available in the My American Girl line alone. And there's more: Bitty Babies and Bitty Twins, and dolls without hair for girls with cancer. The accessories are fantastic, too. An egg chair, straight out of a 1970s California bedroom, retails for $100. At American

Girl stores, there are doll hospitals where you can have your doll repaired, or her ears pierced or fitted with hearing aids. There is a restaurant where you can eat with your doll beside you (the waiter poses riddles for you to solve together) and a photo studio where you can get your picture taken together.

9   Maplelea Girls are sold online, and by phone and mail-order catalogue, which makes them slightly less expensive than their American counterparts, although you can still send your Maplelea Girl to a "spa" to have her repaired. Maplelea is a bit more prudent, more restrained, less hasty, less needy of the miracles of product diversification. Like so much of Canadian culture, Maplelea is an American idea made slightly more virtuous.

10   Before she conceived of Maplelea, Morton ran Avonlea Traditions, which held toy licences for Anne of Green Gables and the RCMP. In the 1990s, the Canadian-identity business changed and Morton changed with it. "Maplelea is how we see ourselves as opposed to how others see us," she says. She designed the Maplelea Girls over three years; the process involved exhaustive consultation with girls, parents, community groups, librarians, and specialty toy stores. This, according to the catalogue, is what they came up with:

> Taryn, Brianne, Alexi, Léonie, Jenna and Saila are all very different—they like different hobbies, sports, school subjects, foods, colours and even have a different personal fashion style! However, there are some things that they have in common—they are all bright, caring, energetic Canadian girls who think Canada is one terrific country.

11   The first thing to notice: geography is everything. The original American Girl dolls... were characters out of American history, often ones who'd lived through national crises: Kaya and her mare, Steps High, from 1764; Caroline Abbott from the War of 1812; Addy Walker, a runaway slave from 1864; Kit Kittredge, who survived the worst of the Great Depression. The Maplelea Girls were not involved in the March West nor, God forbid, the Battle of the Plains of Abraham. They weren't watching quietly from the sidelines at the signing of Treaty Number Six. They emerge from the landscape instead.

12   Jenna is the Maritime doll. She loves to watch the gannets: "I live in Lunenburg, Nova Scotia, right beside the Atlantic Ocean. I have fiery red hair and a personality to match." Taryn is from Banff, which makes her technically Albertan, although spiritually she is closer to British Columbia: "Three things I couldn't survive without are my hiking boots, clean fresh mountain air and butterflies. Can you tell I'm a bit of an environmentalist at heart?" Brianne, from Manitoba, is a blond farm girl: "I love my Welsh pony named Chinook, belong to 4-H and dance in the big Ukrainian Festival in Dauphin every year." Saila, the Inuit girl, eats grandma's bannock and crowberry jam and travels immense distances by boat or by *qamutik* (that is, sled) for bouts of clam digging. There

are two city girls: First there's blond Léonie Belanger-Leblanc, from Quebec City, who plays "outdoor hockey whenever I can" and wears her Québécois pioneer outfit when she goes to visit her cousins at the *cabane à sucre*. (Naturally, the girl from Quebec has the best clothes.) Then there's Alexi, the girl from Toronto, whose skin is a subtle, unidentifiable shade of brown, and who loves computers. Taryn and Léonie are the bestselling dolls in the series; they also have the most common eye- and hair-colour combinations in Canada, according to Maplelea.

13   These energetic girls fill the emptiness of the land with their hearts. It's a century-old archetype, the girl who crowns herself with dandelions. Emily Pauline Johnson had the song her paddle sings. Susanna Moodie and Catharine Parr Traill fought the bush with all their love and contempt. Anne of Green Gables remained wilful in her imagination despite a childhood of indentured servitude. Maplelea, like all iconic Canadiana, reveals the oppression of the landscape and the human response to that oppression.

14   And then there is Alexi. Like the other girls, Alexi comes from a place, but a very specific place—not just a city or a province, but a neighbourhood. She is from Cabbagetown, in Toronto. "People come from all over the world to make Toronto their home. That makes me proud," she writes in her journal. (Every Maplelea Girl comes with her own journal, and each item of clothing comes with new pages.) "Restaurants here are fabulous. Cambodian, Greek, Indian, Italian, Chinese, Caribbean—we have it all." She visits the Royal Ontario Museum and the St. Lawrence Market, and Centre Island for family picnics. She plays piano and wants to be an inventor. Her mother, Emmay, manages IT for a big bank. "My dad, Ben, is an artist and he has a big sunny studio where he says the light is best. He's a stay-at-home dad, and he's always here when I get back from school. He's a terrific cook and an outstanding housekeeper."

15   With all this detail, one absence is glaring: her ethnicity. The images of her parents—Dad's skin is light brown, Mom's is darker—make it impossible to identify any ethnic origin. "We decided to not state what her ethnicity was or her cultural background," Morton tells me. "The girl could make up that aspect herself."

16   Alexi's identity must be hidden for two reasons. The first is market based. She belongs to the category, so prevalent in advertising, known as "ethnically ambiguous." The second is more subtle. The appeal of Alexi, like the appeal of Toronto, is in the impossibility of determining her ethnicity. To put a name on her would be to reduce her, to narrow the possibilities of her being.

17   In the rest of the world, the multicultural impulse—the belief that ethnic diversity is a public good to be celebrated in itself—has come under severe threat. European countries have seen the rise of anti-immigrant parties, from the UK Independence Party to neo-fascist groups in Greece and Hungary. Even Denmark and Sweden have seen dramatic spikes in explicit political xenophobia.

Australia recently unveiled its No Way campaign, in which the phrase *You will not make Australia home* looms over an image of a stormy sea. They released the threat in seventeen languages. In Canada, there is no national anti-immigrant party with a significant voice. The Conservative party, or one of their former splinter parties, might once upon a time have wanted to ban turbans from the RCMP. Now visiting a Sikh temple is the equivalent of visiting a state fair during an American election—a required political ritual for all sides.

18   Canada, alone among the liberal democracies, has kept its idealism about immigration, mainly because its expectations are so low. Canadian culture, unlike French or even American culture, is not an ancient tradition whose symbols are internalized from birth. Immigrants to other countries integrate or fail to integrate into long-standing identities. Canadian multiculturalism demands tolerance and openness in the service of tolerance and openness. Hollowness haunts Canadian multiculturalism, although it can be a comfortable hollowness—the hollowness of a nest, perhaps.

19   The contradiction that Alexi represents is the contradiction of our future. She is ethnic with no ethnicity, a blending of anything with anything. We are mixing ourselves toward... who can say? The absence at the heart of Alexi is a horizon of limitless possibility, blank pages on which anything or nothing can be written.

20   Canada is a country that makes people feel small. That is its gift among nations. Human beings are small. It is good to be reminded of it. A 1980s archeological survey on Axel Heiberg Island, in what is now Nunavut, found among other Dorset artifacts an antler carving of two faces, one of which appears to be European. Not an archeological record of slaughter, as is so often found, but a 700-year-old miniature, the face of a little other. A record of an encounter between peoples, between cultures, on an unimaginably desolate strip of the earth, for the purposes of trade.

21   Dolls are our diminished idols, repositories of longing and fear we keep in children's bedrooms. In this country that makes people feel small, the kids put their wild-hearted dolls to bed at night and wake them up in the morning. Even abandoned, the dolls who sleep or are tucked away or sit in empty rooms around little tables in frozen conversation don't suffer from too little meaning. Dolls have everything that people have. They have names and stories and bodies and houses and people who love them. They have more than most people. They're only missing life.

QUESTIONS FOR DISCUSSION

1. Identify three or four descriptive details in paragraph 1. What is the main point of the paragraph?

2. What strategies does the second paragraph use to develop the point that Maplelea is "one of the most successful toy companies in Canada"?

3. Paragraph 5 focuses on contrasts between Canada and the United States, including Maplelea and American Girl dolls. Identify three international contrasts listed in the paragraph. What are some other differences between the two countries that you've observed?

4. How did Kathryn Gallagher Morton, the owner of Maplelea, develop the Maplelea Girls product line (paragraph 10)? Identify the six dolls she came up with. What is the primary distinguishing characteristic of each doll? (See paragraphs 12–14.)

5. Where is Alexi from? Why do you think Morton defines Alexi as from a specific neighbourhood, rather than a city or province? What does she look like? What does Marche think Alexi represents?

6. In paragraphs 17 and 18, the author contrasts Canada and other "liberal democracies" in terms of attitudes toward immigration. Do you agree with him? Why or why not?

SUGGESTIONS FOR WRITING

1. Did you have a favourite toy as a child? Do you still have it? Describe it and explain why the toy meant so much to you when you were young.

2. Did you play with dolls as a child? If so, what kind of doll was special to you? Do you think the "little girl" identity of Maplelea Girls makes them exclusively toys for girls? If you are male, how did you feel about "girl toys" growing up? Would you permit your son to play with Maplelea dolls? Why?

3. Marche claims that "Canada is a country that makes people feel small. That is its gift among nations" (paragraph 20). Do you agree or disagree? Why?

POINT, CLICK, DATE: THE ONLINE MATCHMAKING PHENOMENON

B. J. Menzel

1   Talia is a poster girl for online dating. At 23, in her last year of college, and about to begin her career, she has been going out with her boyfriend for more than six months. Talia had met men through friends, at work, at bars, and at her gym, and can relate dating experiences that would be hilarious if they weren't so painful. There was the man who lived with his parents and had to sneak out of the house to meet her so his family wouldn't know he was dating. There were the gropers, who seemed all right until they thought it was time to

Reprinted by permission of the author.

get physical, usually about an hour into the first date. There were the slobs, who showed up for a dinner date dressed in a T-shirt, workboots, dirty jeans, even a baseball cap. Then there was the religious nut who spent the evening trying to persuade her to be "born again" and come with him to a church rally in Texas. And that's not counting the potentially nice guys who were too shy to speak or too nervous to shut up or interested only in *World of Warcraft* or cars or zombies or the Canucks. Finally, persuaded by friends who had had success with online dating, Talia signed up with *Zoosk*. She took her time, screened the potential matches carefully, corresponded with a few, narrowed her selection, talked on the phone with just three, and chose to meet two. One was nice, but there was no spark. The other was just right. Talia and Ben hit it off immediately, and six months later they are talking about moving in together after graduation.

2   Online dating now accounts for more than a third of long-term relationships and has become a $1.25 billion industry, clearly enjoying a phenomenal rate of growth considering the industry has existed only since 1995. Last year, more than 80 per cent of North American singles participated in some form of Internet dating. In the five years between 2007 and 2012, the number of people subscribing to online dating sites doubled from about 20 million to around 40 million in the U.S. alone, and this is a worldwide phenomenon. As breathtakingly quick as the acceptance of online dating seems, there's really nothing mysterious about its popularity.

3   We entrust computers with our banking and investing; we work and play online; we select our vacations, electronics, clothing, and just about everything else through commercial websites; and we pay for these choices using an online "pal." It seems only natural that we would turn to the computer to suggest relationship partners. And, used intelligently, it's a far better process than trying to find love at a meat-market bar or selecting from the limited choices available through our personal networks.

4   The range of dating sites is enormous. Some are free while others charge up to five figures to subscribe. Some provide matchmaking algorithms that select profiles the program predicts will have the best chance of success, while others are basically catalogues of singles from which you can choose people who appeal to you. Some are broad-based and open to all ages, interests, and motives, while others provide niches for specific interests, ages, orientations, preferences, and even income levels. Some are easy and intuitive to use; others require some technical knowledge and rely on the user's familiarity with social media. Some use the GPS function built into your smartphone to locate potential dates in your proximity, while others scan the world for dates ("Here's an interesting match in Azerbaijan!") unless you narrow the search. Some, like *eHarmony*, emphasize long-term relationships and marriage. Some are hookup

sites: *Tinder, Get It On,* and *Adult Friend Finder* are well-established sites that belong in this category. There are specific niche sites for members of religious organizations, for gays, for pet lovers, for outdoorsy types, for fans of every kind of music, for Trekkies; and sites for vegetarians, golfers, single parents, equestrians, soldiers, and even millionaires.

5   Sometime in the future, online matchmakers may develop an algorithm that will accurately match two people with a guarantee that they will fall in love. For now, online dating can identify couples with common interests and some assurance of compatibility based on age, education, profession, hobbies, and so on, but those who have met their mates online—even some of the creators of dating sites—agree that long-term relationships are a product of intangibles beyond the computer's most sophisticated program. Dating sites can find lots of people who might enjoy a date or two together, but they can't recognize chemistry.

6   Aware of all this potential and mindful of the limitations, what are the keys to making the process work for you? Many dating sites publish blogs that offer advice on increasing the odds of success, and Internet dating has become a favourite topic for study by social scientists and psychologists, whose observations appear in outlets as diverse as *Canadian Living Magazine, Dr. Phil, Men's Health,* and the *Huffington Post.* These observers agree on several points.

7   First, know what you want—and select a site that meets your needs. If you are new to a town and want to meet other singles for casual dates, then free sites like *Plenty of Fish* or *Zoosk* (and about a hundred others) will help you find people who might share your interests. If you are looking for something more serious, then *eHarmony* and its competitors claim to have a better track record in relationships that lead to marriage. And if a no-strings-attached hookup with someone in your vicinity is what you're after, there are *Tinder* and its ilk. Another approach to finding the right site is to look for those that cater specifically to your demographic: for example, *Christian Mingle* or *JDate* for religious compatibility or *OurTime* for the over-50 set. Using demographic-specific sites means that you will be less overwhelmed with choices, most of which are likely to be inappropriate. There are several Internet sites that compare online dating services, categorizing them according to many criteria, including some that might be suitable for your expectations and motives: datingreviewsguide.com and dating-guide.ca and onlinedatingmagazine.com are among the best.

8   Second, take some care with the profile you post on a site. In online dating, honesty is the best policy: you want to present yourself as your potential dates will actually see you. It's best to avoid the 10-years-ago or 50-pounds-lighter photos. There is no sense raising expectations that will be crushed at the first

meeting. Similarly, don't claim to enjoy activities you're only mildly interested in. One woman tried to attract male attention by describing herself as an enthusiastic hockey fan, and it worked. She more than doubled the number of people interested in her, but every man she met was obsessed with hockey to the exclusion of any other interest. Eventually, she removed the hockey reference from her profile. On the flip side of being honest about yourself, it's also wise to consider the potential for exaggerated and outright misleading content in the profiles you scan. Because it's natural for people to minimize shortcomings and emphasize strengths, it's impossible to know whether what you see in an online profile is an accurate picture, wishful thinking, or an outright lie. Thus, it's a good idea to recognize the profile as the first step of the process, to be followed up by more research.

9   Dating site experts advise that you never go on a date without first communicating directly with the person, preferably by video link. Some sites encourage texting and online chat, while others reserve that function for paying customers. In any case, texting and chatting should be preliminary to a phone or video conversation. This step is necessary to ensure you will be meeting the person whose profile is on the site and not some fictional persona that the profiler wishes he or she was. You'll also discover if you have enough in common to enjoy a conversation and if there's enough attraction to justify spending an hour or two in each other's presence. Of course, even this step is no guarantee. It's important to take first-date precautions, such as meeting in a public place. It is also a good idea to set out limits, if there are any, for the first date. You don't need a formal discussion or contractual agreement, but mentioning, for example, that you need to be home by a certain time because you have an early appointment the next day or suggesting that you aren't interested in people who drink too much or use drugs may short-circuit potential problems.

10   In its short lifetime, the phenomenon of online dating has revolutionized the way people meet and form relationships. More people meet through online sites than in all other ways combined, and that trend will continue. People will still find dates through friends, at school, and at work, but the data tell us that online dating presents more chances for meeting a good match. Remember Talia and Ben, the man she met online? Turns out that he comes from her hometown, went to the same college she did, and even knew some of her friends. But it took a computer to get them together.

QUESTIONS FOR DISCUSSION

1. Who are Talia and Ben? Why are they mentioned in this essay? What does the reader find out about them?
2. What is the topic sentence of paragraph 2? How is its point developed?

3. Paragraph 4 uses examples to illustrate what point? Are there enough examples to support the point?
4. According to paragraph 5, what can an online dating site offer the user? What can't it provide?
5. According to the essay, what are the keys to making an online dating site work for the person using it? Which paragraphs develop these points?
6. Paragraph 8 points out two sides of an important step toward successful online dating. What step is it? What are these two sides of the step?
7. According to paragraph 9, what phase of online dating is similar to (or the same as) traditional dating? Do you agree? Why or why not?

SUGGESTIONS FOR WRITING

1. Do you have any experience with online dating? Has it been a positive or a negative experience for you? Write a short essay outlining your experience.
2. When you are presented with so many online options—hundreds of seemingly attractive people eagerly waiting to meet someone—does it make it harder to "settle" for one of them? Does restlessness set in when people have to spend real time getting acquainted, knowing that so many cyber-possibilities are waiting at the swipe of a cellphone? Write an essay about the effects of so many would-be partners on the potential for a lasting relationship.

DEAR DAD

Jeffrey Moussaieff Masson

1   One reason that so many of us are fascinated by penguins is that they resemble us. They walk upright, the way we do, and, like us, they are notoriously curious creatures. No doubt this accounts for our fondness for cartoon images of penguins dressed up at crowded parties, but as fathers, penguins are our superiors.

2   Unlike mammals, male birds can experience pregnancy as an intimate matter, with the father in many species helping to sit (brood) the egg. After all, a male can brood an egg as well as a female can. But in no other species does it reach this extreme.

3   The emperors usually wait for good weather to copulate, any time between April 10 and June 6. They separate themselves somewhat from the rest of the

Jeffrey Moussaieff Masson, "Dear Dad." Reprinted by permission of the author.

colony and face each other, remaining still for a time. Then the male bends his head, contracts his abdomen, and shows the female the spot on his belly where he has a flap of skin that serves as a kind of pouch for the egg and baby chick. This stimulates the female to do the same. Their heads touch, and the male bends his head down to touch the female's pouch. Both begin to tremble visibly. Then the female lies face down on the ice, partially spreads her wings and opens her legs. The male climbs onto her back and they mate for 10 to 30 seconds.

4   They stay together afterward constantly, leaning against one another when they are standing up, or if they lie down, the female will glide her head under that of her mate. About a month later, between May 1 and June 12, the female lays a single greenish-white egg. French researchers noted that the annual dates on which the colony's first egg was laid varied by only eight days in 16 years of observation. Weighing almost a pound [.45 kg], and measuring up to 131 millimetres long and 86 millimetres wide, this is one of the largest eggs of any bird. The male stays by the female's side, his eyes fixed on her pouch. As soon as he sees the egg, he sings a variation of what has been called the "ecstatic" display by early observers, and she too takes up the melody.

5   She catches the egg with her wings before it touches the ice and places it on her feet. Both penguins then sing in unison, staring at the egg for up to an hour. The female then slowly walks around the male, who gently touches the egg on her feet with his beak, making soft groans, his whole body trembling. He shows the female his pouch. Gently she puts the egg down on the ice and just as gently he rolls it with his beak between his large, black, powerfully clawed feathered feet, and then, with great difficulty, hoists the egg onto the surface of his feet. He rests back on his heels so that his feet make the least contact with the ice. The transfer of the egg is a delicate operation. If it falls on the ice and rolls away, it can freeze in minutes or it might even be stolen. If it is snatched away by a female penguin who failed to find a mate, its chances of survival are slight because the intruder will eventually abandon the egg, since she has no mate to relieve her.

6   With the egg transfer successfully completed, the happy couple both sing. The male parades about in front of the female, showing her his pouch with the egg inside. This thick fold, densely feathered on the outside and bare inside, now completely covers the egg and keeps it at about 95 degrees Fahrenheit [35°C], even when the temperature falls to 95 degrees below zero [−70°C].

7   The female begins to back away, each time a little farther. He tries to follow her, but it is hard, since he is balancing the egg. Suddenly she is gone, moving purposefully toward the open sea. She is joined by the other females in the

colony, who, by the end of May or June, have all left for the ocean almost 100 kilometres away. The females have fasted for nearly a month and a half, and have lost anywhere between 17 to 30 per cent of their total weight. They are in urgent need of food.

8   The female must renew her strength and vitality so that she can return with food for her chick. Going to the sea, she takes the shortest route to reach a polynya (open water surrounded by ice). Penguins appear to be able to navigate by the reflection of the clouds on the water, using what has been called a "water sky."

9   The male penguin, who has also been fasting, is now left with the egg balanced on his feet. The first egg was laid on the first of May; a chick will emerge in August. Since the seasons are reversed south of the equator, full winter has arrived, with many violent blizzards and the lowest temperatures of the year. Emperor penguins are well adapted to the almost unimaginable cold of these 24-hour Antarctic nights: Their plumage is waterproof, wind-proof, flexible and renewed annually. They may not need tents, but as soon as the bad weather starts, generally in June, the males need some protection from the bitter cold, and nearly all of them find it by forming a *tortue*, which is a throng of very densely packed penguins. When the storms come they move in close to one another, shoulder to shoulder, and form a circle. The middle of the tortue is unusually warm and one would think that every penguin fights to be at the epicentre of warmth. But in fact what looks like an immobile mass is really a very slowly revolving spiral. The constantly shifting formation is such that every penguin, all the while balancing that single precious egg on his feet, eventually winds up in the middle of the tortue, only to find himself later at the periphery.

10   What early French explorers noticed during the two- to three-month incubation period is an almost preternatural calm among the males. This is no doubt necessitated by the long fast that is ahead of them. Many of them have already fasted, like the females, for two months or more, and must now face another two months of fasting. And moving about with an egg balanced on one's feet is difficult at the best of times.

11   The only time a father will abandon an egg is if he has reached the maximum limit of his physiological ability to fast, and would die if he did not seek food. Not a small number of eggs are left for this reason, and it would seem that in each case the female is late in returning.

12   In July or August, after being gone for almost three months, the female emperor returns from the sea, singing as she penetrates various groups of birds, searching for her mate and her chick or egg. The males do not move, but make small peeping noises. When she finds her partner, she sings, she makes

little dance steps, then she goes quiet and both birds can remain immobile for up to 10 minutes. Then they begin to move around one another. The female fixes her eyes on the incubatory pouch of her partner, while her excitement grows visibly. Finally, if it is the right bird, the male allows the egg to fall gently to the ice, whereupon the female takes it and then turns her back to the male, to whom, after a final duet, she becomes completely indifferent. The male becomes increasingly irritated, stares at his empty pouch, pecks at it with his beak, lifts up his head, groans, and then pecks the female. She shows no further interest in him and eventually he leaves for the open sea, to break his long fast. The whole affair has lasted about 80 minutes....

13   The miracle is that the mothers usually return on the day their chicks hatch. How is it, one wonders, that the female emperor penguin is able to return just in time for the birth of her chick? As Alexander Skutch notes in his wonderful book, *The Minds of Birds*, it is improbable that she has consciously counted the 63 days or whatever the exact number is between the laying of her egg and the hatching of her chick. "Some subconscious process, physiological or mental, was evidently summing the days to prompt the birds to start homeward when the proper number had elapsed."

14   If the egg has hatched before her arrival and the male already has a chick between his legs, the female is even more excited to hear it peep, and quickly removes it from the male. She immediately regurgitates food to the chick. If she is late in coming, the male, in spite of his near starvation, has a final resource: He regurgitates into the beak of his peeping newborn a substance known as penguin milk, similar to pigeon's milk, or crop milk, which is secreted from the lining of his esophagus. The secretion is remarkably rich, containing essential amino acids, much like the milk of marine mammals such as seals and whales. These feedings allow the young birds to survive for up to two weeks after hatching. Many of these males have now fasted for four and a half months, and have lost up to half of their body weight. It is a sight to see the well-nourished, sleek, brilliantly feathered, healthy-looking females arrive, and the emaciated, dirty, tired males leave.

15   How difficult it is for us to understand the emotions involved in these events. Yet it is hard to resist the anthropomorphic urge. Obviously the male emperor is aware of the loss of what has, after all, been almost a part of his body for two to three months. Is he disappointed, bewildered, relieved, or are his feelings so remote from our own (not inferior, mind you, just different) that we cannot imagine them? We would groan, too, under such circumstances, but the meaning of a penguin's groan is still opaque to us. Yet we, too, are fathers and mothers with babies to protect and comfort, negotiating meals and absences and other obligations, just like our Antarctic cousins. Sometimes, when we are

overwhelmed by an emotion, we are hard-pressed to express ourselves. If penguin fathers could speak about this moment in their lives, perhaps they would be at a similar loss for words. Perhaps the songs and groans of the male penguin are all the expression they need.

QUESTIONS FOR DISCUSSION

1. What kind of hook does the author use in the introduction (paragraphs 1 and 2)? (See "Writing Introductions and Conclusions" in Chapter 25 for a discussion of hooks.)
2. Masson's thesis is implied but not stated in this essay. In your own words, write a thesis statement for this piece.
3. Which paragraphs are developed primarily by means of numerical facts and statistics? Why is this an effective way of supporting the main ideas of these paragraphs?
4. The language of this essay combines scientific terms with words and phrases associated with human emotions, such as "happy couple" in paragraph 6 and "increasingly irritated" in paragraph 12. That is, Masson implies similarities between penguins and humans. Why do you think he chooses these kinds of phrases? What does the word *anthropomorphic* in paragraph 15 mean?
5. What is the author's attitude toward the emperor penguins? Identify three or four examples to support your opinion.

SUGGESTIONS FOR WRITING

1. Write an essay about a father's role in his young child's life (birth to 24 months). What are the essential responsibilities of a father?
2. Write an essay about being a caregiver. Describe a situation in which you have cared for someone on an ongoing basis. How did you feel about the responsibilities you assumed?

Two versions of the same essay follow. The first is an example of a short research paper formatted in MLA style. The annotations point out some features of MLA format and documentation. (If your instructor requires a separate title page, ask for guidelines.) The second is the same short research paper, formatted in APA style, with annotations that identify features specific to APA documentation and format. (A title page is required in APA style.)

Read the essay your instructor specifies. Then answer the questions at the end.

LEARNING A NEW LANGUAGE: WHY IS IT SO HARD?
Dahlia Rodriguez

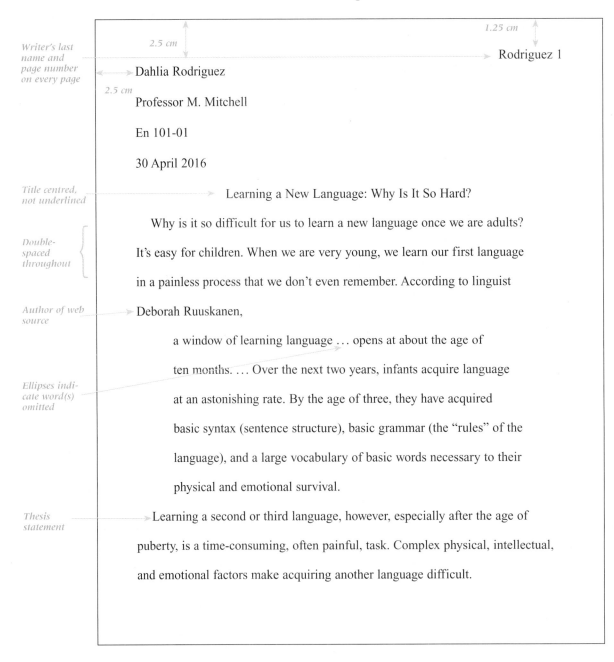

Writer's last name and page number on every page

1.25 cm

2.5 cm

Rodriguez 1

Dahlia Rodriguez

2.5 cm

Professor M. Mitchell

En 101-01

30 April 2016

Title centred, not underlined

Learning a New Language: Why Is It So Hard?

Double-spaced throughout

Why is it so difficult for us to learn a new language once we are adults?

It's easy for children. When we are very young, we learn our first language

in a painless process that we don't even remember. According to linguist

Author of web source

Deborah Ruuskanen,

a window of learning language ... opens at about the age of

ten months. ... Over the next two years, infants acquire language

Ellipses indicate word(s) omitted

at an astonishing rate. By the age of three, they have acquired

basic syntax (sentence structure), basic grammar (the "rules" of the

language), and a large vocabulary of basic words necessary to their

physical and emotional survival.

Thesis statement

Learning a second or third language, however, especially after the age of

puberty, is a time-consuming, often painful, task. Complex physical, intellectual,

and emotional factors make acquiring another language difficult.

Rodriguez 2

An important part of acquiring a language is learning to speak, which is a physical skill, like walking or dancing or riding a bicycle. As any athlete will tell you, it is an advantage to start learning a physical skill at a young age. There are hundreds of muscles used in human speech: mouth, lips, tongue, larynx, vocal cords, and throat. A young child who babbles her way to articulate speech is practising the physical skills of her native language. Young children have a vast capacity for sound production, for mimicry, that is gradually lost as they mature. Hence, even adults who become fluent in another language are likely to retain an accent that is a vestige of their first language. Anne Merritt points out the reasons for the persistence of an accent in adult language learners: "[younger learners are] better … at mimicking new sounds and adopting pronunciation. The brain is more open to new sounds and patterns in pre-adolescence, so it is very difficult for older language learners to speak without an accent."

An adult has intellectual and cognitive skills that a child lacks. An adult can think abstractly and is able to memorize vocabulary and learn grammar (Crystal 373). These skills might seem to make it easier to learn a new language, but in fact the opposite is true. An adult already has a firmly established first language in his or her intellectual repertoire, and the native language interferes with mastering the second language. An academic study entitled "When It Hurts (and Helps) to Try:

Quotation introduced by complete sentence + colon

Square brackets indicate word(s) changed or added

Paragraphs indented 1.25 cm

Quotation introduced by complete sentence + colon

Rodriguez 3

The Role of Effort in Language Learning" researched adult language learners and concluded that effort and concentration on linguistic details can actually impede learning: "a learner with less attentional capacity … would have less interference and better learning outcomes" (Finn et al.). Thus children, who learn grammar by osmosis rather than memorization, are more effective language learners than adults.

Emotional factors also complicate the process of learning a second language. Young children are naturally open and lack the self-consciousness that leads to inhibition. Adults, on the other hand, have a highly developed language ego; their control of language is bound up with self-esteem. Making mistakes, as any learner must do, makes an adult anxious, shy, and reluctant to communicate in the new language. These emotions make the process of mastering it even more difficult. Interestingly, a healthy level of self-esteem and the ability to take appropriate risks are valuable assets for adult language learners (Kazumata).

Many linguists argue that humans are born with an innate capacity for learning language, that we have what is known as a "language acquisition device (LAD) hard-wired into our genetic makeup" (Crystal 234). This LAD is what makes it possible for us to learn our native language with ease. Knowing more

Ellipses indicate word(s) omitted

Summary (with author's name)

Quotation integrated into writer's sentence

Author and page reference of source

Rodriguez 4

than one language is, of course, a valuable skill. Yet acquiring another language

is a complex and demanding process for most people, especially if they

undertake it as adults. Language and identity are tightly interwoven; learning

another language necessarily implies the struggle to lose one identity in

order to acquire another. This struggle is often painful. In her essay, "Lost in

Translation," Eva Hoffman writes movingly about the emotional upheaval that

accompanied her struggle to master English and transfer her identity, so to

speak, from her native Polish language:

> What has happened to me in this new world? I don't know. I don't
>
> see what I've seen, don't comprehend what's in front of me. I'm not
>
> filled with language anymore, and I have only a memory of fullness
>
> to anguish me with the knowledge that, in this dark and empty state, I
>
> don't really exist. (126)

Long quotation set off 2.5 cm from left margin

Source author and title named in sentence, page number follows long quotation

Rodriguez 5

Works Cited

Crystal, David. *The Cambridge Encyclopedia of Language.* Cambridge UP, 1992.

Finn, Amy S. et al. "When It Hurts (and Helps) to Try: The Role of Effort in
Language Learning." *PLoS ONE,* vol. 9, no. 7, 2014, dx.doi.org/10.1371/
journal.pone.0101806.

Hoffman, Eva. "Lost in Translation." *Canadian Content,* 7th ed., edited by Nell
Waldman and Sarah Norton, 2012, pp. 123-28.

Kazumata, Keiko. "Roles of Self-Esteem in Second Language Oral Production
Performance." *Temple University Japan Studies in Applied Linguistics,*
vol. 27, 1999, www.tuj.ac.jp/tesol/publications/studies/vol-27/kazumata.html.

Merritt, Anne. "Are Children Really Better at Foreign Language Learning?"
The Telegraph, 18 Sept, 2013, http://www.telegraph.co.uk/education/
educationopinion/10315238/Are-children-really-better-at-foreign-language
-learning.html.

Ruuskanen, Deborah. "Ask a Linguist FAQ." *The Linguist List,* International
Linguistics Community Online, http://linguistlist.org/ask-ling/career.cfm.

QUESTIONS FOR DISCUSSION

1. In your own words, identify the subject and main points of this essay.
2. How many different kinds of research sources does the essay rely on? How
   many are used in each paragraph? Are they all quotations?
3. What kind of concluding strategy does this essay use? Is it effective?

SUGGESTIONS FOR WRITING

1. Have you ever learned (or tried to learn) a new language? Were you successful? Why?
2. What is the value of learning another language as an adult? Why do
   people choose to make the effort to do so?

Readings

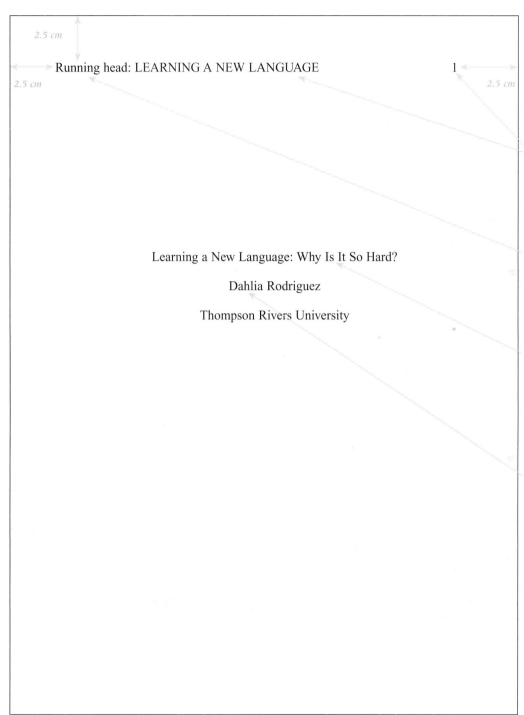

2.5 cm

Running head: LEARNING A NEW LANGUAGE   1

2.5 cm   2.5 cm

Learning a New Language: Why Is It So Hard?

Dahlia Rodriguez

Thompson Rivers University

Abbreviated title in caps and page number to appear in running head on every page

Include words "Running head" before title on first page only

Essay title, author's name, and institutional affiliation centred in upper half of the page

Other information (such as course, instructor's name, and date) optional (ask your instructor)

LEARNING A NEW LANGUAGE   2

Double-spaced throughout

Learning a New Language: Why Is It So Hard?

Why is it so difficult for us to learn a new language once we are adults?

It's easy for children. When we are very young, we learn our first language

in a painless process that we don't even remember. According to linguist

Author of source and date of publication (n.d. = no date listed)

Deborah Ruuskanen (n.d.),

Long quotation (more than 40 words) block-indented 1.25 cm

> a window of learning language … opens at about the age of ten months. …
> Over the next two years, infants acquire language at an astonishing rate. By
> the age of three, they have acquired basic syntax (sentence structure), basic
> grammar (the "rules" of the language), and a large vocabulary of basic
> words necessary to their physical and emotional survival.

Ellipses indicate word(s) omitted

Learning a second or third language, however, especially after the age of

puberty, is a time-consuming, often painful, task. Complex physical, intellectual,

and emotional factors make acquiring another language difficult.

Thesis statement

An important part of acquiring a language is learning to speak, which is a

physical skill, like walking or dancing or riding a bicycle. As any athlete will tell

you, it is an advantage to start learning a physical skill at a young age. There are

hundreds of muscles used in human speech: mouth, lips, tongue, larynx, vocal

cords, and throat. A young child who babbles her way to articulate speech is

practising the physical skills of her native language. Young children have a vast

capacity for sound production, for mimicry, that is gradually lost as they mature.

LEARNING A NEW LANGUAGE   3

Hence, even adults who become fluent in another language are likely to retain an

accent that is a vestige of their first language. Merritt (2013) points out the

reasons for the persistence of an accent in adult language learners: "[younger

learners are] better … at mimicking new sounds and adopting pronunciation. The

brain is more open to new sounds and patterns in pre-adolescence, so it is very

difficult for older language learners to speak without an accent."

An adult has intellectual and cognitive skills that a child lacks. An adult can think

abstractly and is able to memorize vocabulary and learn grammar (Crystal, 1992).

These skills might seem to make it easier to learn a new language, but in fact the

opposite is true. An adult already has a firmly established first language in his or her

intellectual repertoire, and the native language interferes with mastering the second

language. An academic study (Finn, 2013) researched adult language learners and

concluded that effort and concentration on linguistic details can actually impede

learning: "a learner with less attentional capacity … would have less interference

and better learning outcomes." Thus children, who learn grammar by osmosis

rather than memorization, are more effective language learners than adults.

Emotional factors also complicate the process of learning a second language.

Young children are naturally open and lack the self-consciousness that leads to

inhibition. Adults, on the other hand, have a highly developed language ego; their

control of language is bound up with self-esteem. Making mistakes, as any learner

Quotation introduced by complete sentence + colon

Square brackets indicate word(s) changed or added

Paragraphs indented 1.25 cm

Electronic source has no page or paragraph numbers

Short quotation introduced by complete sentence + colon

LEARNING A NEW LANGUAGE   4

must do, makes an adult anxious, shy, and reluctant to communicate in the new

language. These emotions make the process of mastering it even more difficult.

Author and date of publication Interestingly, a healthy level of self-esteem and the ability to take appropriate risks

are valuable assets for adult language learners (Kazumata, 1999).

Summary (with author's name and date of publication)   Many linguists argue that humans are born with an innate capacity for learning

language, that we have what is known as a "language acquisition device (LAD)

Quotation integrated into sentence hard-wired into our genetic makeup" (Crystal, 1992, p. 234). This LAD is what

makes it possible for us to learn our native language with ease. Knowing more

than one language is, of course, a valuable skill. Yet acquiring another language is

Author, date of publica- tion, and page source of reference a complex and demanding process for most people, especially if they undertake it

as adults. Language and identity are tightly interwoven; learning another language

necessarily implies the struggle to lose one identity in order to acquire another.

This struggle is often painful. In her essay, "Lost in Translation," Eva Hoffman

(2012) writes movingly about the emotional upheaval that accompanied her

struggle to master English and transfer her identity, so to speak, from her native

Long quota- tion set off 1.25 cm from left margin Polish language:

What has happened to me in this new world? I don't know. I don't

see what I've seen, don't comprehend what's in front of me. I'm not

filled with language anymore, and I have only a memory of fullness

Author and date given in sentence, page number follows long quotation to anguish me with the knowledge that, in this dark and empty state, I

don't really exist. (p. 126)

LEARNING A NEW LANGUAGE   5

References

Crystal, D. (1992). *The Cambridge encyclopedia of language.* Cambridge,

England: Cambridge University Press.

Finn, A. (2014). When it hurts (and helps) to try: The role of effort in language

learning. *PLoS ONE, 9*(7), e101806. doi:10.1371/journal.pone.0101806.

Hoffman, E. (2012). Lost in translation. In N. Waldman & S. Norton (Eds.),

Canadian content. (7th ed., pp. 123–128). Toronto, ON: Nelson Education.

Kazumata, K. (1999). Roles of self-esteem in second language oral production

performance. *Temple University Japan Studies in Applied Linguistics, 27.*

Retrieved from http://www.tuj.ac.jp/tesol/publications

Merritt, A. (2013, September 18). Are children really better at foreign language

learning? *The Telegraph.* Retrieved from http://www.telegraph.co.uk/

education/educationopinion/10315238/Are-children-really-better-at-foreign

-language-learning.html

Ruuskanen, D. (n.d.) Ask a linguist FAQ. *LinguistList.org.* Retrieved from

http://linguistlist.org/ask-ling/biling.cfm#first

Heading is centred and bold-faced

Use DOI = digital object identifier (if available) for online sources (not URL)

Use URL if no DOI is available from source

Retrieval dates not required

QUESTIONS FOR DISCUSSION

1. In your own words, identify the subject and main points of this essay.
2. How many different kinds of research sources does the essay rely on? How many are used in each paragraph? Are they all quotations?
3. What kind of concluding strategy does this essay use? Is it effective?

SUGGESTIONS FOR WRITING

1. Have you ever learned (or tried to learn) a new language? Were you successful? Why?
2. What is the value of learning another language as an adult? Why do people choose to make the effort to do so?

Appendixes

A The Fundamentals

Sentences: Kinds and Parts
Function: Four Kinds of Sentences
Structure: Basic Sentence Patterns
The Parts of a Sentence

Parts of Speech
1. Nouns
2. Verbs
3. Pronouns
4. Adjectives
5. Adverbs
6. Prepositions
7. Conjunctions
8. Articles
9. Expletives

Numbers
When to Use Words
When to Use Figures
When to Use Both Words and Figures

B List of Useful Terms

APPENDIX A

The Fundamentals

This appendix contains a brief overview of the basic building blocks of the English language. At the very least, you should know the kinds and parts of a sentence and the parts of speech before you tackle the complex tasks involved in correcting and refining your writing.

SENTENCES: KINDS AND PARTS

A sentence is a group of words expressing a complete thought. Sentences can be classified in two different ways: by function and by structure.

FUNCTION: FOUR KINDS OF SENTENCES

1. The *declarative* sentence makes a statement or conveys information.

George Clooney starred in *O Brother, Where Art Thou?*, a Coen brothers' film.
He played a character named Ulysses Everett McGill.

2. The *interrogative* sentence asks a question.

Did George Clooney do his own singing in *O Brother, Where Art Thou?*
Was Pete really turned into a frog, or was he turned in to the police?

3. The *imperative* (command) sentence gives an order or a directive.

Be quiet!

The *request* is a modified form of imperative sentence. Its tone is softer:

Let's watch *O Brother* on Netflix tonight.

4. The *exclamatory* sentence is a strong statement of opinion or warning.

The scene in which Clooney insists on wearing a hair net to bed is hilarious!

Don't answer the phone! This is my favourite part of the movie!

STRUCTURE: BASIC SENTENCE PATTERNS

Every sentence can be classified into one of four patterns, depending on the number and kinds of clauses the sentence contains. (In the examples below, subjects are underlined with one line, verbs with two.)

1. A *simple sentence* consists of one independent clause. It has one subject and one verb, either or both of which may be **compound** (multiple).

a. Matt plays hockey for McGill. (single subject, single verb)

b. Matt and Caro play hockey with their friends on weekends. (compound subject, one plural verb)

c. Matt and Caro play hockey and watch movies with their friends on weekends. (compound subject, compound verb)

2. A **compound sentence** is made up of two or more independent clauses. The clauses may be joined by a **coordinating conjunction** or by a semicolon. (See Chapters 7, 10, and 18.)

Geoff paid for the flight to Cuba, *and* Kendra paid for their accommodation.

Either or both clauses in a compound sentence may contain a compound subject and/or a compound verb:

Geoff and Kendra flew to Cuba; Matt and Caro stayed home and worked.

3. A **complex sentence** has one independent clause and one or more dependent clauses introduced by **subordinating conjunctions** (see page 54) or relative clauses introduced by relative pronouns (see pages 106–107).

We flew to Cuba for our vacation *while* my brother stayed home to take care of our dogs.

Matt and Caro stayed home *because* they couldn't afford the trip.

4. The **compound-complex sentence** combines the features of sentence patterns 2 and 3 above. That is, it contains two (or more) independent clauses, together with one or more dependent clauses.

Geoff and Kendra flew to Cuba, *but* Matt and Caro stayed home *because* they couldn't afford the trip and *because* someone needed to care for the dogs.

THE PARTS OF A SENTENCE

Every sentence or independent clause can be divided into two parts: subject and predicate. The subject half contains the **subject** (simple or compound), together with its modifiers. The predicate half contains the **verb** (simple or compound), with its modifiers and any other words or phrases that complete the sentence's meaning. These predicate completers may be **direct objects**, **indirect objects**, or **complements**.

1. The **subject** of a sentence is a noun/pronoun (or phrase or clause used as a noun).

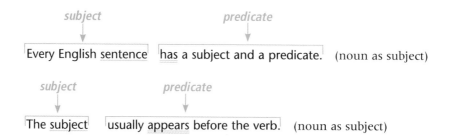

subject	predicate	
Every English sentence	has a subject and a predicate.	(noun as subject)

subject	predicate	
The subject	usually appears before the verb.	(noun as subject)

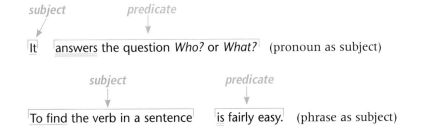

subject *predicate*

It answers the question *Who?* or *What?* (pronoun as subject)

subject *predicate*

To find the verb in a sentence is fairly easy. (phrase as subject)

How sentences are constructed fascinates grammar geeks. (clause as subject)

2. The **verb** is the word or phrase that tells the reader what the subject is or does.

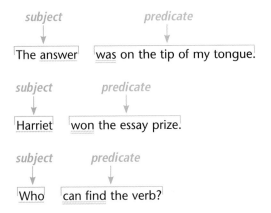

subject *predicate*

The answer was on the tip of my tongue.

subject *predicate*

Harriet won the essay prize.

subject *predicate*

Who can find the verb?

In the following examples, direct objects are indicated by a triple underline; indirect objects by a dotted underline; and complements by a broken underline.

3. The **direct object** is the noun or pronoun that names the receiver of the action of the verb.

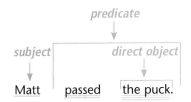

predicate

subject *direct object*

Matt passed the puck.

4. The **indirect object** is a noun or pronoun that tells to whom something is (was/will be) done. The indirect object comes before the direct object.

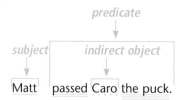

5. An **object of a preposition** is a noun or pronoun that follows the preposition in a prepositional phrase.

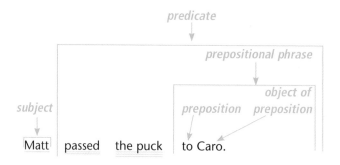

6. A **complement** is a noun, pronoun, or modifier that explains, renames, or describes the subject of a linking verb (e.g., *is, seems, appears, smells, tastes*).

Caro is the captain of the team. (noun complement)
The goal and the game are ours! (pronoun complement)
The crowd went wild. (adjective complement)

PARTS OF SPEECH

The words that make up sentences can be classified into nine grammatical categories or word classes. The function of a word in a sentence determines what part of speech it is. The word *rock*, for example, can belong to any one of three categories, depending on its context.

We stopped to rest in the shadow of an enormous *rock*. (noun)

The baby will usually stop fussing if you *rock* her. (verb)

I used to listen only to *rock* music, but now I prefer rap. (adjective)

Here's another example, illustrating three functions of the word *since*.

We haven't seen Lucy *since* Saturday. (preposition)

We haven't seen Lucy *since* she left. (subordinating conjunction)

We haven't seen Lucy *since*. (adverb)

1. NOUNS

A noun is a word that names a person, place, object, quality, or concept.

A. **Common nouns** are general names for persons, places, and objects: for example, *artist, politician*; *city, suburb*; *train, computer*.

- **Concrete** nouns name things that can be seen and touched: *tablet, sister, puppy*.
- **Abstract** nouns name thoughts, emotions, qualities, or values—things that cannot be seen or touched: for example, *ambition, success, honesty*.

B. **Proper nouns** name specific persons, places, and things and are capitalized: for example, *Queen Elizabeth, Homer Simpson, Bugs Bunny, CN Tower, Calgary, General Motors*.

C. **Collective nouns** name groups of people or things that act as a single unit: for example, *jury, class, committee, herd*.

2. VERBS

A. A verb is a word or phrase that tells what the subject of the clause is or does.

- **Action verbs** tell what the subject does: The driver braked suddenly.

- **Linking** (or copula) **verbs** connect the subject to a word or phrase identifying or describing the subject of a sentence: The driver was my older brother. He felt sleepy.

B. All verbs have different forms (called **tenses**) to indicate past, present, or future time.

Our team played badly last night. (action verb in past tense)

Mario thinks that we will win tonight. (present tense, future tense)

I am not so confident. (linking verb in present tense)

C. **Auxiliary** (or **helping**) **verbs** are used with a main verb to show tense or voice.

The auxiliary verbs are *be, have, do, may, can, ought, must, shall, will,* and their various forms.

By November, we will have been in Canada for six months. (future perfect tense)

D. The way verbs interact with their subjects is shown through a quality called **voice**. Active-voice and passive-voice verbs give different messages to the reader.

- **Active-voice** verbs show the subject doing or being:

A woman in a BMW took my parking place.

I was furious.

- **Passive-voice** verbs show the subject being acted upon:

My parking place was taken by a woman in a BMW.

My afternoon was ruined by her lack of courtesy.

(See Chapter 11, pages 83–85, for instructions on when to use passive-voice verbs.)

3. PRONOUNS

Pronouns are words that substitute for nouns. They can act as subjects or objects.

There are seven classes of pronouns:

a. Personal pronouns	*Singular*	*Plural*
	(Subject/Object)	(Subject/Object)
1st person	I/me	we/us
2nd person	you/you	you/you
3rd person	he, she, it/him, her, it	they/them

We would like *you* to come with *us*, but *they* can fit only four people in the car.

b. Possessive pronouns	*Singular*	*Plural*
1st person	mine	ours
2nd person	yours	yours
3rd person	his, hers, its	theirs

The wonton soup is *yours*; the chicken wings are *hers*; the spareribs are *mine*; and the spring rolls are *ours* to share.

c. Indefinite pronouns	*Singular*	*Plural*
	any, anyone, anybody, anything	some, all, many
	everyone, everybody, everything	some, all, many
	someone, somebody, something	some people, some things
	no one, nobody, nothing, none (*sing.*)	none (*pl.*)
	one	several
	each	both
	either, neither	few, several, many

Is *no one* curious about *anything someone* is doing for the good of us *all*?

**d. Demonstrative
pronouns**

	Singular	*Plural*
	this	these
	that	those

This paper is mine; *these* papers are yours.

That is my journal; I've read *those*, so you can have them if you wish.

e. Relative pronouns

Singular and plural
(Subject/Object)

who/whom; whoever/whomever;
which/whichever; what/whatever;
that; whose

The Order of Canada, *which* was created in 1967, is awarded each year to Canadians *who* have distinguished themselves in the arts and sciences, politics, or community service, and *whose* contributions in *whatever* field are deemed worthy of national honour.

f. Interrogative pronouns

Singular and plural
(Subject/Object)
who?/whom?
which?/which?
what?/what?

Jan is the leader on *whom* the team depended. *Who* could take her place? *What* can the team do now?

**g. Reflexive/Emphatic
Pronouns**

	Singular	*Plural*
1st person	myself	ourselves
2nd person	yourself	yourselves
3rd person	himself, herself, itself	themselves

We had planned to go by *ourselves*, but since Sharon invited *herself* along, Leo and Jon should have included *themselves* on the outing, too.

4. ADJECTIVES

An **adjective** is a word that modifies or describes a noun or pronoun.

- Adjectives usually answer one of these questions: *What kind? Which? How many?*

    what kind?   which? how many? what kind?

The exhausted young mother carried her two screaming toddlers.

- Pay special attention to the possessive pronoun adjectives: *my, our, your, his, her, its, their.* These words follow the same rules for agreement that govern the possessive pronouns listed above. See Chapter 15, pages 101–104.
- Most adjectives have the following three forms:
    1. **positive (base) form:** *short, brief, concise*
    2. **comparative form:**
        - Add *-er* to one-syllable words: *shorter, briefer*
        - Use *more* + base form for adjectives of two or more syllables: *more concise*
    3. **superlative form:**
        - Add *-est* to one-syllable words: *shortest, briefest*
        - Use *most* + base form for adjectives of two or more syllables: *most concise*

A few adjectives such as *bad* have irregular comparatives (*worse*) and superlatives (*worst*). Your dictionary will list these irregular forms.

5. ADVERBS

An **adverb** is a word that modifies or describes a verb, an adjective, or another adverb.

- Adverbs commonly answer the questions *When? Where? How?*
- Adverbs often—but not always—end in *-ly.*

Rocco *foolishly* challenged the police officer. (adverb modifies verb)

The baby is an *extremely* fussy eater. (adverb modifies adjective)

My elderly father drives |*very slowly.*| (adverb modifies another adverb; adverb phrase modifies verb)

6. PREPOSITIONS

A preposition is a word (or words) such as *in, on, among, to, for, according to,* and *instead of* that introduces a prepositional phrase. A **prepositional phrase** = preposition + object of the preposition (a noun or pronoun).

Prepositional phrases can function as adjectives, adverbs, or nouns.

Celeste is an old friend |*of mine*| |*from Paris.*| (prepositional phrases as adjectives modifying noun *friend*)

I'll wait |*until seven o'clock.*| (prepositional phrase as adverb modifying verb *wait*)

We all hope |*for a better world.*| (prepositional phrase as noun object of verb *hope*)

7. CONJUNCTIONS

Conjunctions are connecting words used to join two or more words, phrases, or clauses.

- **Coordinating conjunctions** (*and, but, or, for, so, nor, yet*) join grammatically equal elements in a sentence (e.g., the two parts of a compound subject; two independent clauses).

  Moreen *and* Luca are coming, *but* James is not.

- **Subordinating conjunctions** are dependent clause cues: *because, although, when, since,* etc. They link dependent (or subordinate) clauses to independent clauses.

  Tom must go home early *because* he promised to cook dinner.

- **Conjunctive adverbs** are transitional expressions (e.g., *however, therefore, nevertheless, in fact*) usually used after a semicolon to join two independent clauses.

  I would like to go to the club tonight; *however,* I have no money.

- **Correlative conjunctions** are conjunctions used in pairs: for example, *both ... and, not only ... but (also), either ... or, neither ... nor.* These constructions are intensifiers. They make the meaning of a statement more emphatic by focusing the reader's attention on each element separately.

  Eva is beautiful *and* intelligent. (coordinating conjunction = statement)

  Eva is *both* beautiful *and* intelligent. (correlative conjunctions = emphatic statement)

  Luca invited all his friends to the party *and* gave everyone a gift. (coordinating conjunction = statement)

  Not only did Luca invite all his friends to the party, *but* he (*also*) gave everyone a gift. (correlative conjunctions = emphatic statement)

8. ARTICLES

An article precedes the noun it modifies. The **definite article**, *the,* may be used with a singular or a plural noun; it denotes a particular person or thing. The **indefinite article** *a* or *an* is generally used with a singular **count noun** and signals an unspecified one of others. (Use *an* before vowel *sounds,* not just vowels: e.g., *an apple, an honest person.*)

The student sitting next to you is asleep. (a particular student)

A student in the back row is snoring. (one of a number of students)

A number of factors determine the use or non-use of articles. For a summary of rules governing articles, refer to Chapter 31.

9. EXPLETIVES

Here and *there* are expletives, which are words used at the beginning of a sentence to postpone the subject until after the verb, thus emphasizing the subject.

Here is your mail. (= Your mail is here.)

There are hundreds of copies still available. (= Hundreds of copies are still available.)

See Chapter 5, page 45.

NUMBERS

Numbers may be expressed as words (*one, four, nine*) or as figures (*1, 4, 9*), depending on the kind of assignment you are writing and what the numbers refer to. In a few circumstances, a combination of words and figures is required. In scientific and technical papers, numbers are normally given in figures; in humanities papers, numbers that can be expressed in one or two words are spelled out. For college and university papers, ask your instructor which style he or she prefers. For general purposes, including most business writing, follow the four guidelines given in this chapter.

WHEN TO USE WORDS

1. Use words to express whole numbers one through nine and simple fractions. Use figures for numbers 10 and above.

The novel's *three* parts chronicle the *nine*-week journey of the *five* Acadian teenagers.

China and India together account for more than *one-third* of the Earth's population.

Approximately *45* years ago, Paul Henderson scored the most famous goal in the history of Canadian hockey.

There are two exceptions to this general rule:

A. Spell out any number that begins a sentence, or rewrite the sentence so that the number does not come first.

Incorrect: 157 students submitted essays to the awards committee.

Correct: *One hundred and fifty-seven* students submitted essays to the awards committee.

Preferable: The awards committee received essays from *157* students.

B. Use either figures *or* words to express numbers that modify the same or similar items in one sentence. (That is, be consistent within a sentence.)

Canada has *ten* provinces and *three* territories. (*not* 10 *and* three)

Only *9* of the *55* applicants had both the qualifications and the experience we required. (*not* nine of the 55 applicants)

2. Treat ordinal numbers (*first, second,* etc.) as you would cardinal numbers (*one, two,* etc.).

Up to its *sixth* or *seventh* month, an infant can breathe and swallow at the same time.

In 1904, Sir Wilfrid Laurier declared that the *20th* century would belong to Canada. Canadians in the *21st* century are still waiting.

WHEN TO USE FIGURES

As a general rule, you should use figures when you are presenting technical or precise numerical information or when your sentence or paragraph contains several numbers.

3. Use figures to express dates, specific times, addresses, and percentages; with abbreviations or symbols; and with units of currency.

Dates	April 1, 2015, *or* 1 April 2015
Times	8:45 a.m. *or* 08:45, 7:10 p.m. *or* 19:10 (Use words with *o'clock*: e.g., *nine o'clock*.)
Addresses	24 Sussex Drive, 2175 West 8th Street
Percentages	19 percent a 6.5 percent interest rate (Use the % sign with figures only in tables and diagrams.)
With abbreviations or symbols	7 mm, 293 km, 60 km/h, 40 g, 54 kg, 18°C, 0.005 cm, 1.5 L, 8 1/2, p. 3
Amounts of money	79 cents *or* $0.79, $2, $100, $30 000, $20 million, $65 billion (Use words if the unit of currency follows whole numbers one through nine: e.g., *two dollars*, *seven euros*, unless the number includes a decimal: e.g., *1.5 trillion dollars*.)

WHEN TO USE BOTH WORDS AND FIGURES

4. When one number immediately follows another, spell out the one that makes the shorter word.
5. For numbers over a million, express the introductory numbers in figures and the quantity (e.g., *billion*, *trillion*) in words.

The Grey Cup is contested by *two 12-man* teams of heavily padded and helmeted warriors.

Our local car dealers sold more than *200 four*-wheel-drive vehicles the day after our first big storm.

The human stomach contains more than *35 million* digestive glands.

Light from the most distant stars in our galaxy takes *4 billion* years to reach Earth.

APPENDIX B

List of Useful Terms

abstract noun	See **noun**.
action verb	A verb that tells what the subject is doing. See **verb**.
active voice	See **voice**.
adjective	A word that modifies (describes, restricts, makes more precise) a noun or pronoun. Adjectives answer the questions *What kind? How many?* and *Which?* For example, the *competent* student, *five* home runs, my *last* class. When two or more adjectives modify a noun, they may require commas between them. See Chapter 17 for the differences between **coordinate** and **cumulative adjectives**. See also Parts of Speech in Appendix A.
adverb	A word that modifies a verb, adjective, or other adverb. Adverbs answer the questions *When? How? Where? Why?* and *How much?* For example, Matt talks *loudly* (*loudly* modifies the verb *talks*); he is a *very* loud talker (*very* modifies the adjective *loud*); he talks *really* loudly (*really* modifies the adverb *loudly*). Adverbs often—but not always—end in *-ly*. See also Parts of Speech in Appendix A.
agreement	Grammatical correspondence in person and number between a verb and its subject, or in person, number, and gender between a pronoun and its antecedent.
anecdote	A short account of an event or incident, often humorous, that is used to catch the reader's interest and illustrate a point.
antecedent	The word that a pronoun refers to or stands for. Literally, it means "coming before, preceding," and the antecedent usually does come before the pronoun that refers to it: My sister thinks she is always right (*sister* is the antecedent of the pronoun *she*).
article	A determiner that precedes a noun. *A/an* is the **indefinite article** that signals an unspecified one of others: *a* stockbroker, *an* accountant, *a* village, *an* animal, *an* opportunity.

Use *a/an* with a singular count noun when making a generalization: *A stockbroker's job is stressful.*

The is the **definite article** that signals a particular person, place, or thing that has been singled out from others: *the* stockbroker next door; *the* accountant who audits our books; *the* village where I was born. *The* is used when the speaker or writer and the audience are thinking about the same specific person(s) or thing(s). *The* is also used when an unspecified noun is mentioned a second time: I bought a box of chocolates, and my roommate ate half *the* box.

No article (**zero article**) is used in general statements with non-count and plural nouns unless the noun is particularized or made specific in some way: *Tea* contains less caffeine than *coffee*. *Diamonds* are a girl's best friend. (Contrast: *The diamond* in this ring weighs .50 carats.)

audience	The writer's intended reader or readers. Knowledge of your audience's level of understanding, interests, attitude toward the subject, and expectations of you as a writer is essential to successful communication. Your level of vocabulary, sentence structure, organization of material, the amount of specific detail you include, and tone should all reflect the needs of your audience.
auxiliary verb	See **helping verb**.
chronological order	Events or ideas that are arranged in order of time sequence.
clause	A group of words containing a subject and a verb. If the group of words can stand by itself as a complete sentence, it is called an **independent** (or *main*) **clause**. If the group of words does not make complete sense on its own but depends on another clause, it is called a **dependent** (or *subordinate*) **clause**. Here's an example: The porch collapsed. This group of words can stand by itself, so it is called an independent clause. Now consider this clause: When Kalim removed the railing with his tractor. This group of words has a subject, *Kalim*, and a verb, *removed*, but it does not make complete sense on its own. For its meaning, it depends on the porch collapsed; therefore, it is a dependent clause.
cliché	A phrase that has been used so often it no longer communicates a meaningful idea. See Chapter 1.

climactic order	The arrangement of key ideas in order of importance. The most important or strongest idea comes last. Thus, the paper builds to a climax.
clincher	A memorable statement that brings your conclusion to a definitive and satisfactory close. It is often preceded by a concise summary of your main points or a restatement of your thesis.
coherence	The logical consistency and stylistic connections between ideas, sentences, and paragraphs in a piece of writing. See Chapter 25.
collective noun	A noun that names a group (e.g., group, audience, team, committee).
colloquialism	A word or phrase that we use in casual conversation or in informal writing, but not in formal writing.

> Max *flunked* his accounting exam.
> *Did* you *get* what the teacher said about job placement?
> I can't believe that *guy* is serious about learning.

command	A sentence that tells the listener or reader to do something. In this type of sentence, no subject appears, but "you" is understood. See Chapter 5.

> Look up unfamiliar words in the dictionary.
> Be all that you can be.
> Sit!

comma splice	The error that results when the writer joins two independent clauses with a comma.

> The comma splice is an error, it is a kind of run-on sentence.

common noun	See **noun**.
comparison	Writing that points out similarities, showing how two different objects, people, or ideas are alike.
comparison and contrast	Writing that identifies both similarities and differences.
complement	A word or phrase that completes the meaning of a verb. Also called a *subjective completion*, a complement can be a noun, pronoun, or adjective that follows a linking verb.

> Ramani is the *manager.* (noun complement)
> The winner was *she.* (pronoun complement)
> The president's speech was *encouraging.* (adjective complement)

compound	A compound construction is made up of two or more equal parts. Examples: Walter and Pieter are brothers. (compound subject) Walter came late and left early. (compound verb) Pieter is quiet and studious. (compound complement)
compound complement	See **compound**.
compound sentence	A sentence consisting of two or more independent clauses. We had no time to warm up, but we won the game anyway. (See Sentences: Kinds and Parts in Appendix A.)
compound subject	See **compound**.
compound verb	See **compound**.
concrete noun	See **noun**.
conjunction	A word that links two or more words, phrases, or clauses. Conjunctions come in three types: coordinating, correlative, and subordinating. There are seven **coordinating conjunctions:** *and, but, so, or, nor, for,* and *yet.* The **correlative conjunctions** include *either … or, neither … nor, not only … but also,* and *both … and.* Use a coordinating or correlative conjunction when the items being linked are of equal importance in the sentence. When you want to show that one idea is secondary to another, you should use a **subordinating conjunction**, such as *although, because, since, so that, though,* or *while.* See page 54 for a more comprehensive list of subordinating conjunctions.
conjunctive adverb	A transitional expression usually used after a semicolon to join two independent clauses (e.g., however, therefore, nevertheless, in fact).
consistency	In pronoun use, the maintenance of number, person, and gender. For example, a sentence that begins in the first person but shifts to the second person is incorrect: *We* chose not to drive to Calgary because, these days, *you* just can't afford the gas.
contraction	The combining of two words into one, as in *they're* or *can't.* Contractions are common in conversation and in informal written English. See Chapter 2.

contrast	Writing that points out dissimilarities between things, showing how two objects, people, or ideas differ.
coordinate adjectives	Adjectives that can be arranged in any order and can be separated by the word *and* without changing the meaning of the sentence. Commas come between coordinate adjectives not joined by *and*.
coordinating conjunction	A linking word used to join two or more words, phrases, or clauses of equal importance: *and, but, so, or, nor, for,* and *yet.*
correlative conjunctions	Linking words that appear in pairs and that join two or more words, phrases, or clauses of equal importance: *either ... or, neither ... nor, not only ... but also,* and *both ... and.*
count noun	A common noun that has a plural form and can be preceded by an indefinite article (*a/an*) or a quantity expression such as *one, many, several, a few, hundreds of* (e.g., car, letter, dollar).
cumulative adjectives	A series of adjectives in which each adjective modifies the word that follows it. No commas are placed between cumulative adjectives.
dangling modifier	A modifier that cannot sensibly refer to any specific word or phrase in the sentence. See Chapter 8.
definite article	See **article**.
dependent clause	A group of words containing a subject and a verb but not expressing a complete idea. It depends on an independent clause for its meaning. Also called a *subordinate clause.* See Chapter 6.
dependent clause cue	A word or phrase that introduces a dependent clause: for example, *when, because, in order that, as soon as.* Also called a **subordinating conjunction**.
direct object	See **object**.
editing	The correction of errors in grammar, word choice, spelling, punctuation, and formatting.
fused sentence	The error that results when the writer joins two independent clauses without any punctuation between them. See Chapter 7. The fused sentence is an error it is a kind of run-on sentence.

general level of Standard English	The level of language of educated persons. General-level English is used in college and professional writing. It is non-technical and readily understood by most readers. It uses few if any colloquial expressions, no slang, and few contractions. See Chapter 1.
helping verb	A verb form that adds further meaning to the main verb. Some helping verbs, also called **auxiliary verbs**, show when an action took place (e.g., *be, do/did, have/had, will*), and some suggest possibility or probability (e.g., *can, could, may, might, must, should, would*). See Chapter 5 and Chapter 29.
homonyms	Two or more words that are identical in sound (e.g., bear, bare) or spelling (e.g., beat—to strike; beat—a rhythmic unit of time in music or poetry) but different in meaning. See Chapter 2.
hook	One or more sentences that come before the **thesis statement** and that are designed to get the reader interested in what you have to say.
indefinite article	See **article**.
indefinite pronoun	See **pronoun**.
independent clause	A group of words containing a subject and a verb and expressing a complete idea. Also called *main clause*. See Chapter 6.
indirect object	See **object**.
infinitive	The base form of the verb, usually expressed with *to*. Infinitives can function as nouns (*To stay up* all night is foolish), adjectives (That is no way *to study*), or adverbs (I stayed up all night *to study*). See Chapter 5.
informal level of Standard English	The level of language most of us use in conversation and in personal writing. It is casual, includes some slang and colloquial expressions, commonly uses contractions, and is written in first and second person. See Chapter 1.
irregular verb	A verb whose simple past and past participle form are not formed by adding *-ed*: for example, eat (ate, eaten), lay (laid), ride (rode, ridden). See list on pages 79–82.
linking verb	See **verb**.
logically linked order	A pattern of organization that depends on causal connections among the main points. One point must be explained before the next can be understood.

main verb	The verb that follows the helping (auxiliary) verb and tells the action in the sentence. See Chapter 5.
misplaced modifier	A modifier that is next to a word or phrase that it is not meant to modify. A misplaced modifier can change the meaning of your sentence. See Chapter 8.
modal auxiliary	A type of **auxiliary verb** that does not change form regardless of person or number. The modal auxiliaries are *may, might, must, can, could, will, would, shall, should,* and *ought to.*
modifier	A word or group of words that adds information about another word (or phrase or clause) in a sentence. See **adjective**, **adverb**, **dependent clause**, and Chapter 8.
non-count noun	A common noun that cannot be preceded by an indefinite article (*a/an*) or by a quantity expression, such as *one, several, many, a couple of,* and that has no plural form (e.g., traffic, mail, money).
noun	A word that names a person, place, thing, or concept and that has the grammatical capability of being possessive. Nouns are most often used as subjects and objects. There are two classes of nouns: concrete and abstract.
	Concrete nouns name things we perceive through our senses; we can see, hear, touch, taste, or smell what they stand for. Some concrete nouns are **proper**: they name people, places, or things and are capitalized—for example, Sir John A. Macdonald, Beijing, Canada's Wonderland. Other concrete nouns are **common** (e.g., woman, city, car, coffee); still others are **collective** (e.g., group, audience, crowd, committee).
	Abstract nouns name concepts, ideas, characteristics—things we know or experience through our intellect rather than through our senses: for example, truth, pride, prejudice, self-esteem.
object	The "receiving" part of a sentence. The **direct object** is a noun or noun substitute (pronoun, phrase, or clause) that is the target or receiver of the action expressed by the verb. It answers the question *What?* or *Whom?*

Jess threw the *ball.* (Jess threw *what?*)
He wondered *where the money went.* (He wondered *what?*)
Munira loves *Abdul.* (Munira loves *whom?*)

The **indirect object** is a noun or pronoun that is the indirect target or receiver of the action expressed by the verb in a sentence. It is always placed in front of the direct object. It answers the question *To whom?* or *To what?*

> Jess threw *me* the ball. (Jess threw *to whom?*)
> Calvin forgot to give his *essay* a title. (Give *to what?*)

The **object of a preposition** is a noun or noun substitute (pronoun, phrase, or clause) that follows a preposition—for example, after the *storm* (*storm* is a noun, object of the preposition *after*); before *signing the lease* (*signing the lease* is a phrase, object of the preposition *before*); he thought about *what he wanted to do* (*what he wanted to do* is a clause, object of the preposition *about*). Notice that what follows a preposition is always its object; that is why the subject of a sentence or clause is never in a prepositional phrase.

parallelism Consistent grammatical structure. In a sentence, for example, all items in a series would be written in the same grammatical form: words, phrases, or clauses. Julius Caesar's famous pronouncement, "I came, I saw, I conquered," is a classic example of parallel structure. The symmetry of parallelism appeals to readers and makes a sentence read smoothly and rhythmically. Lack of parallelism, on the other hand, is jarring: My favourite sports are *water-skiing, swimming*, and *I particularly love to sail.* See Chapter 9.

paraphrase The rephrasing of another writer's idea in your own words. A good paraphrase reflects both the meaning and the tone of the original; it is usually about the same length as or shorter than the original. When you paraphrase, you must acknowledge your source.

participle The form of a verb that can be used as an adjective (the *starving* artist, the *completed* work) or as part of a verb phrase (am *working*, have *purchased*).

The **present participle** of a verb ends in *-ing*.
The **past participle** of a regular verb ends in *-d* or in *-ed*. For a list of **irregular verbs**, see pages 79–82.

passive voice See **voice**.

past participle See **participle**.

person A category of pronouns and verbs. *First person* refers to the person who is speaking (*I, we*). *Second person* refers to the person being spoken to (*you*). *Third person* is the person or thing being spoken about (*he, she, it, they*). Regular verb forms remain constant except in the present tense third-person singular, which ends in *-s*: *I* run; *you* run; *he/she/it* runs; *we* run; *they* run.

person agreement

The consistent use of the first-, second-, or third-person pronoun throughout a sentence or a paragraph.

phrase

A group of meaning-related words that acts as a noun, a verb, an adjective, or an adverb within a sentence. Phrases do not make complete sense on their own because they do not contain both a subject and a verb.

> Please order *legal-size file folders.* (phrase acting as noun)
> I *must have been sleeping* when you called. (verb phrase)
> *Sightseeing in Ottawa*, we photographed the monuments *on Parliament Hill*. (phrases acting as adjectives)
> Camping *in this weather* is no fun. (phrase acting as adverb)

plagiarism

Using someone else's words and/or ideas in your writing without acknowledging their source.

plural

A term contrasting with **singular** (e.g., mother) in the number system of English. Plural nouns (e.g., mothers) and pronouns (e.g., they) refer to more than one person or thing.

Verbs have singular and plural forms, too, and must be matched in number with any grammatically linked nouns or pronouns (e.g., mother calls; mothers call).

possession

Ownership, as denoted in writing by the addition of *'s* to a singular noun or just an apostrophe (') to a plural noun ending in *s*. See Chapter 2.

> The writer's goal was to tell as many fallen soldiers' stories as she could in one book.

possessive pronoun

A group of words that are already in the possessive form and do not require *'s*. The possessive pronouns are *my, mine, your, yours, his, her, hers, its, our, ours, their, theirs,* and *whose*. See Chapter 3.

prefix

A meaningful letter or group of letters added to the beginning of a word to change either (1) its meaning or (2) its word class.

> 1. *a* + moral = amoral
>   *bi* + sexual = bisexual
>   *contra* + diction = contradiction
>   *dys* + functional = dysfunctional

2. *a* + board (verb) = aboard (adverb, preposition)
    con + temporary (adjective) = contemporary (noun, adjective)
    dis + robe (noun) = disrobe (verb)
    in + put (verb) = input (noun)

Some prefixes require a hyphen, as here:

all-Canadian
de-emphasize
mid-morning

preposition	A word that connects a noun, pronoun, or phrase to some other word(s) in a sentence. The noun, pronoun, or phrase is the **object** of the preposition. I prepared the summary *of the report.* (*of* relates *report* to *summary*) One *of the parents* checks the children every half hour. (*of* relates *parents* to *One*)
prepositional phrase	A group of grammatically related words beginning with a **preposition** and having the function of an adjective, adverb, or noun. See the list on pages 48–49.
present participle	See **participle.**
pretentious language	Sometimes called *gobbledygook* or *bafflegab*, pretentious language is characterized by vague, abstract, multi-syllable words and long, complicated sentences. Intended to impress the reader, pretentious language is sound without meaning, and, rather than impress readers, it annoys them; after a few sentences, they stop reading. See Chapter 1.
principal parts	The verb elements we use to construct the various tenses. The principal parts are the infinitive form (*to* + the base verb), the simple past, the present participle (*-ing*), and the past participle. See Chapter 11.
pronoun	A word that functions like a noun in a sentence (e.g., as a subject or as an object of a verb or a preposition). Pronouns usually substitute for nouns, but sometimes they substitute for other pronouns.

He will promote *anything that* brings in money.

Everyone must earn *her* bonus.

There are several kinds of pronouns:

personal: *I, we; you; he, she, it, they; me, us; him, her, them*

possessive: *mine, ours; yours; his, hers, its, theirs*

demonstrative: *this, these; that, those*

relative: *who, whom, whose; which, that*

interrogative: *who? whose? whom? which? what?*

indefinite: all *-one, -thing, -body* pronouns, such as *everyone, something*, and *anybody*; also *all, any, each, neither, either, few, none, several*

Note: Possessive pronouns also have adjective forms: *my, our; your; his, her, their*. Possessive adjectives follow the same rules for agreement that govern pronouns. They must agree with their antecedents in person, number, and gender.

Every young *boy* wants to be the goalie on *his* team. (not *their* team)

pronoun form	Determined by the pronoun's function in a sentence: subject or object. See Chapter 14.

Subject Pronouns		Object Pronouns	
Singular	*Plural*	*Singular*	*Plural*
I	we	me	us
you	you	you	you
he, she, it, one	they	him, her, it, one	them

proofreading	The correction of errors in typing or writing that appear in the final draft.
proper noun	See **noun**.
random order	A shopping-list kind of arrangement of main points in a paper. The points could be explained in any order. Random order is appropriate only when all points are equal in significance and are not chronologically or causally connected to one another.
regular verb	A verb whose simple past and past participle form are formed by adding *-ed* or just *-d* when the verb ends in *-e*. See Chapter 11.
relative pronoun	See **pronoun**.

run-on	A sentence with inadequate punctuation between clauses. The two kinds of run-on sentences are **comma splices** and **fused sentences**.
sentence combining	A technique that enables you to produce correct and pleasing sentences. Sentence combining accomplishes three things: it reinforces your meaning; it refines and polishes your writing; and it results in a style that will keep your reader alert and interested in what you have to say. See Chapter 10.
sentence fragment	A group of words that is punctuated like a sentence but either does not have both a subject and a verb or does not express a complete thought. See Chapter 6.
singular	One person or thing. See **plural**.
slang	Nonstandard language used in conversation among people who belong to the same social group. See Chapter 1.
subject	In a sentence, the person, thing, or concept that the sentence is about (see Chapter 5). In an essay, the person, thing, or concept that the paper is about (see Chapter 22).
subordinating conjunction	A word or phrase that introduces a dependent clause: for example, **when, because, in order that, as soon as**. See page 54 for a more comprehensive list of subordinating conjunctions.
suffix	A letter or group of letters that is added to the end of a word to change (1) its meaning, (2) its grammatical function, or (3) its word class.

1. king + *dom* = kingdom
   few + *er* = fewer
   tooth + *less* = toothless
2. buy (base form) + *s* = buys (third-person singular, present tense)
   eat (base form) + *en* = eaten (past participle)
   instructor + *s* = instructors (plural)
   instructor + *'s* = instructor's (possessive singular)
3. your (adjective) + *s* = yours (pronoun)
   act (verb) + *ive* = active (adjective)
   active (adjective) + *ly* = actively (adverb)
   ventilate (verb) + *tion* = ventilation (noun)

Some words add two or more prefixes and/or suffixes to the base form. Look at *antidisestablishmentarianism*, for example. How many prefixes and suffixes can you identify?

summary statement	A sentence that concisely restates the key ideas of an essay; part of the conclusion, it appears before the clincher.

tense	The form of the verb that indicates past, present, or future time. The verb ending (e.g., plays, played) and any helping verbs associated with the main verb (*is* playing, *will* play, *has* played, *had* played, *will have* played) indicate the tense of the verb.

There are simple tenses:

present: ask, asks
past: asked
future: will ask

and perfect tenses:

present: has (have) asked
past: had asked
future: will (shall) have asked

The simple and perfect tenses can also be **progressive:** *am asking, have been asking,* etc.

thesis	A thesis is the idea or point about a subject that the writer wants to explain or prove to the reader. A summary of the writer's thesis is often expressed in a **thesis statement**. See Chapters 22 and 23.
thesis statement	A statement near the beginning of a paper that states the paper's subject and scope.
tone	A reflection of the writer's attitude toward his or her topic. For instance, a writer who is looking back with longing to the past might use a nostalgic tone. An angry writer might use an indignant tone or an understated, ironic tone, depending on the subject and purpose of the paper. Most research papers require an objective or neutral tone.
topic sentence	A sentence that identifies the main point or key idea developed in a paragraph. The topic sentence is usually found at or near the beginning of the paragraph.
transition	A word or phrase that helps readers to follow the writer's thinking from one sentence to the next or from one paragraph to another. See Chapter 25.
vague reference	A pronoun without a clearly identifiable antecedent. See Chapter 15.
verb	A word or phrase that says something about a person, place, or thing and whose form may be changed to indicate tense (or time). Verbs may express action (physical or mental), occurrence, or condition (state of being). See Chapter 5.

Jamie *hit* an inside curve for a home run. (physical action)
Laurence *believed* the Blue Jays would win. (mental action)
Father's Day *falls* on the third Sunday of June. (occurrence)
Reva eventually *became* interested in English. (condition)

Some verbs are called **linking verbs**: they help to make a statement by linking the subject to a word or phrase that describes it.

William Hubbard *was* Toronto's first Black mayor.
(*was* links *William Hubbard* to *mayor*)
Mohammed *looks* tired. (*looks* links *Mohammed* and *tired*)

In addition to *am, is, are, was, were,* and *been,* some common linking verbs are *appear, become, feel, grow, look, taste, remain, seem, smell,* and *sound.*

Another class of verbs is called **auxiliary** or **helping verbs**. They show the time of a verb as future or past (e.g., *will* go, *has* gone) or as a continuing action (*is* reading). They also show the passive voice (*is* completed, *have been* submitted).

voice

Verbs may be **active** or **passive**, depending on whether the subject of the verb is *acting* (active voice) or *being acted upon* (passive voice).

In 2015, the government introduced a new set of tax reforms. (active)
A new set of tax reforms was introduced in 2015. (passive)

wordiness

The use of more words than necessary. Wordiness results when information is repeated or when a writer uses a phrase when a single word would do. See Chapter 1.

zero article

See **article**.

INDEX

Note: Information found in footnotes is indicated by an *n* following the page number.

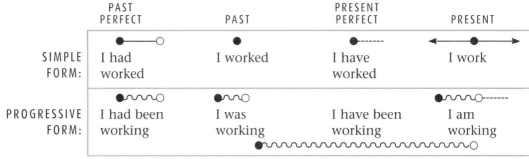

	PAST PERFECT	PAST	PRESENT PERFECT	PRESENT
SIMPLE FORM:	I had worked	I worked	I have worked	I work
PROGRESSIVE FORM:	I had been working	I was working	I have been working	I am working

▲ NOW

▲ indicates *now*, the present moment.

● represents *a completed action or state of being.*

○ indicates *an event that occurred or will occur sometime after the action represented by the black dot took place.*

˜ represents *a continuing action or condition*, both of which are expressed by the progressive forms of a verb.

--- indicates that *the action or condition may continue into the future.*

SIMPLE	PROGRESSIVE
Simple Present	**Present Progressive**
Expresses an action or condition that regularly or usually exists. It exists now, has existed in the past, and will probably exist in the future.	Expresses an action or condition that is in progress or that is taking place at this moment.

I *work* all week. Sami *does* his homework every day.	I *am working* on the project. Sami *is doing* his homework now.
Simple Past	**Past Progressive**
Expresses an action or condition that began and ended in the past.	Expresses an action or condition that began, continued for a period of time, and ended in the past.

I *worked* last night. Sami *did* his homework yesterday.	I *was working* all night. Sami *was doing* his homework when I called.
Simple Future	**Future Progressive**
Expresses an action or condition that will happen some time after the present moment.	Expresses an action or condition that will begin some time in the future and will continue for a period of time.

I *will work* hard on the project. Sami *will do* his homework tomorrow. (Alternative form: I *am going to work* hard on the project. Sami *is going to do* his homework tomorrow.)	I *will be working* next week. Sami *will be sleeping* during tomorrow's class.

FUTURE	FUTURE PERFECT
I will/am going to work	I will have worked
I will be working	I will have been working

The Time Line

PERFECT

Present Perfect

Expresses an action or condition that occurred at some unspecified time in the (recent) past and persists in the present.

I *have worked* hard all my life.
Sami *has done* his homework.

Past Perfect

Expresses an action or condition that was completed in the (distant) past, or one that occurred before another event took place.

I *had worked* for the company since 1990.
Sami *had done* his homework before he left.

Future Perfect

Expresses an action or condition that will be completed in the future before another future event occurs.

I *will have worked* for hours by the time you get home.
Sami *will have done* homework for hours before he goes to bed.

PERFECT PROGRESSIVE

Present Perfect Progressive

Expresses an action or condition that began in the past and has continued up to the present moment.

I *have been working* for many years.
Sami *has been doing* his homework for hours.

Past Perfect Progressive

Expresses an action or condition that happened over a period of time in the past, or that was in progress until another event occurred.

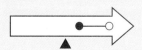

I *had been working* hard on the project.
Sami *had been doing* his homework until you arrived.

Future Perfect Progressive

Expresses an action or condition that will be in progress before or until another event in the future occurs.

I *will have been working* here for 12 years this summer.
Sami *will have been doing* homework for hours before he goes to bed.